ESSAYS ON
POLITICAL MORALITY

ESSAYS ON

POLITICAL MORALITY

R. M. Hare

CLARENDON PRESS · OXFORD

Oxford University Press, Great Clarendon Street, Oxford OX2 6DP

Oxford New York

Athens Auckland Bangkok Bogotá Buenos Aires Calcutta
Cape Town Chennai Dar es Salaam Delhi Florence Hong Kong Istanbul
Karachi Kuala Lumpur Madrid Melbourne Mexico City Mumbai
Nairobi Paris São Paulo Singapore Taipei Tokyo Toronto Warsaw

and associated companies in
Berlin Ibadan

Oxford is a registered trade mark of Oxford University Press

Published in the United States by
Oxford University Press Inc., New York

First published 1989
First issued as paperback 1998

British Library Cataloguing in Publication Data
Data available

Library of Congress Cataloging in Publication Data
Data available

ISBN 0-19-824995-0
ISBN 0-19-824994-2 (Pbk)

Printed in Great Britain
on acid-free paper by
Biddles Ltd, Guildford and King's Lynn

PREFACE

THIS is the second of a series of volumes in which, for the convenience of readers, I am collecting essays of mine that now are scattered, inaccessible or as yet unpublished. I have been gratified to see how well they are fitting together. The first volume was called *Essays in Ethical Theory*; the others will apply to further areas of practice the theory advocated there and in my main books: a combination of what I think to be true in the theories of Kant and the utilitarians. I have in preparation two more volumes to be called *Essays on Religion and Education* and *Essays on Bioethics*. Since I am still hard at work writing, there may be, if I am spared, more to come on both theory and practice.

Throughout my career I have been looking for a method of thinking rationally about practical moral questions. That was what brought me into philosophy in the first place. I have been publishing papers on practical questions since 1955, and I have written more as my confidence in my understanding of the theoretical issues has grown. Over half of my output is now on applied ethics. I am happy that more moral philosophers are now doing the same; the view, which I never shared, that philosophy cannot contribute to the solution of practical problems is not heard so much these days. Indeed, we are now in a position to help a great deal, if the philosophy is well done and the public can be got to recognize this, and distinguish the serious philosophers from those who are only confusing the issues.

The essays in this volume fall into sections. The first (papers 1 to 3) deals with laws: how philosophers can help in improving them, the basis of the obligation to obey them, and when this obligation can be overridden. The topic of violence thus introduced is pursued in the next section (papers 4 to 6), which deals with the morality of acts of terrorism and war.

Papers 7 to 9 deal in general with rights and how they can be argued for on Kantian-utilitarian grounds (the only grounds, so far as I can see, which can support them adequately). Particular rights are then discussed in papers 10 to 13: equality, liberty, both political and personal, with

vi *Preface*

especial attention to the rights of trade unions and their members, and to slavery. The proposed method is then applied at length to the situation in South Africa.

Papers 14 and 15 deal with the particular problem of justice, distributive and retributive, showing how a Kantian-utilitarian theory can resolve it. The last two papers apply the same method to problems of environmental planning, which have been at the centre of my interest throughout my career, although I have not written much about them in the philosophical journals.

The easiest papers to start with are probably numbers 1, which surveys the field open to the applied philosopher in politics, and 9, which introduces fairly simply the topic of rights and their grounds. I have tried deliberately to make it possible for the papers to be read singly. Keeping them free-standing has involved leaving in some repetitions, because essentially the same moves are made in nearly all of them when clarifying the different particular problem that each deals with. But to have cut out these repetitions would not have made the volume appreciably shorter, because I should then have had to add at the beginning a general introduction (such as paper 11 or 13 of *Essays in Ethical Theory*) to explain the theoretical background. Those who want fully to understand this background will in any case have to consult my main books, starting with *Moral Thinking*, which gives the needed references.

These collections could never have been produced so soon if my wife, assisted by my secretary Mrs Dawson, had not been so unsparing in her efforts to collect the material from many journals in different styles and sizes and present it in a form that could just decently be given to the Press, and in checking the proofs. The Oxford University Press has been extremely kind in encouraging me to get these volumes together. They are my attempt to show how a unified and self-consistent theory can illuminate practice. If others can do better, I wish them luck; what I feel most need of are collaborators (of whom there are already a few, but very few) who have both a clear grasp of the theoretical issues and a serious desire to help with practical problems.

R. M. H.

Ewelme, Oxford
September 1988

CONTENTS

1

The Role of Philosophers in the Legislative Process

SINCE Plato it has often been mooted whether philosophers ought to be concerned in government—though the roles proposed for them have varied. But before discussing the possibilities I should utter a warning. Looking for political salvation from philosophers is a bit like looking for national salvation from a return to religion. It all depends on what religion one is supposed to return to. I doubt if we could expect much good to come from a mass conversion to the religion of the Aztecs, for example, or to the Islamic fundamentalism of the Ayatollah Khomeini. One has to choose one's philosophers with equal discrimination.

Let me mention a few classes of philosophers who might do harm if they had anything to do with the legislative process or with government generally. First, the romantics, who had almost a monopoly of philosophy in Germany from the beginning of the nineteenth century until recently. I say 'almost', because there were Frege, and Leonard Nelson, and adherents of the Vienna Circle, and a few others; and I say 'until recently', because with the return of democracy to Germany there is now growing up there a very good school of rigorous philosophy. But the history of Germany is not a good advertisement for romantic philosophy; I do think that if they had had philosophers of the calibre of Bentham and the Mills during that period, and they had listened to them, history might have been very different. Both Ulrike Meinhof and Klaus Barbie were students of philosophy. If philosophers are going to do good rather than harm in politics they must value clarity and rigour above excitement. If anybody is made to feel good by something he does not understand, just because

Not published before. Given to a conference with the same title at the University of Florida, Gainesville, 1983.

he does not understand it, that is where the danger begins. To a true philosopher the most (perhaps the only) exciting thing is to become clear about an important point that was unclear before.

However, one does not have to be a romantic to be worse than useless as a help in government. I can think of some very good analytical philosophers on both sides of the Atlantic who, when they turn from their own speciality of logic to have a fling in politics, subordinate their reason to their emotions. I do not say that they give up producing arguments; often their analytical training has made them good at it. What I say is that the arguments are not what lead them to their political positions; they are merely weapons for defending them. If they happened to be stirred by different political feelings, they would defend them with equal skill.

Leaving all these people aside, we come to the class of serious philosophers who are genuinely trying to shed light on political issues by rigorous argument. Thank goodness there are now a lot of these. But even here we have to exercise discrimination. We may distinguish three broad classes, according to whether someone has a considered ethical theory, and if so, what theory. By 'an ethical theory' I mean a theory, in the first place, about the character of the moral concepts or the meanings of the moral words, or about what one is asking when one asks a moral question, for example about some issue in politics; and in the second place, a theory about the rules or canons of valid moral reasoning which the understanding of those concepts dictates. Anyone who lacks such a theory has nothing to discipline his arguments—no way of telling a good from a bad one.

First of all, there are those who have no ethical theory, and often are proud of it. They are prepared to produce arguments—sometimes quite rigorous ones—about particular matters of detail; but they have no idea about how one should conduct a moral argument—what are the kinds of considerations which can be appealed to. Commonly their arguments are of the form 'Here is something which everybody would agree to; but if you agree to that you must also agree to this, since the principle involved is the same.' This is often a legitimate move. But it depends on two assumptions which are not argued for; first, that the thing which everybody would agree to is something that they ought to agree to; and secondly, that the principle really is the same, which can hardly be determined without a close investigation of what the principle is. Even then we have been given no reason why we should not reject the principle, and with it both judgements.

Such philosophers are appealing to our intuitions, in the hope that these will agree. This hope that there will be a consensus of moral convictions is unlikely to be fulfilled if the question is a controversial one. Try appealing to people's moral convictions about abortion, for example, or about the duty to fight for one's country. The same trouble afflicts my second class of serious philosophers these have a theory, but an intuitionist one. I shall call them for short 'intuitionists', though they often do not acknowledge the name.

A typical intuitionist position is this; more sophisticated versions of it may be found in Rawls (1971), who got it from Ross (1930; see H 1973*a*); it is sometimes wrongly fathered on Aristotle. In its simplest form, which I am not attributing to any of these writers, it goes roughly as follows. There are certain almost universal moral convictions which we can treat as the raw data of moral reasoning, about politics or anything else. Any general theory, whether ethical or moral, has to square with these data. We can, as indeed we do in science, question the data in the light of theory (scientists do not treat all experimental results as sacrosanct, because there may have been mistakes in the conduct of the experiment, or unrecorded disturbing factors). But in the end, after much reflection, an equilibrium will be reached, in which we have both a corpus of detailed moral convictions, and a supporting theory, with which we are content.

This is in essence a coherence theory of moral reasoning. I will not spend time pointing out its defects, since I have done so elsewhere (*MT*), and so has Richard Brandt to telling effect (1979: 16 ff.). The trouble is that such an intuitionist theory can be used to justify absolutely anything. I need only instance the case of Rawls and Nozick (see p. 106). The truth is that if one puts philosophers of this sort in some role in the legislative process, they will only do what my first class of analytical philosophers would do, namely dress up as philosophy the political convictions which they had prior to any of their philosophical reasoning. I do not deny they might do some good if their political opinions were sound ones; but they have no means of telling whether they are sound.

The only way of telling this is to have an ethical theory which is independent of prior moral and political commitments. I do not rule out the possibility that there might be different theories which meet this requirement. But I must confess that I do not know of any which is not consequentialist in character (that is to say, which does not tell us to evaluate carefully the consequences of alternative courses of legislative and other political action, and make our political decisions on that basis). And in assessing the consequences, it has to use some scale of values. Again, different scales are in principle possible; but I do not know of any way of assessing them that is acceptable in the light of my understanding of the nature of the questions we are asking, except one which takes good or evil consequences to any of those affected as having an equal bearing on the decision; that is to say, it is impartial between the interests of all. I will not now try to justify such a way of thinking; I have tried to do it elsewhere in this volume and in *MT*. But the philosopher who thinks in this way is the one who is most likely to fill a useful role in the legislative process. I am judging from my knowledge of what has been affected in the past by sound philosophical thinking.

But what role? I can think of a number of roles. The first is educational. In past times in Britain, the majority of top civil servants and a very substantial number of politicians had been to Oxford and read the course known as 'Greats', consisting of classics, Greek and Roman history, and philosophy. Later, other courses were added, and many of them still include philosophy. This is on the whole a good thing. But the people who have had this training are not now so much in demand.

Although I have been hard on philosophers of other persuasions than my own, I would not dream of excluding them from the schools, provided that they were prepared to exercise a similar restraint (but I should not like it if the Marxists conspired to exclude everybody else, as has happened in some philosophy departments in Western countries). At the student level, provided that there is a training in rigorous thinking available, I agree with Mill and with Gamaliel that we can leave students to shop around. Much more harm than good is likely to come of any attempt at thought-policing. The excellent British civil servants I have spoken of were at certain periods brought up on the idealist disciples of Hegel; and they were none the worse for it, perhaps because their main diet was Plato and Aristotle, and there were always some hard-nosed philosophers around who knew a bad argument when they saw one. It was all a good training of the mind.

But when we come to actual involvement in the legislative process, entirely different considerations apply. There are several roles to be distinguished here. First, that of elected legislators. These are chosen on quite different grounds, and in a democratic polity have to be. It is good if the legislators are well educated; and an education in philosophy is one of the best kinds; but in a democracy we cannot demand it. Next, we have the civil servants, and among these we might include the secretariats, more amply funded in the United States than in Britain, which serve legislative assemblies and their members. Here I am convinced that philosophical training and skills have a useful part to play alongside, for example, scientific, historical, legal, or linguistic training and skills; this is only to say that people in these jobs ought to have had some sort of training in rigorous thinking.

Next, consider the committees and commissions and working parties that governments, and also churches and other less official organizations, set up when they want a problem gone into in depth. Sometimes they do it simply in order to put off making decisions; sometimes they shelve the report of a committee after it has been produced at a high cost in labour and money. But often such reports do have a great and beneficial effect on legislation. I have sat on a number of such committees, only one of them governmental (and that was axed shortly after I joined it). When there were philosophers on them (even if they disagreed, as often happens) I do think that they improved the reports by deepening the arguments and making them more rigorous, by questioning the assumptions of the other members and their own, and at least by getting the report into a clearer form. I recently went to a seminar to discuss a report on what was called 'The Ethics of Conservation' (a subject on which philosophers should have something to say, and to some extent have had) by a committee containing no philosopher. The report was, it seemed to me, almost valueless for lack of these necessary attentions.

Next, what about philosophers as expert witnesses before public hearings such as have long been held in the US Congress, and have recently and to good effect been imitated in the British Parliament? Here it is very important what philosopher one gets. I am ashamed to say that many philosophers are no more clear-headed than anybody else who holds forth in public about legislative proposals. And there is a danger that philosophers will speak, often quite ably, to a political brief, arguing for causes which they support on political grounds. They may heighten the level of argument, but the dangers may outweigh the advantages. And philosophers as such are not experts in anything else but philosophy. If they are any good, they should know how to take an argument to pieces and construct a better one. But that is all their proper skill runs to.

What then about philosophers in the media? Here they can do good. I know several instances recently of philosophers who have run highly successful television discussion programmes in which they have used their skills to bring out the crucial issues. They have thus done a lot indirectly to pave the way for improvements in the laws. I think, from this experience, that philosophers are probably, as a class, the best people there are at this job. I would not say the same about articles by philosophers in the newspapers; sometimes they are good, but sometimes they are a disgrace.

Lastly, of course, philosophers contribute to the legislative process by their own strictly philosophical writings, some of them about practical issues and some about the theoretical issues that lie beneath them. There has recently been a boom in applied philosophy, especially in the field of medical ethics. Some years ago I heard it referred to as 'the garbage explosion'. But since then we have perhaps got better at sorting out the useful bits from the garbage. All the faults that I mentioned at the beginning have been distressingly apparent; but it is perhaps not too much to hope that people are getting wise to them.

2
Political Obligation

THIS paper is one of a number of essays which I have written in recent years on the application of ethical theory to practical issues. These include, besides papers in this volume, *FR* 203 ff., H 1972*c*, 1973*b*, 1975. The objects of all these have been the same; first to do something for the morally perplexed, including myself—the aim with which I originally became a moral philosopher; secondly, to gain greater insight into the theory itself by seeing how it works in practice; and thirdly, to convince the prejudiced and obtuse majority of my profession that a formal ethical theory about the logical properties of the moral concepts, which itself begs no questions of moral substance, and can therefore be accepted by people of differing moral opinions, can shed light on practical questions, and lead in practice to their solution. It is not my purpose here to defend my views about these logical properties, but only their relevance to practice if true. Those readers who question my theoretical assumptions will have to look elsewhere for their justification (see *MT* and refs.).

The expression 'political obligation', although it conveniently delimits my topic, ought not to be used (though it often is) without an awareness of its dangers. As I shall use the term, political obligation is not (as perhaps legal obligation is) a species of the genus obligation, co-ordinate with moral obligation; it is, rather, a sub-species of moral obligation, co-ordinate with other sub-species such as social and parental obligations. Just as parental obligations are the *moral* obligations which we incur when we become parents (for example to feed our children) and social obligations the *moral* obligations that we have because we are members of a society, so political obligations are the *moral* obligations that lie upon us because we are citizens (*polītai*) of a state with laws. To think that political obligations are not a sub-species of moral obligations,

From *Social Ends and Political Means*, ed. T. Honderich (Routledge, 1976).

but a species of the genus obligation (if there is one) co-ordinate with moral obligations, might lead someone to do highly immoral acts in the name of a 'political obligation' conceived of as overriding morality; but, if we ask what such a 'political obligation' could be, or what could be its source, the resulting darkness may persuade us that this way of using the terms is radically misconceived. Be that as it may, I shall myself be speaking only of those *moral* obligations that we have because we are citizens, and of how they arise.

Does the fact that I am a citizen of the United Kingdom lay upon me moral obligations which I should not have if I were not? Most people think that it does: obligations, not only to obey the laws of the United Kingdom in general (there may be exceptions) but to take part in the political process in order to improve those laws if they need it, to defend them if they do not, and, in general, to perform the 'duty of a citizen' (see also p. 72). I shall be concentrating in the main on one of these kinds of obligation, the moral obligation to obey the laws— although I acknowledge that this obligation may lie not only on citizens but also on anybody, even an alien, who finds himself within the jurisdiction (most people think that foreign visitors too have a moral obligation not to steal). This moral obligation to obey the laws must of course be distinguished from legal obligations (i.e. the requirements, morality aside, of the laws themselves). That there is a legal obligation in a certain country to serve in the army does not entail that there is a moral obligation to obey the law imposing this legal obligation; a person who said that there was not would not be contradicting himself, even if he admitted that that was the law.

One source of confusion must be removed at the outset. It might be argued that, because moral principles have to be universal, the expression 'the United Kingdom' cannot occur in one. And from this it might be concluded that I cannot have any duties *qua* citizen of, or resident in, the United Kingdom. This is a simple mistake. The moral principle involved does not contain any singular terms like 'The United Kingdom'; it contains universal relational terms such as 'resident in' or 'citizen of'. Such a principle might be, for example, the following: 'One ought to obey the laws of the country of which one is a citizen, unless one or other of the following conditions is satisfied, etc.'. From this, in conjunction with the premiss that I am a citizen of the United Kingdom, I can derive the conclusion that I have a duty to obey the laws of the United Kingdom, unless, etc.; but the moral principle itself does not contain this singular term (see also p. 69).

How, then, do political obligations arise? Attempts have been made in the past to show that they arise because we have assumed contractual obligations through becoming citizens. It is now generally acknowledged that the social contract is a fiction to which no reality corresponds; there has been no contract. However, as a matter of philosophical history, Rousseau, who put forward such a theory, greatly influenced the moral philosophy of Kant, who gave as helpful an account of the nature of morality as anybody could who wrote in such an impenetrably obscure style. My own view, which owes a lot to Kant, might therefore be said to contain traces of Rousseau, as does that of Professor Rawls.[1]

Sooner than speak of a fictitious or hypothetical contract, however, it is clearer to start directly from the logical properties of the moral concepts. If I am right about these, to ask what obligations I have as citizen is to ask for a universal prescription applicable to all people who are citizens of a country in circumstances just like those in which I find myself. That is to say, I have to ask—as in *any* case when faced with a question about what I morally ought to do—'What universal principle of action can I accept for cases just like this, disregarding the fact that I occupy the place in the situation that I do (i.e. giving no preferential weight to my own interests just because they are mine)?' This will lead me to give equal weight to the equal interests of every individual affected by my actions, and thus to accept the principle which will in all most promote those interests. Thus I am led to a form of utilitarianism.[2]

---

[1] For the analogies and differences between Rawls's theory and my own, see p. 47, H 1973a, and Barry 1973: 12 f. Barry is right in his conjecture that my *Freedom and Reason* was not directly influenced by Rawls's views; I did not see the similarity between them and it until after it was written, and in particular after reading in typescript, Richards, 1971.

[2] Rawls would be led to the same conclusion by his own method if he abjured intuitions which are not justified by the method; see H 1973a.

For political, as for other, obligations we could ask this universal-prescriptive question directly of each individual case, and no general principles would be required, although, in deciding on each case, we would be accepting some *universal* principle.[3] Thus in theory no distinction between 'prima facie' obligations (which are expressed in simple, general rules) and 'actual' obligations is needed. But in practice it is not only useful but necessary to have some simple, general, and more or less unbreakable principles, both for the purposes of moral education and self-education (i.e. character-formation), and to keep us from special pleadings and other errors when in situations of ignorance or stress. Even when we have such principles, we *could* disregard them in an individual case and reason it out *ab initio*; but it is nearly always dangerous to do so, as well as impracticable; impracticable, because we are unlikely to have either the time or the information, and dangerous, because we shall almost inevitably cheat, and cook up the case until we reach a conclusion palatable to ourselves. The general principle that we ought to obey the law is a strong candidate for inclusion in such a list, as I shall be trying to show; there may be occasions for breaking it, but the principle is one which in general there is good reason for inculcating in ourselves and others.

In order to apply all this to politics, let us start with a very simple model of the political situation. Suppose that a hundred of us are cast away on a desert island. At once moral questions will arise owing to the fact that our actions affect the interests of the others. The answers to these questions will be given by what will most promote the interests of those affected by our actions (including ourselves, but not giving ourselves a privileged position). It will be seen that some of these questions can be answered without bringing in any reference to politics or to laws—which may not yet exist. For example, I have a duty to observe hygiene, because, if I do not, people will die of diseases as a result of my negligence, and the satisfaction of interests will therefore not be maximized. To take a specific instance; I have a duty to wash and delouse

---

[3] For the too much neglected distinction between universality and generality in principles, see H 1972*a*. For the terms 'prima facie' and 'actual' see Ross 1930: 19 f.

myself regularly to prevent the spread of typhus. On the other hand, some obligations arise only because of the existence or possible existence of laws. I shall call those obligations which arise independently of laws or of a state, *social* obligations; they arise if people are living together in a society, whether or not that society is organized politically into a state with laws. And I shall call the obligations which arise only because there is a state with laws, *political* obligations.

As an example of the latter kind of obligations, consider obligations relating to the possession of goods (obligations which would concern matters of property and ownership, *if* we had the legal institution of property on our island). Let us suppose that I have in my possession enough food for myself and to spare for a few weeks, and so have a number of others; but some people have nothing. We might well say that if no laws are in contemplation, I shall be best serving the interests of people in general if I allow my own store to be divided up. But I shall then have no assurance that this benevolent action of mine will be imitated by others who have food. And, I might reason, what is my little store among so many? I should promote people's interests still more if I could bring it about, by an exercise of leadership, that there is set up a law, enacted perhaps by acclamation at a town meeting and enforced by volunteer policemen, *regulating* the distribution of the available food. It is not self-evident that the law will, if the people at the town meeting decide rationally and impartially in the interests of all, require the *equal* distribution of food. It may be that, because of the difficulty of enforcing the law and avoiding concealment, they will agree to those who have stores keeping part of them so long as they hand over part for distribution. It may be, also, that extra food will be allowed to those who need it in order to preserve their strength so that they can go out fishing or cultivate the land. Or it may be that extra rations will be offered as an incentive to suitable people to get them to produce food in these ways. It may even be that a system of competition, with currency and a market, will be adopted in order to spur people on to maximize their production of food. Such a system relies on laws, both to establish the currency (though barter might do, and this is in any case not the most important reason), and to secure to people the property which they have got for themselves by competition (for otherwise there will be no incentive to compete).

It is not my intention to attempt a comparative evaluation of these different economic systems. But I take it as obvious that the general interests of people in society will be promoted by having *some* laws regulating property and the distribution of goods. Some legal systems will promote these interests better than others; but almost any system of laws that has much chance of getting adopted is likely to promote them better than having no laws at all. And the same holds good of other laws relating to such matters as hygiene (which I have mentioned already), the settlement of disputes and the avoidance of violence. Anarchy, as those know who have experienced it, is seldom in the general interest. But one can also have *too many* laws.

I could have mentioned other laws too. There would probably be one requiring the able-bodied to arm themselves as well as they can and turn out to repel aggressors from neighbouring islands. But the points I now wish to make can best be illustrated by reference to hygiene. We saw that even without any laws I had some obligation to observe cleanly habits. But the enactment of hygiene laws adds to this obligation. If we can see why it adds to it, we shall understand a great deal about the obligation to keep the law. It adds to it, not because the mere enactment by the town meeting of a law lays any moral obligation on me directly, but because it alters the conditions under which I am asking my moral question.

How does it alter these conditions? Primarily by bringing it about that observance of hygiene by me has more chance of achieving its purposes, because other people, who would not of their own accord observe hygiene, are being coerced into doing so. Before the law is enacted and enforced, if I keep myself clear of lice I am not making very much difference to the number of lice biting other people. This is because, owing to general apathy, there are a great many lice about. I may not be very successful in getting even myself deloused, if we are living at close quarters. But if there is an enforced law which makes nearly all the others, from fear of the penalty, delouse themselves, *my* delousing or not delousing myself makes a much bigger difference to the hygiene of people in general. Consider the extreme case: everyone else has deloused themselves for fear of the penalty, and I alone have lice, and for some reason think I can escape detection. Let us suppose that besides having lice I am a typhus carrier, or that there is one sleeping near me. Then it is obvious that my failure to delouse myself will make a *very great* difference to the likelihood of people getting typhus; and thus my obligation to do so (because it is in the general interest) will be much greater than it would be if there were no law, and therefore little delousing, and therefore the epidemic was going to spread whatever I did.

We may now sum up the results of this unsavoury discussion by listing the reasons which I have so far acquired for obeying the hygiene laws. There are, first of all,

A. *Prudential Reasons* (ignored in what follows)
    A.1. My own interest in not getting bitten by lice or catching typhus;
    A.2. My own interest in not incurring the legal penalty for lousiness, with the public opprobrium entailed.

Note that *A.1* owes nothing to the existence of the law, whereas *A.2.* owes something but not everything.

B. *Moral Reasons not related to the existence of the law*
    B.1. The fact that failure to delouse myself will, law or no law, harm people's interests by making them *a little* more likely to get lice or typhus;
    B.2. The fact that if I myself get typhus I shall be a burden to others;

C. *Moral Reasons related to the existence of the law*
    C.1. The fact that, because there is an enforced law, resulting in general delousing, failure to delouse myself will harm people's interests much more, by making them *very much* more likely to get lice or typhus;
    C.2. The fact that, if I break this law, it will cause trouble to the police in catching me, thus rendering necessary the employment of more policemen, who therefore cannot grow yams instead, and so harming the interests of the people who could have eaten the yams;

C.3. The fact that, if I break this law, it may encourage people to break this or other laws, thereby rendering a little more likely (*a*) the removal of the benefits to society which come from the existence of those particular laws, and (*b*) the breakdown of the rule of law altogether, which would do great harm to the interests of nearly everybody.

Only the reasons given under *C* (the last three) lay upon me *political* obligations; and of them, the second and third are subsidiary, but have the important property that (except for *C.3(a)*) they might survive even if the law in question were a bad or unnecessary one whose existence did not promote the general interest. To these must be added at least one other kind of political obligation, mentioned already, namely the obligation to further the enactment and enforcement of good laws—an obligation which arises because it is in the interests of people in general, including myself, that I should do this. I leave out of consideration the case of the person in whose interest it is that there should not be laws (because he can do better for himself without them). He is not relevant, because we are considering the question, what I morally ought to do, and to answer *this* question I have to treat others' interests as of equal weight to my own. If this fortunate person does that, he will come to the same answers as we have come to.

I have listed one major, and two subsidiary, moral reasons for obeying the law. There may well be others. And the hygiene example may not be typical. Do the same considerations apply, for instance, to laws about property? It might be argued that they do not, as has been suggested to me by Dr Honderich.

It must at any rate be allowed that, if there were no laws of property, there could be no theft; for theft can only be of property, and there is no property without laws—at least customary laws—about possessions. So *if* there is a moral obligation not to steal, it owes its existence to law, as a necessary constitutive condition of the institution of property. The question is, however, whether, given the existence of this institution and its constitutive laws, there is in general a moral obligation to abstain from breaking them. According to the utilitarian there will be, if breaking them is in general likely to harm the interests of people in society.

It might be thought that thefts do not harm the interests of anybody except the victim, and that if he is rich and the thief poor, the diminishing marginal utility of goods will in most cases bring it about that the theft creates a net gain in utility. But this is to leave out of account the side-effects of stealing. The more thefts there are, the more precautions people and the state will take against theft; and the cost, both financial and other, of the precautions (the cost of the police force, of locks and banks, the inconvenience and unpleasantness of having to watch one's property or go in fear of losing it, and the growth of general mistrust) is likely to outweigh the utilities created by theft. On the other hand, if precautions are not taken, theft will become so general that the whole institution of property will collapse. Only those, therefore, who think this institution unnecessary for the general welfare will be able to prescribe that everybody who wants to should steal.

But this in itself does not quite restore the analogy with the hygiene case. It is true that we could represent the spread of theft as analogous to an epidemic; but a single theft could never have the same effect in spreading it as a single typhus-carrying louse in my clothing might. Readers of such books as Professor Lyons's *Forms and Limits of Utilitarianism* (1965) will be familiar with examples in which one person can, by breaking a law, secure for himself an advantage at the cost of no comparable disadvantage to others, because he knows that they are all going to keep the law, and it takes quite a large number of breaches of it to produce any substantial disutility. A common example is that of the person who uses electricity for space-heating contrary to government orders in a power shortage, knowing that others are too law-abiding to do likewise, and that he will not be detected. He gets the warmth, and no power stations break down, because he is one of only a very few delinquents. Utility is therefore increased by this action which most of us would condemn; and so utilitarianism seems to be at odds with received opinion.

In dealing with such cases, a theory which arrives at a sort of 'utilitarianism' by asking the universal-prescriptive question has an advantage over the more standard sorts. It is not difficult to understand why few of us are prepared to prescribe universally that people, and therefore that we ourselves, should be imposed upon, even without our knowledge, in this way. The 'disutility' involved, which escapes the net of utilitarianisms couched in terms of present pleasures or pains, is that of having a desire frustrated which nearly all of us have, namely the desire not to be taken advantage of, even unknown to us. And there are good utilitarian reasons for encouraging people to have this desire (H 1971b: 128 ff., 1976).

This manœuvre enables us to distinguish neatly between two kinds of case which seem superficially similar, but in which we normally give different verdicts. One is the 'electricity' case just mentioned; the other is the case of the person who picks the primroses in the woods, knowing that others will not (because they have no desire to). In both these cases, we are at first inclined to argue that, if everybody acted likewise, the results would be very bad (no electricity for anybody; no primroses; perhaps no woods), and that therefore we cannot prescribe that anybody should do it. This seems absurd in the 'primrose' case; and in the 'electricity' case Lyons has shown that the universal prescription, that anybody should use it who knows that the others will not, is not open to the same objection, since everybody's acting on *that* prescription will not lead to a power breakdown. I have already shown why, all the same, we are not prepared to prescribe that people should do this in the 'electricity' case; it remains to notice why the objection that the desire not to be taken advantage of will be frustrated does not apply in the 'primrose' case. It does not, because only a very few people *want* to pick the primroses; and therefore, if those who do, pick them in moderation, leaving the roots unharmed, those who do not will not feel that they are being taken advantage of, even if it comes to their notice. If a universal desire developed to pick primroses, those who now do it would have a duty to stop unless they could somehow justify the privilege; but, failing such a universal desire, we can readily prescribe that anybody who wants to pick them, and knows that the others do not want to, should pick them.

Applying all this to the case of theft, we see that the thief is asking for a privilege for himself without giving a justification for it. We have seen that if theft became widespread, the institution of property would break down, and have supposed that this would be a sufficiently bad outcome to justify the rejection of the prescription that everybody should steal who wants to. The thief, if he wishes to win the argument, will have to have recourse to the move made by Lyons in the 'electricity' case: he will have to say that it is all right for him to steal, because he knows that not enough other people will do it to lead to a breakdown in the institution of property. But this move we have now shown to be illegitimate; the others all have the desire not to be taken advantage of, and will be taken advantage of if the thief steals while they, out of law-abidingness, do not. They would all like to be able to take other people's property, just as in the 'electricity' example everybody would like to consume more electricity. The 'disutility' inflicted by the thief consists not merely in the harm to the person whose goods he takes, but in the harm to all those who would like to have other people's things, were it legal, but do not take them because it is not, and are therefore taken advantage of by the thief's act. The sum of these 'disutilities' is large enough to make us condemn the thief's act in spite of its utility to him.

If stealing became widespread enough to approach what Lyons calls the 'threshold' (i.e. the point at which any further stealing really would cause the property institution to break down), then the considerations in the 'typhus' example would apply. The 'typhus' example is one in which the threshold has already been reached by even the first man who has lice, if the others have not. The manœuvre which we have performed in the stealing case was therefore not required in the 'typhus' case, though it would be applicable in that case too.

We have, then, to add the following item to our list of reasons for obeying the law:

> *C.4.* The fact that, if I break the law, I shall be taking advantage of those who keep it out of law-abidingness although they would like to do what it forbids, and thus harming them by frustrating their desire not to be taken advantage of.

The original list was phrased in terms of the 'typhus' example; but since it is obvious how the whole table would have to be generalized to omit specific references to the 'typhus' example, I shall spare the reader this exercise. The result would be a list containing a number of reasons for obeying the law, not all of which will apply in all cases. Our moral obligation to obey the law, therefore, has complex grounds; and I am sure that I have not exhausted their complexity in this paper.

I will end with two questions which have puzzled me. First of all, does the fact that a law is unenforced remove the moral obligation to obey it? We have to distinguish the case in which the law is unenforced but nevertheless generally obeyed out of law-abidingness, from that in which it has become a completely dead letter which makes no difference to anybody's behaviour. In the latter case, reasons *C.1*, *C.2*, *C.3* and *C.4* all go by the board. If the law makes no difference to people's behaviour, the situation in which I am contemplating breaking it is no different in any material respect from what it would be if there were no law; *C.1* therefore collapses into *B.1*. *C.2* is obviously inapplicable to an unenforced law. *C.3* lapses, because if everybody is already breaking the law when it suits them, their law-abidingness is unlikely to be diminished by seeing *me* also breaking it. *C.4* goes because, if breaking of this law is general, nobody is constrained by it to do what he does not want, and nobody, therefore, is taken advantage of if I break it. On the other hand, if the law is unenforced but still widely respected out of law-abidingness, reasons *C.1*, *C.3* and *C.4* apply, but not *C.2*.

The second question is this. Suppose that, in the 'typhus' case, the number of people who delouse themselves when there is a law is identical with those who would have done so had there been no law; and suppose that this is not, as in the previous case, because the law is not enforced (it *is* the case that *if* anybody failed to delouse himself, he would be punished), but because they are all middle-class Americans of cleanly habits and would delouse themselves, law or no law. In that case, by delousing myself I shall be observing the law; but have I any *extra* moral obligation to do this which arises because of the existence of this law? Since other people's behaviour is not affected by the law, the existence of the law has made it no more likely that failure on my part to delouse myself will lead to a typhus epidemic; any increase in the likelihood of this will have been already allowed for under *B.1*, and *C.1* lapses. On the other hand, in this situation reasons *C.2* and *C.3(b)* will remain applicable, but not *C.3(a)* (I shall not be inclining people to break this *particular* law, because they have no disposition to do so). Reason *C.4* will, as it stands, lapse; for if it is not out of law-abidingness that people are doing what the law enjoins, there can be no question of their law-abidingness being taken advantage of. However, the place of *C.4* may be taken by an analogous reason, falling under *B*, if the motive for other people's cleanly behaviour is in part moral: in that case I shall be taking an advantage of their good moral behaviour and thus harming them. This presupposes that they have some desire to save themselves the trouble of delousing themselves, but do it from moral scruple. If, on the other hand, their motive is purely prudential, and they have no desire to do what the law forbids (i.e. be lazy and lousy), then the case becomes like the 'primrose' case in this respect, that I should not be taking advantage of them if I failed to delouse myself (though, in contrast to the 'primrose' case, other reasons for conformity would remain).

These complexities could no doubt be extended by asking further questions. But I have perhaps done enough to show that moral reasons can be given, in terms of a formal theory about the logical properties of the moral concepts, for obeying the law in general, and that some but not all of these reasons are weakened or disappear if a law is unenforced but still widely respected, or if it is observed only because people have motives independent of the law for doing what it enjoins. We have to go on, as I begin to do in the next paper, to ask what are the conditions under which these reasons for obeying the law in general can be defeated by reasons for breaking it in particular cases—the exceptional cases in which there is a moral justification for crimes or acts of rebellion.

3
Rebellion

THIS third paper is in the nature of an appendix to the second, which I had used in my lectures at the University of Michigan in 1968. I thought that I should add something about the right attitude to the unrest that was at that time affecting almost all universities. It is something of a period piece, and was not published at the time; but it may interest the reader to know what I felt it right to say to disaffected students at the height of the radical movement. I must express my admiration for the students I had in my class, who taught me a lot. Maybe their quality made me too optimistic about the future. But I have not cut out any of the political thoughts that I then had, contenting myself, as throughout this volume, with minor stylistic changes, and adjustments to relate the philosophical argument to my later more developed theory.

In the preceding paper I discussed the basis of political obligation—that is to say, the duties we have as citizens, and the reasons for them. Now I am going to discuss the limits of our duty to obey the law. There are certainly occasions on which we ought to break the law. I shall try to say just what conditions have to be fulfilled before this becomes the case. We must not, however, think that our duty as citizens, and our duty to obey the law, are the same thing. Many people think—and I cannot say that they are wrong—that it may sometimes be someone's duty to *break* the laws of his country, if they are bad ones and breaking them is a way of getting them changed or of diminishing their evil effects. Examples of this will occur to everyone. But the philosophical task is to try to say clearly just when it is right to do this.

First let us distinguish between the positions of two people whom I am going to call the *criminal* and the *rebel*. Both of these are disposed to break the law; but they are different sorts

Not published before.

of people. We must be clear, to start with, that the important distinction is not that the word 'criminal' carries unfavourable evaluation, whereas 'rebel' does not. Both can on occasion be used either pejoratively or neutrally. Even a person who looked on criminals and rebels with equal disfavour, and therefore used both words as terms of condemnation, would have to distinguish between the two kinds of people.

There seem to be two possible ways of making the distinction, and they are not precisely equivalent. The first is to say that the criminal breaks the laws for his own personal advantage or for those of a comparatively narrow group to which he belongs (for example his family); whereas the rebel breaks them for some altruistic political reason. The reason need not be universally altruistic—that is to say, the law-breaking need not be done for the benefit of all people, or even of all the citizens, equally; for minority groups (for example ethnic groups) can rebel in their own interests against those of the rest of society. But there are limits to this. I think that if a single nuclear family took to law-breaking in its own interests, we should call them criminals, though if a clan or a tribe does it, we commonly call it a rebellion.

The other way of making the distinction would be to say that a rebel always has the object of getting the law or its administration changed in some way, whereas the criminal is content that the law he is breaking should remain a law; indeed, it is often to his advantage that it should. For if, for example, there were no law against taking other people's things, there would be no advantage in—indeed no possibility of—stealing, only universal looting, because there would be no such thing as property. I shall not discuss which of these ways of making the distinction is the best. It would be interesting, as no doubt we could, to think up some borderline cases, and cases in which the two distinctions cut opposite ways. My purpose in making the distinction is simply to enable us to concentrate on the question, 'When is *rebellion* justified?', and leave aside the question, 'When is *crime* justified?' (which perhaps it sometimes is).

In defining rebellion I have not said anything about *violence*. Rebellions are of course often violent, and it would be in accord with the etymology of the word if we made it part of its definition that violence should occur. It would also be in accord with the implications of such phrases as that in the Anglican prayer book, 'From all sedition, privy conspiracy and rebellion, good Lord deliver us', where, obviously, rebellion is being distinguished from sedition by being violent, and from privy conspiracy by being open. However, the distinctions we need for our present purposes are fairly gross; and so, although I recognize the finer distinctions I have just made, I shall use the word 'rebel' to cover the entire class of politically motivated law-breakers. It is, I think, often now used in this looser way.

I might have used the word 'revolutionary', but this would have obscured another important distinction. A revolutionary is one who is trying by illegal means to alter, not merely particular laws or the administration of them, but the entire regime or system of government of his country. Rebellion is usually against laws or administrative measures, revolution against governments. The person who protests violently against the Vietnam war is a rebel; the person who is trying to overthrow by violence the government of his country is a revolutionary (though there can also be non-violent, bloodless revolutions, to say nothing of *coups d'état*). Although there is a wide penumbra of activities which could be called either rebellious or revolutionary, it is a very crucial question for anybody tempted to engage in them to ask of himself, of which sort his own motives are.

Our main question then is, 'When is rebellion justified?' We might start by asking, 'Why is it not justified whenever one finds oneself in disagreement with what the government is doing?' Why not, for example, rebel (violently or non-violently) whenever a law is passed of which one disapproves? People have often in the past rebelled against the imposition of taxes that they thought unjust (for example the Americans against the British); why should not *any* group of people which thinks that it is being taxed unfairly take violent or non-violent illegal action to get the tax removed? The answer to that question is implicit in what I said in the preceding paper. We (very wisely) value the stability provided by government too highly to disturb it for any but the strongest of reasons. If I may, with apologies, use an unpopular expression, we value law and order too much to be willing to cause it to break down except in an attempt to right the most grievous wrongs.

There is another distinction to be made here. Often people take illegal political action in the hope that they will succeed in bringing pressure to bear on the government, and so altering its policies, without causing the general fabric of law and order to break down, or at least without harming it very much. They think that they can go on the streets and call policemen pigs and have fracas with them, and then, when it is all over, go away and buy themselves a cup of coffee. Well, perhaps they can. Perhaps it is possible—and perhaps it is sometimes right—to give law and order a jolt in the hope of getting things changed, taking care not to jolt it too much, so that one can go on enjoying its benefits. But I am afraid that to achieve this requires a nicer political judgement and a firmer discipline than many demonstrators possess. What I fear is that, since human beings do not like being called pigs, the end of it all may be that these rebels get the kind of police force that they deserve. And perhaps they will give law and order one jolt too many.

It should not be difficult—least of all in America—to see that social order is a fragile thing. There is enough purely criminal violence going on below and above the surface of that country to make one frightened of what would happen if the police lost what control they now have of the situation. When President Kennedy was assassinated, he was the last of a very large number of shooting casualties to be treated that day in the local hospital. Certainly it is easy to explain the votes that there are in the cry 'Law and Order'. However, I am not yet trying to determine the exact limits of justifiable political law-breaking, but just claiming that there are *some* limits. Only anarchists think otherwise; and only those who have not actually *seen* anarchy become anarchists.

So now it is time to address what is always the first question to ask whenever one is confronted with a moral problem. This question is 'What should I be doing if I did the thing proposed?' Whenever anybody is thinking of breaking the laws of his country in a particular situation, he should ask himself in some concrete detail, and not merely in terms of highly general principles, what he would be doing (which includes what he would be bringing about) if he broke them in that particular situation in that particular way. As Aristotle said (1110a 12), actions are to be chosen 'then, when they are done, and the end of the action is relative to the occasion'. Though general principles are good things to have, they cannot always tell one what one ought to do in unusual situations: that is, in ones in which the political consequences of one's acts may be very different from what they would be in a normal case. But in a matter like this there is one very valuable general principle which is simple: to look at what one is doing.

We must not fall into the trap of thinking that all demonstrations are, or ought to be, illegal. It is not even the case that all violence is illegal. However, what actions are illegal is a question that has to be decided by the courts. It is always illegal (though not necessarily immoral) to 'take the law into one's own hands'. Therefore, even if demonstrations are *illegally* banned, those who wish to hold them have no legal redress except through the courts. And this means, unfortunately, that they are faced with a choice of either defying the ban illegally, or else going through a lengthy legal procedure to obtain their rights. If they take the first alternative, they will be assisting in the decline of law and order. I do not say that it is always wrong to do this; but I do say that those who do it should consider carefully what they are doing, as with all moral decisions.

We have to ask, then, what could be a sufficient reason for engaging in illegal political activity, whether violent or non-violent, such as is likely to impair the stability of the social order, on which (however unpopular it may be to say so) we all depend for our safety and for such justice in the regulation of our conflicting interests as the law is able to provide— which may not be as much as we should desire, but is better than no justice at all. It is obvious that the reason has to be a grave one.

The first condition which has to be satisfied is that the end which is to be achieved cannot be achieved by any legal means. It is easy to think of situations in which this might be the case. There frequently occur cases of countries ruled by corrupt oligarchies, which have got the judicial machinery and the legislature and executive too in their pockets. In such countries, if the poor are oppressed, they have no recourse but rebellion; and if the oppression is bad enough, and they have a good hope of setting up a better alternative government, they do right to rebel. This is a consequentialist and utilitarian argument: the rebellion is justified by what it can achieve, *if* it can achieve it.

But the hypothetical clauses in the last two sentences bring us to two other conditions that have to be fulfilled. The oppression has to be bad enough, and there has to be a hope of setting up a better alternative government. Let us take first the question, 'When can we say that conditions are bad enough in a country to justify its citizens in engaging in illegal political activity which is likely to impair law and order?' This is a question which it is really impossible to answer in the abstract. I should, if I tried to answer it, have to give one of those very general principles which, as I have said, may not always be of help in unusual particular cases. Perhaps the only way of answering it generally is by making it a question of balance. The conditions are bad enough to justify rebellion if the evils (that is to say the sufferings) that are caused by the existing state of affairs are greater than the sum of those which are likely to result during the course of a rebellion or a breakdown of law and order, and in the subsequent convalescent period. I said 'are likely to result'; this warns us that we are dependent on exceedingly shaky judgements of probabilities; and this should make us cautious. I am no great historian; but it is my impression that, judged by this criterion, some rebellions have been justified, but that more have been quite unjustified; but of course the leaders of all of them *thought* that they were justified.

We are thus required to make a *utilitarian* judgement about the justification of rebellions. We are balancing the evils which result from inaction with those which result from illegal action. In my books I have tried to show how the principles of moral argument which my account of the moral concepts generates lead to a kind of utilitarianism. The present case is an illustration of this. If we ask what we can prescribe universally to be done in a case when people are suffering under an oppressive regime, the answer is that we can prescribe the action which maximizes the safeguarding of the interests of all those affected, treating the interests of each individual as of equal weight. So if the suffering that is likely to be relieved is greater than the suffering that is likely to be caused, the rebellion is justified. Of course, in practice, one cannot strike in any scientific way the immensely complicated balance of sufferings and probabilities of sufferings that is needed; but all the same, this is the sort of judgement that I should try to guess at, guided by such general principles as I had gleaned from my reading of history.

That, then, is my somewhat unsatisfactory answer to the question, 'When are conditions bad enough to justify rebellion?' My answer has already implicit in it an answer to the other question, 'How good a hope has there to be of a better alternative administration?' For this is included in the other side of the balance I have already set up. I said that the suffering that is to be relieved has to be greater than the suffering that will be caused, first of all in the actual course of the rebellion or of the breakdown of law and order, and secondly during the convalescent period, if, as is normal, the government that is set up does not at first make a very good job of governing. The French and the Russian Revolutions (both of which started as rebellions) give us plenty of illustrations of all these points.

I will now try to sum up the conditions under which rebellion, or more generally illegal political activity which is likely to result in the breakdown of stable government, is justified. It is justified when (1) the good results sought cannot be achieved by legal means; (2) it is probable that the evils that will be removed by the rebellion are greater than those which will be caused by it.

There is a complication here which I must mention briefly, though I think that it is of more theoretical than practical importance. It has practical importance only because people are beguiled by it when they should not be. This is the complication introduced by the fact that the immediate sufferings caused by, and remedied by, rebellions have in theory to be balanced against the benefits or the sufferings caused to what is called 'posterity'—i.e. the generations for ever thereafter whose lives are different because the rebellion has happened. Undoubtedly people (especially revolutionaries) often *think* that this is a factor that has to be given great weight. But this is because they think they can predict what *will* be the effects of their actions on later generations. But this is an assumption that is nearly always false. The future is so imponderable—and in no case more so than when there has been a rebellion—that it is nearly always practically impossible to predict what the results of such action will be for more than the immediate future. So in practice the effects of rebellions for more than a few years ahead ought to be discounted in our calculations. I suppose that things might get so bad that people would be justified in saying, 'Anything would be more tolerable than this; so let us give the political system a stir to see if something better turns up.' But such occasions must be extremely rare.

And now, if I may be forgiven as a complete outsider, I will leave these general questions and ask a particular one. Is the situation in the United States so bad that, according to these criteria, rebellion, or illegal political action likely to lead to a breakdown of stable government, is justified? I ask the question, because obviously some people think that it is justified, and because I should be blamed if I did not apply the general reasoning to the case which most concerns us. But I do it with some diffidence, because my factual knowledge about the American political situation is quite inadequate, and I shall be going only on my impressions. I have, however, the additional excuse for giving my opinions, that what happens in the United States affects the future of the entire world more than what happens in any other country. And I have one advantage as a foreigner, that it is perhaps easier for me to see things in proportion.

I do not suppose that any competent and honest political doctor would give the United States a clean bill of health; but the same could be said of my own country and any others I can think of—at least among medium-sized and large ones. And I think it is obvious that the larger a country is, the more difficult it is to devise a way of governing it satisfactorily. With the doubtful exception of India, the United States is the only country which has devised a way of governing a really large territory and population both democratically and stably. I am myself a firm believer in democracy (see p. 124). I believe that it is the best way of securing, not only the various freedoms, but (in spite of what some people say) efficiency. The Nazi political system was less, not more, efficient, even in fighting, than that of Britain and America, and that is one reason why the Germans lost the Second World War. I should therefore expect the United States, if it became less democratic than it is, to become, not only less free and generally less pleasant to live in, but also less efficient economically and in every other way. It could even sink to a level of efficiency comparable to that of the Soviet Union. By 'efficient' I mean 'efficient in securing the ends at which its citizens aim'.

However, the American political system is extremely rigid and resistant to change. In some ways American politics are like British industry, and vice versa. British industry is too set in its ways, and as a result lethargic and backward compared with the American. And in the same way the American political system has got into a rut from which it has proved difficult to budge it. The political scene in the United States takes my memory back irresistibly to the British political scene in the 1930s; there are many of the same attitudes on both sides: both the Blimpish conservatives and the woolly left-wingers make the same noises as they did then in Britain. We emerged from that political atmosphere after the War, via a dramatic shift to the left, into a situation very different from that in America, and in some respects, though by no means all, an improvement on what had gone before. Many of the old problems were solved, to be succeeded by intractable new ones. I should expect the same to happen in the United States, given patience.

Nearly all the troubles there come from one single cause: the inbuilt conservatism of the political system (which, however, is also the source of its stability). This has two main supports: the power of existing political machines and the power of money. The party and electoral systems put immense leverage into the hands of those who have worked their way into the strategic points of the network (Mayor Daley for example). But even they could be fairly easily dislodged but for the fact that to do anything in politics requires an enormous amount of money, which is only forthcoming from those who have it. It is an unhealthy thing that to do much in American politics one almost has to have a personal fortune; and even then one needs powerful financial backers.

However, though these are great obstacles to change, they are not insuperable. Even financial oligarchies are apt to be divided among themselves; and it is not beyond the bounds of possibility that quite large sums of money might find their way into left-wing politics. Indeed, this has already happened to a certain degree. The mass media are to some extent independent of the financial establishment; they have a lot of money themselves, and their interests do not wholly coincide with those of the rest of big business. The television coverage of the 1968 Democratic Convention in Chicago was startlingly objective. It was quite different from what a fascist government would have arranged. In the upshot, the voters were not offered a very significant choice; but it could be different next time, and I should not be surprised to see, one day soon, a marked shift to the left in American politics.

The chief obstacle to this is really not any of those I have mentioned. It is that, for all the talk there has been, nobody has produced a credible left-wing platform. Those who dislike the present state of affairs have not convinced me that they are able to offer a viable alternative. I am not thinking only of changes in the electoral system (which, though desirable, are not absolutely necessary). I am thinking of specific programmes in particular fields of policy, such as education, urban problems, poverty, race, conservation, air and water pollution, crime prevention, prisons, the tax structure, and military and foreign policy. One of the troubles with the American party system is that, as it seems, it is impossible to get any clear idea of what a party stands for (American parties do not stand for anything definite) and difficult even to tell what an individual stands for (if he is wise, he keeps it dark). It really would be a good thing if it were possible for the voters to vote between two parties with more or less concrete programmes that were different, and know roughly the names and the faces of the ministers who would be implementing them. To achieve this requires a revision of the party system; but it also requires something else: the elaboration of programmes to present to the electorate, which takes a great deal of research, continuing over the years, by coherent groups of people who are seeking the votes of the electorate. Otherwise the electorate has nothing to go on except how much it likes the faces on television of the presidential and vice-presidential candidates.

The American political system could be improved in these ways; but how? One thing is certain, and that is that it is only going to be improved by *people*. What makes me relatively optimistic is that America contains a lot of very admirable people, especially those in the younger generation. The generation that comes into positions of political power in the next twenty years in the United States is going to be better educated, more politically aware, better informed, and more enlightened, as well as more selflessly dedicated than any which has preceded it. Therefore I am fairly confident that things will change for the better. The more educated people are, the less becomes the power of money over the mind. We have already seen the beginnings of an educated electorate, and this will make a difference.

However, that will not overcome the problems of the next few years, which are most intractable. There is a great paucity of enlightened people at the top, and I cannot see the United States being very well governed in the immediate future. Still, it will probably survive. Dangers threaten from both political directions. The forces of conservatism are unduly frightened of political change; and the forces of the left are too undiscriminating in their choice of means of bringing about reform. Violence on the left has produced a reaction of violence on the right (for violence has never been far below the surface, as I said). If this got out of hand, the right would almost certainly win, and then there would be a fascist America. But it will not happen unless everybody is a great deal stupider than I think they are. It is more likely that the admittedly creaking political machinery will produce the necessary changes before it is too late.

In making all these political judgements I have strayed far outside my competence as a philosopher. I may be quite wrong. But in order to bring moral philosophy to bear on any practical problem one has to make certain assumptions about the facts, and I have made what I think are the most likely ones. If they are right, what bearing do they have on the moral question of whether it is right to rebel—i.e. to engage in illegal and possibly violent action for political purposes? Earlier I said that the two conditions for justifying a rebellion were these: (1) the results sought cannot be achieved by legal means, and (2) it is possible that the evils that will be removed by the rebellion are greater than those which will be caused by it. It seems to me that at the present time neither of these conditions is satisfied.

First of all, the results sought can be achieved, with patience and political skill, by legal means. One has to have a clearer idea than most people on the left have, *what* results one is seeking. So the first thing to do is to clarify one's political thought—and philosophy ought to be able to help with this. Then we need more political skill, a better understanding of the way the existing political machinery works, and thus a greater ability to make it work the way one wants. Demonstrations and all that certainly help if they are judged just right, and do not lead to violence on one side or the other or both. Even a little violence can do more political harm than good—though it often does more harm to those who use it than to those who suffer it. But in setting the scene for violence one is playing with fire, and one had better keep off it unless one has much sounder political judgement than is possessed by anybody on the right or left in the United States, so far as I can see.

If there are a lot of people taking up politics these days who are determined to acquire these qualities of clear thought about what is needed and the political skill to bring it about, then illegal political action is not called for; it will do more harm than good. It may be that the people who are taking up politics are not the ones who will have these qualities. If not, then one cannot be so optimistic. Admittedly, the people who are most in evidence are both foggy-minded and politically unskilled. But this was so in Britain in the thirties too; yet all the time there were some quite able and enlightened people who in due course came to the top. I hope it is so in the United States.

I conclude that the first condition for the justification of rebellion is not satisfied there. It is possible, with patience, to achieve the results sought by other means; and, though things have moved much too slowly in the recent past (hence the current impatience) they have moved a lot, and will soon begin to move faster. The second condition was that it should be probable that the evils which will be removed by the rebellion are greater than those which will be caused by it. I am quite sure that illegal violence in the United States is much more likely to result in a public demand for increased police powers, used with even less restraint, than in anything that would please the left-wingers. It could produce a very violent situation indeed, which would do nobody any good. The present structure of American society, though far from ideal, is better for even its least fortunate members than any revolutionary or anarchic situation would be. A relapse into anarchy or into fascism would put an end to any improvement for decades.

As an outsider, I should like to express another and purely selfish wish. I hope that, in spite of disillusionment with the war in Vietnam, America is not going to get so wrapped up in its own problems that it forgets about the rest of the world. Admittedly the world has not been nearly grateful enough for all the good that America has done in it; I do not think that any nation has such a record. And it would be quite understandable if Americans got fed up with people like de Gaulle and decided to retire into their own ample skin. But the periods in which they have done this have not been good either for America or for the world.

4
On Terrorism

THE ECONOMIST magazine of 5 January 1974 ends an article called 'Your Neighbourhood Terrorist' with the following sentences.

Kidnappers cannot operate without safe houses where they can hide their victims. Even the most transient of assassins need to borrow cars and money and perhaps weapons as well. There are people in Britain who have been prepared to supply that sort of logistical support to the bombers of the Angry Brigade and the IRA. Their motives are various and often confused, but to explain the climate that makes it possible for the modern terrorist to breathe one has to fall back on the truth of an old Turkish proverb; fish rot from the head downwards. To the extent that some academics and communicators can still be found who will defend the fashionable apologies for violence, they are helping to make the terrorist possible.

I do not know what kind of intellectual rottenness *The Economist* had in mind; but it seems to me a good proverb. I will try to explain what kind *I* have in mind. I wish to do so without presupposing that terrorism is in all cases unjustified, as perhaps *The Economist* does. 'Defending the fashionable apologies for violence' is only one of the possible philosophical sins (if it is a sin), and perhaps not the most damaging of them.

The first thing to be clear about is that philosophy can do nothing to help in practical affairs unless it is devoted to producing cogent arguments. I can think of three kinds of philosophers whose efforts to help with practical problems (as philosophers certainly should) have been quite useless. The first kind consists of those who do not aim at rigour at all, but are most interested in producing exciting rhetoric. The second kind consists of those who are perfectly capable of writing rigorously about some other branch of philosophy (say mathematical logic), but, when they come on to talk about

From *Journal of Value Inquiry* 13 (1979).

politics or morality or any other practical question, leave all that behind them—perhaps because, like Plato's sailors (*Republic* 488b), they do not think there can be any discipline of the intellect in practical affairs. The third kind consists of those who do claim to be producing arguments, and indeed closely meshed systems of argument, about practical affairs, but who rest the crucial, or as Rawls (1971: 261) has it the Archimedean, points of their systems (what we might term their fulcra) upon nothing but private intuitions or prejudices.

The tragedy is that these kinds of people, often with the best of intentions, do real and lasting harm (perhaps more harm than those philosophers, sometimes good ones, who make little attempt to say anything of immediate practical relevance). I think that there are German philosophers who bear much more blame than Frege for the flow of thought one of whose results was Hitler. If philosophy is to make its own peculiar and distinctive contribution to practical affairs, it can do it only by insisting always on rigour in practical argument; and rigour can be achieved only by careful attention to what we are saying—to the concepts we are using, their logical properties, and hence to the validity of arguments in which they occur. And that is why the study of these concepts and their logical properties, their analysis or their meaning, must be the centre and foundation of the philosopher's work on practical problems. Any philosopher who despises this kind of investigation is condemning himself to competing with politicians and journalists, lacking perhaps their skills and contributing nothing special of his own.

I have therefore devoted most of my effort as a moral philosopher to conceptual studies, although my aim was always to do something for practical problems. Aristotle said that we enquire into what goodness is, not in order that we may know, but in order that we may become good men, but he did enquire into what goodness is, as the necessary means to that end; that is what the *Ethics* are all about (1103b 27, 1105b 19; the second passage shows that the first cannot mean what most translations of it seem to imply; Lambinus's translation is correct). I will try to say how the conceptual study of the moral words helps in understanding, and might even help in preventing, terrorism. For it is conceptual misunderstandings and the unwillingness to think that lie at the root of much terrorism, as of other violence.

In my view (an unpopular one) the only method of reasoning which can import any adequate rigour into thought about practical affairs has at least strong affinities with utilitarianism. I do not say that the method I am advocating *is* utilitarian, because there are many different kinds of utilitarianism, which the ignorant often confuse; and therefore to call any method utilitarian is to expose it to the fashionable vilifications of those who do not feel the need to identify their target very accurately. Better to say what the method is as clearly and precisely as possible. I have tried to do this in various places (p. 49 and *MT*), so I will not attempt it here. I claim that the method is consistent with, and practically equivalent to, versions of Kantianism, the Golden Rule, the ideal observer theory, the rational contractor theory (though not Rawls's version), and rule-utilitarianism; and that it can be grounded on the view about the logical properties of the moral concepts which I have advocated. This too I shall have to leave unexplained.

Briefly, according to this view, if we are asking whether we ought to do a certain action, we are asking for a universal prescription for situations exactly like this one, hypothetical as well as actual, to be applied no matter what individuals occupy what roles in them. Since, in the various possible hypothetical situations, I would occupy the roles of all the other persons affected, this way of putting the question makes me give equal weight to the equal interests of all these parties; and this is one way of putting the utilitarian principle.

I shall be discussing in the main the moral question of what can *justify* terrorist acts; but there is another question that I shall touch on from time to time, and which we must not confuse with the first question. I mean the question of what arguments might, if he accepted them, stop a terrorist from doing these acts. The two questions are not the same, because if a terrorist did not have moral reasons for his acts in the first place (if, for example, he was doing them on purely self-regarding nationalistic grounds), to convince him that he had no *moral* justification for them might make no difference to his actions. The same two kinds of question have to be distinguished in the case of those who start wars. I have argued elsewhere (H 1966) that the roots of war lie in two alternative but combinable states of mind which may be called nationalism and fanaticism. Nationalism, if we extended the sense of the word 'nation' somewhat, could include the self-centred pursuit of the interest of any individual group. The logical task of defining what I mean by 'individual group' is too complex to be undertaken here; but, roughly, those who are fighting for 'the Palestinian people', and whose motives would not make them do the same for any other people having precisely the same universal properties, are nationalists. I argued in the same place that, since the prescriptions of the nationalist were not universalizable, they could not count as moral prescriptions. The fanatic, on the other hand, is fighting for a cause which can be specified in strictly universal terms; his prescriptions can therefore, so far as their form goes, count as moral ones; we cannot exclude them from the arena of moral argument on that score (*FR* 161 ff.; *MT* 170 ff.).

Turning aside for a moment to the question of arguments that might stop wars, as opposed to merely showing them to be immoral: I argued in the paper referred to that, because only nations have the ability to make wars of the conventional kind, major wars (as opposed to limited ones) can start only if nationalism and fanaticism are combined; in modern conditions not enough of those who control national policies are going to be fanatics for them to start a major war for purely fanatical reasons; and, since national interests (again in modern conditions) cannot be advanced by a major war, nobody is going to start one on nationalistic grounds alone, if he knows the facts about military technology and is clear about where the interests of his nation really lie. A major war would benefit nobody. There have been some less than major wars recently; of these, the Vietnam war (which was not *much* less than major) could be argued to have been the result of nationalism combined with fanaticism on both sides, whereas the war in the Middle East has been almost exclusively nationalist in origin. One of the reasons (there are of course others) why the great powers have not got involved in it to the degree that the US did in Vietnam is that no cause has emerged which could engage fanatical sentiments on their

part, and the pursuit of national self-interest has not seemed
to them to justify large-scale intervention. We might have had
a Vietnam-type situation in the Middle East if the Arabs had
been more homogeneously revolutionary, and if, therefore, the
opposite kind of fanatic in the US had felt moved to oppose
them with military force. The only kinds of fanaticism that
have united each side in the Middle East have been religious
kinds; and fortunately these have not struck enough of an
answering chord elsewhere to lead to military intervention, as
opposed to aid, by non-Arab countries.

Because of this inhibition on war in the conventional sense,
people who cannot command the co-operation or the resources
to wage it often take to terrorism. To some extent terrorism is
a substitute for conventional war. This might be a merit, if it
were not the case that the two kinds of violence are so easily
combinable, and so often connected—it was an act of
terrorism which sparked off the First World War.

I shall not be able, as a full-scale treatment of terrorism
would, to include a definition of it and a classification of its
kinds. I will mention one broad division: that into terrorist
acts committed by the nationals of a country against their own
government or fellow-nationals, and those committed by the
nationals of one country against another. I am not going to
deal with coercion by fear in general, or violence in general;
nor with a kind of political violence which I do not classify as
terrorism, namely the attempt by violence to depose a
government in *coups d'état* and revolutions of the ordinary kind.
Terrorism is engaged in when there is no immediate hope of
deposing the government; it may be intended as a prelude to
revolution, but it *is* not revolution. The attempted assassination
of Hitler was not terrorism, because it was hoped immediately
to set up a new government which would end the war; on the
other hand many of the activities of the Resistance in German-
occupied territories were terroristic as I understand the term,
even if they were directed only against the German forces. This
may remind us that the question whether terrorism can ever
be morally justified at least *arises* for those of us who approved
of the activities of the Resistance.

After these preliminaries, let us now apply what I said
about nationalistic and fanatical motives for making war to

the kindred question about terrorism. I think that by parity of reasoning it could be shown that purely nationalistic terrorism cannot normally be justified on moral grounds. Unless we are prepared to say that anybody should terrorize or make war on us in an identical situation in which the roles were reversed, we cannot justify such acts morally. There will, however, be exceptions in both cases. Defensive wars (if the term could ever be satisfactorily defined) might get through this test; and so might acts of terrorism in cases where the terrorists are acting on behalf of an oppressed section of the population which has absolutely no alternative means of securing redress of its just grievances. Such people might claim that they were prepared to have anybody do the same to them in a like case. There will be problems about what are to count as just grievances; these I shall not have space to deal with. It will have to be shown that there are no other means. Those who seek to justify terrorism in Northern Ireland claim that it was the only means open to the Catholic minority of securing equal treatment. I do not believe it; I believe, in fact, that terrorism on both sides has done more to delay progress towards political equality there than to hasten it, though I would not say the same about demonstrations and the like; but these are factual questions which are beyond the scope of this paper. In general, I am inclined to say that an adequate moral defence for nationalistic terrorism will very seldom be found, and that such defences would seldom be even offered unless they were stiffened by an element of fanaticism, namely the fanatical pursuit of 'liberation' for its own sake, whoever is being 'liberated'.

Fanatical motives for terrorism are more difficult to handle. The fanatical terrorist is a person who attaches so much importance to some ideal, that he is prepared to prescribe that he himself should be murdered, kidnapped, tortured, etc., if it were necessary in order to advance the cause which he has embraced. He is not seeking self-centred ends—indeed the true fanatic is the most unselfish and self-sacrificing of people.

But before we come to the fanatic, let us ask how the ordinary person who is not a fanatic should reason about the justification, if any, of acts of terrorism. He will first of all ask what, in actual fact, the terrorist is doing when he commits a particular act. He is, say, killing a lot of people in an airport lounge with a sub-machine-gun; he is bereaving their children and spouses (and bereavement is very often the greatest of human ills); he is wounding others; he is disrupting air travel, which may have far reaching though hard-to-measure consequences if people who ought to go to places decide not to for fear of such attacks; he is causing governments and airlines to spend a lot of money on precautions against terrorism, and so increasing taxes and the price of air travel; and so on. On the other hand, he is also (or so he thinks) helping to produce a state of affairs in which the cause he has embraced (say the expropriation of capitalists' wealth) is likely to be advanced.

All these things that he is doing are consequences or hoped-for consequences of his pulling the trigger. If anybody wishes to label me a 'consequentialist' for taking such things into consideration, then let him. Perhaps he might also like to suggest how a serious discussion of terrorism could be carried on *without* taking them into consideration (are we perhaps to discuss the nature and quality of the act of trigger-pulling or of finger-crooking *per se*?).

More important is to decide how we should assign weight, in the moral argument, to these various consequences of the act. We shall do it, if my view is correct, by first asking *how much* the interests of the various victims or beneficiaries are going to be affected by various possible outcomes of the act, and secondly *how likely* each of these various outcomes is. We are thus landed with a complicated calculus of utilities and probabilities whose resulting balance can in practice be only estimated (which does not prevent it being extremely obvious in many cases whether it is favourable or unfavourable). Cost–benefit analyses are not popular now in some quarters; and they have indeed been misused, by failing to include very important costs and benefits (often because they are not measurable in terms of money). However, I cannot see any rational way of approaching questions like this except by asking how people's interests are likely to be affected. After all, what makes terrorism wrong in most cases is that people do not want to be killed or bereaved.

All the same, the fact that these very difficult judgements of probability are nearly always involved leads in practice to a necessary modification of the procedure I have so far outlined. Since in particular cases we cannot be sure how the balance will turn out, and since, if we try to do the calculations, we shall often deceive ourselves (because of self-interest or fanaticism), most of us use general principles for judging such questions. The status of these principles is something that it is very easy to be confused about. They are principles for assessing, not the rightness of acts, but their moral rationality at the time at which they are done. The archangel Gabriel, who knows the whole history of the world, will be able to tell which acts were, in the event, right; but we do not have this knowledge, and therefore we have to make do with trying to do the act which is most *likely* to be right—the act which is morally rational as I shall say (H 1976: 125). And that is where these general principles come in. What we have to do in practice is to form for ourselves, in the light of our own and other people's experience, general principles whose general acceptance (there are two senses of 'general' here, neither of which is equivalent to 'universal' as I have been using it (H 1972*a*)) is most likely to lead to people doing the acts which turn out to have been right. And we shall be most likely to do what is right if we stick to the principles, not indeed, as Moore (1903: 162) thought, on absolutely all occasions, but at least unless we have a pretty cast-iron reason, based on firm knowledge that the case is an unusual one, for breaking them.

Coming back now to our argument with the terrorist: we have to ask whether the act which he is proposing is most likely to be in the greatest interest of all those affected by it. We have principles for judging this, and their effect will almost certainly be to show that it is not. The terrorist, on the other hand, may claim that we are wrong about this. What sort of difference are we then having with him?

It may be that he has rival general principles which he claims to be more likely than ours, if generally accepted, to lead to acts which are in the greatest interests of those affected. He may, for example, say that the furtherance of the revolution is of such great advantage to posterity that principles giving free rein to acts of terrorism with this aim, although initially they lead to suffering, are most likely to promote people's interests in the long run. If he takes this line, our difference with him is a factual one. For it is a factual question what states of affairs will result in the future from different alternative actions; and it is also a factual question how much the people affected will like them.

It is, indeed, possible to dream up cases in which acts of terrorism could be justified on utilitarian grounds. I have mentioned one already: I have no doubt that *some* of the acts of members of the Resistance against the Germans could be so justified. And in a different world it might be the case that principles enjoining the commission of acts of terrorism on a wide variety of types of occasion would, if generally accepted, lead to the furtherance of people's interests. The question is, though, whether such particular cases are *likely* to be encountered in the world as it is, and whether, therefore, the world in general *is* such that the principles of the terrorist have a higher acceptance-utility than those which most of us embrace.

This, as I said, is a factual question, but not one that can easily be settled. The best way of settling it is to look at history; to see what results terrorist acts have had in the past: whether they have led to the good results hoped for by the terrorists, and whether these have outweighed the obvious sufferings and other evils caused. My own answer would be, 'Very seldom'. And then we should ask whether the situation of our own society at all resembles those situations in which terrorism did yield a balance of good, in the respects which made it do so. Again, my answer would be that it does not. Professor Peter Singer (1973) has argued that the fact that a society is democratic does make a difference to the morality of breaking its laws—although he also acknowledges that imperfections in democracy may make this argument no longer hold for a particular society. He would, I hope, agree that a democracy has to be *very* imperfect before acts of real terrorism, as opposed to other forms of political law-breaking, become permissible.

The arguments so far have been factual—arguments about what will actually result from the acceptance of certain principles. The terrorist might now, however, seize on what looks like a weak point in my exposition, and produce an argument which is not factual. We spoke of a balance of good

over evil (both evaluative terms); and it might be claimed that
although it is a factual question what the consequences will
be, it is not a factual question whether those consequences will
be good or evil on balance. The terrorist might say that he
disagrees fundamentally with us about what is a good state of
society. So, although he admits that the results which would
be produced by his acts of terrorism are as we predict, and
that they would be bad by *our* standards, they are by his
standards better than the existing state of society. But if he
says this he may be misconceiving our arguments so far. We
were not saying that *our own* preferences were to live in a
society like the existing one rather than in the one that he
seeks to bring about. We may indeed prefer this, but that was
not our argument; it was, rather, that *the people affected* would
prefer it. That is why I called it a factual argument, because
that they would prefer it is a matter of fact. If the terrorist is
saying that even though they would prefer things as they are,
or as they would be without terrorism, the world would be a
better place if things were different (say, if there were no more
private property and everybody had to live in communes),
then he is showing his colours as a true fanatic, and we can no
longer argue with him on the former basis (even if, as is highly
unlikely, he is sincere and clear-headed in what he says). For
he is maintaining that the ideal of the propertyless society is so
important that it ought to override all the actual desires of
people, even of himself if he were in their situations and had
their desires.

Before we discuss this kind of fanaticism, however, it may
clarify matters if we first put aside certain spurious kinds
which are very much more common. Of course most terrorists
are not as clear-thinking as is required in order to engage in
the sort of argument we have been having. They have an
extremely selective view of the facts; they do not pay much
attention to the facts on which we have been relying, such as
the suffering that they are inflicting on others, and the rather
dubious and over-optimistic nature of their own predictions.
They give play to particular emotions to an extent which
makes them incapable of logical thought. The philosopher
cannot say anything that will help further an argument with
such people; for he can only reason, and they will not. The

argument will have to shift, instead, to the much more difficult moral question of what measures society can legitimately take in order to protect innocent people against them. But, putting aside such less pure-blooded fanaticisms, let us consider the logically possible case of the man who says that his ideal of a propertyless society is so important that all these sacrifices are worth while in order to attain it, even if they were his own sacrifices.

I have given reasons in other places (H 1976; *MT* 170 ff.) for saying that we are never likely to meet such a person. Briefly, he can only say what he says if the importance he attaches to his ideal is great enough to outweigh all the sufferings caused by its pursuit and its realization. This means (to dramatize the argument in a manner suggested by C. I. Lewis, 1946: 547) that, were he to know that he was going to occupy, in random order, in a succession of qualitatively identical universes, roles corresponding to those of all his victims (major and minor) and of all the beneficiaries in succession, and not discount the future, he still thinks that this is what should be done in them. Suppose that he is going to kill ten people and wound twenty and bereave thirty and deter hundreds of thousands from travelling, and that others, moved by his example, will do the same in scores of cases; suppose that the resulting disruption is such that the propertyless society is really brought about, and that the people in it do not like it nearly as much as the present state of affairs. All these sufferings and dislikes have then to be added up and they have not to outweigh the importance which he and a very few others attach to having a propertyless society. I am claiming that nobody is going in fact to value what is in the two sides of the scale in such a way as to be a true fanatic. People *appear* to be true fanatics because they have not paid attention to the facts or have not thought about them clearly. And the rotten fish-heads of the proverb are all those who talk in a way which impedes people from doing these two things.

5

Rules of War
and Moral Reasoning

THIS paper does no more than add a few methodological
notes to the consideration of the rules of war by Brandt (1972)
and Nagel (1972). My reason for wishing to do so is that I find
the contrast between the methods of the two writers both
striking and instructive, and am convinced that a decision
between the two methods is of immense practical importance,
because what philosophy has to contribute to practical
questions *is* simply a method of discussing them rationally;
and on the soundness of the method will depend the
rationality of the discussion. When I formed the intention of
replying to Professor Nagel's paper, I had not seen Professor
Brandt's. The basis of Brandt's argument is so like that which
I should have adopted, and his conclusions coincide with my
own with so few exceptions that it would be pointless for me to
go over the argument again, even if I could rival Brandt's
clarity.

I have the same difficulty as Brandt evidently had in
believing that Nagel is really wedded to the 'absolutism' that
he expounds in his article; but since it is a kind of position
which undoubtedly has adherents, and indeed has superficial
attractions, it is worthwhile trying to be clear what is wrong
with it. For brevity, I shall be referring to the 'absolutist'
whose views are set out in Nagel's paper as 'Nagel'. But before
I start doing this, some remarks about what I take to be the
predicament of the real Nagel may be in place.

This real person seems to be torn between two ways of
moral thinking which he dubs 'utilitarian' and 'absolutist'.
That is to say, he wants sometimes to use utilitarian
arguments, with all their consideration of the consequences
for good or ill of alternative courses of action; but sometimes

From *Philosophy and Public Affairs* 1 (1972).

he wants to override such considerations with an absolute ban, founded upon simple general rules, on certain kinds of actions. We must note that Brandt also wishes to operate both with simple general rules and with calculations about consequences; both the real Nagel and he, therefore, have on their hands the problem of reconciling the two ways of thinking (which might, it seems, come into conflict). My verdict will be that, whereas Brandt has a way of dealing with this problem, the real Nagel has conspicuously failed to provide one. That is why, although halfway through his paper, when flirting with the law of double effect, he claims it as a merit of that device that it avoids the problem that in certain cases 'nothing one could do would be morally permissible', at the end of the paper he admits that his own position has this same consequence. Absolutism, or an impure absolutism which tries to incorporate utilitarian elements without coherently relating them to its own absolutist structure, is bound to have this trouble.

It may help to clarify these obscure remarks if I start by summarizing five theories about the basis of moral thought which have been current recently, one of which I have advocated myself. I shall argue that *for practical purposes* there is no important difference between these theories as regards the method of moral thinking which they generate—that they are, if I may be allowed to use a deplorably vague expression, practically equivalent. If, as I think, the version which I have advocated can be shown to have a basis in the logic of the moral concepts themselves (MT) and if this basis needs the addition of no substantial *moral* assumptions, this will provide equally strong support for all the other versions, since they do not differ from it in any respect which would deprive them of this support. I hope to show that the conclusions which Brandt has reached could be that much more firmly based if they were to rest on this foundation.

I shall call the five positions: (1) the ideal observer theory; (2) the rational contractor theory; (3) specific rule-utilitarianism; (4) universalistic act-utilitarianism; (5) universal prescriptivism. My bald summaries of these positions will be far from representing accurately the views of any particular thinkers (even Brandt's and my own). (1), (2), and (3), as I shall summarize them, bear a certain relation (which is not one of identity) to theories which Brandt has advocated (1955; 1959; 1972), and (4) is, as I have argued elsewhere (*FR* 135; H 1972*a*), and as Professor David Lyons (1965) has argued more rigorously, equivalent to (3). Mr David Richards (1971) has expounded a theory of type (2), and he, in turn, is heavily influenced by Professor Rawls's views, although I hesitate even to summarize the latter until I have read *A Theory of Justice* (1971), which at the time of writing is still unpublished. Many other writers both in the past and recently have put forward theories which approximate to one or another of these types. A clear display of their practical equivalence would therefore be of some significance for moral philosophy, and have practical moral implications far beyond the issue of war and massacre raised by Nagel.

The ideal observer theory (as I shall summarize it) holds that in considering what we ought to do, we have to conform our thought to what would be said by a person who had access to complete knowledge of all the facts, was absolutely clear in his thinking, was impartial between all the parties affected by the action, and yet equally benevolent to them all. That is to say, we are to think like a person who gives equal, and positive, weight to the interests of all the parties and to nothing else, and in serving these makes no factual or conceptual errors.

The rational contractor theory (in the version I shall discuss) holds that what we ought to do is to follow those principles which would be adopted by a set of rational people, each prudently considering his own interest, who were seeking agreement with each other on the principles which should govern their conduct in a society of which they were to be members; these rational contractors are presumed to have complete knowledge of all facts about the society and the environment in which they are to live, *except* the particular role which is to be played by each individual one of them.

It is easy to see that these two theories are practically equivalent. For, firstly, the requirement of knowledge of the facts is common to both theories. The ideal observer, it is true, has access to one sort of fact of which the rational contractors have to be ignorant—namely the role which each individual plays. But this will make no difference, because the ideal observer, being required to be impartial between individuals, can make no use of this extra piece of knowledge in his moral thinking. Secondly, we may presume that the rational contractors, being rational, will, like the ideal observer, make no conceptual errors. Thirdly, the requirement that the ideal observer be impartial between individuals is exactly matched by the requirement that the rational contractors be ignorant of the individual roles which they are to play. For to be impartial (in the sense in which I shall be using the term) is to take no account of individuals *qua* those individuals; and it makes no difference whether this is done because of a direct requirement that no account be taken, or because no account *can* be taken owing to ignorance of which individual is to play which role. And lastly, the requirement that the ideal observer be benevolent is matched by the requirement that the rational contractors be prudent. We have already seen that both will give equal weight to the interests of all parties; that this equal weight will be positive is guaranteed in the one case by express stipulation, and in the other by the requirement that the rational contractors be prudent, i.e. consider their own interests. This, in conjunction with equality of weight, entails impartial *benevolence*.

It might be objected that the rational contractor theory introduces the notion of *principles* to be followed, whereas the ideal observer theory does not. But it does by implication. If no account is to be taken of individual (as opposed to qualitative) differences, the ideal observer will have to make his moral judgements in the form of principles expressed in purely universal terms; any individual name that occurred in them would have to be excluded as an irrelevancy. We see here how the feature of moral judgements which position (5) makes explicit, namely universalizability, is implicitly, but essentially, a feature of (1) and (2). As we shall see in a moment, it is also a feature of (3) and (4), which we must consider next.

I mean by *specific* rule-utilitarianism a type of rule-utilitarianism whose rules (or principles, as I prefer to call them) are allowed to be of unlimited specificity provided that

they do not cease to be universal.[1] It is thus the practical
equivalent of (4), namely an act-utilitarianism which accepts
the meta-ethical view that moral judgements are universalizable. Positions (3) and (4) are practically equivalent,
because (4), in accepting universalizability, admits that moral
judgements made (on a utilitarian basis) about individual acts
commit their maker also to principles applying to all precisely
similar acts; and this is tantamount to accepting *specific* rule-
utilitarianism. I shall therefore not deal with (4) separately.
(3) holds that we ought on any occasion to do that act which is
required by the set of principles whose universal observance
would best serve the interests of all. For reasons given by
Lyons, it will be possible for an act-utilitarian to force such a
rule-utilitarian, since his principles *can* be as specific as he
pleases, to *make* them specific enough to suit the particularities
of each individual case; thus, again, (3) collapses into (4), as
well as vice versa.

It now looks plausible to say that (3) and (4) come for
practical purposes to the same thing as (1) and (2). I think
that this is so, although the problem of distributive justice, to
be mentioned shortly, might make me qualify this claim. The
similarities, in any case, are obvious. The requirements of
factual knowledge and of conceptual clarity are there as
before; for one cannot successfully undertake utilitarian
calculations without both of these. This is not to say that it is
no use *trying* to do them unless one is perfect in these respects;
here, as in the case of the first two theories, we are told what
moral thought would be if done correctly, and enjoined to aim
at this (though, as we shall see, a big practical qualification is
needed here). The requirement of impartiality has been a part
of utilitarianism at least since Bentham's 'Everybody to count
for one and nobody for more than one'; and these varieties are
no exception, since impartiality is guaranteed by the stipulation
that the principles must be universal. They cannot even
mention individuals. The requirement of benevolence is
secured by the reference to serving the interests of all.

Coming now to the universal prescriptivist theory, we can
see that it exhibits, in perhaps the clearest form of all, the

---

[1] For the distinction between generality (the opposite of specificity) and
universality, see *FR* 38 f.; H 1972*a*.

essential features of the other four theories. It holds, on the basis of its analysis of the moral concepts, that when I am making up my mind what I ought to do, I am making up my mind what to prescribe for all cases exactly like this one in their universal properties. It should be evident that if this is what I am doing, I shall have to find out, first of all, just what I *am*, in effect, prescribing. This entails arming myself with the factual knowledge of what I should be bringing about if I acted upon one or another of the prescriptions between which I am deciding. It is part of this theory, too, that conceptual clarity is a necessary condition of rational moral thought. Impartiality is guaranteed by the fact that my prescription has to apply to all cases resembling this one in their universal properties; since these will include cases (hypothetical or actual) in which I myself play the roles of each of the other parties affected, I am put by this theory in exactly the same position as the rational contractors. And benevolence is secured by the element of prescriptivity. Since I am prescribing actions which will affect the interests of myself and of others, and am bound to treat the interests of others as of equal weight to my own, we may presume that this weight will be at least positive. I shall not inquire here whether this last presumption could be defended a priori.

This is hardly the place to elaborate and defend the five theories that I have been trying to merge with one another. Nor shall I even ask what other theories might also be merged with them, though it is obviously tempting to suggest that by making God the ideal observer (as in effect Butler does) some varieties of theological ethics could be brought in. It is worth mentioning, however, that there are at least four difficulties which all five of these theories have to face, and that this lends some support to my proposed merger. Three of these difficulties I shall simply list; but I shall deal at greater length with the fourth, since it has a close bearing on the dispute between Brandt and Nagel.

The first difficulty is that presented by the problem of distributive justice. So far, we do not know what the ideal observer, or the rational contractors, or I when I am universally prescribing will do when we are faced with a choice between maximizing benefits and distributing them in other ways which, though reducing their total, might be thought preferable for other reasons (for example, on grounds of fairness). Various such ways have been suggested—e.g. equality, the Pareto principle, and the maximin principle. Mr Richards has not convinced me that there is a unique answer to the question of what the rational contractors would do when faced with such a choice (it might depend on how much gambling instinct they had); and the ideal observer is in the same trouble, as is the universal prescriber.

It has been traditional among utilitarians to say that benefits should be maximized whatever their distribution; and this puts them at variance not only with common opinion but with some exponents of the other kinds of theory—(1), (2), and (5)—that I have been summarizing. It might therefore be objected to my proposed merger that the five theories are not even practically equivalent, since (3) and (4)—the utilitarian theories—are committed to a particular answer to the question about distributive justice, whereas for the other theories the question at least remains open. My own tentative view is that it will not remain open once the implications of the three non-utilitarian theories have been fully understood, but that they too will be bound to accept the answer which requires maximization of benefits, though this answer will be qualified, and at the same time brought more into accord with received opinion, by the moves which I shall shortly make in discussing the fourth difficulty. I shall not try to defend this view here (see paper 14).

The second difficulty is that of justifying the enterprise of moral thought in the first place: What are we to say to the amoralist who just will not use the language whose logic requires him to reason in this way? The third difficulty is that presented by the fanatic who is prepared to prescribe universally that some particular ideal or goal of his should be realized at the expense of all other interests of himself and others. Both these difficulties affect all five theories—the second difficulty obviously, the third less obviously. But we can see that the third does affect the other four as much as it affects universal prescriptivism, if we consider that to have a fanatical ideal is to have an interest in its realization. If the

fanatic's interest in the realization of his ideal is great enough
to trouble the universal prescriptivist, it will be great enough
to claim a preponderant weight in the calculations of all the
other four theories. All five theories will have to be content to
say that fanatics of such heroic stature are unlikely ever to be
encountered (see *MT* 170 ff.). But I shall not pursue this
argument here.

The fourth difficulty, however, is one which must be dealt
with at greater length, although an adequate treatment of it
will have to wait for another occasion. All these theories,
unless they take precautions, will appear to have consequences
which run counter to the intuitions of the ordinary man. Nagel
is the latest of many thinkers to try to take advantage of this
apparent weakness in utilitarianism and related theories. It is
easy for him to think up cases in which a utilitarian calculation would seem to justify actions contrary to principles which
most of us, at least when we are not philosophizing, hold
sacred. On careful inspection it will turn out that these
cases are either fictitious or at least highly unusual, or else
that the utilitarian calculations are very sketchily done,
leaving out considerations which in practice would be most
important. Nagel himself refers to 'the abyss of utilitarian
apologetics', and a utilitarian can readily admit that it is
possible by a too superficial or facile application of utilitarian
arguments to justify courses of action which a more thoroughgoing utilitarianism would condemn. But all the same, many
have been put off utilitarianism by this move, which takes a
good deal of methodological sophistication to counter.

Brandt, with his 'two-level' approach, has given a clear
indication of the way in which a utilitarian can defend himself
against this attack. I wish, however, to set this defence within
a more general framework of ethical theory, without claiming
that Brandt would agree with all that I say. The 'sacred
principles' of the ordinary man, and the rules of war which are
a crude attempt to apply them to a particular practical sphere,
have an established place in any complete utilitarian theory;
unfortunately utilitarians have not sufficiently emphasized
this, and therefore 'absolutists' have some excuse for ignoring
it. Confusion has resulted on both sides from a failure to make

clear what this established place is. The best *name* for it is that chosen by the deontologist Ross: 'prima facie'. Indeed, it would have been better for Nagel to use, to describe the view which he expounds, the old name 'deontologist', instead of adopting the term 'absolutist', which invites confusion with the kind of absolutist who is the opponent of relativism (whatever that may be). I trust that Nagel does not think that his utilitarian opponents are relativists. But although 'prima facie' is a good name for these principles, it does not do much to explain their nature.

The defect in most deontological theories (and this would seem to apply to Ross, Anscombe, and Nagel) is that they have no coherent rational account to give of any level of moral thought above that of the man who knows some good simple moral principles and sticks to them. He is a very admirable person; and to question his principles (at any rate in situations of stress and temptation) is indeed to 'show a corrupt mind'.[2] But if philosophers do no more thinking than he is capable of, they will be able to give no account, either of how we are to come by these admirable principles, or of what we are to do when they conflict.

To achieve such an account, we have to adopt a 'two-level' approach. We have, that is to say, to recognize that the simple principles of the deontologist, important as they are, have their place at the level of character-formation (moral education and self-education). They are what we should be trying to inculcate into ourselves and our children if we want to stand the best chance, amid the stresses and temptations of the moral life, of doing what is for the best. Moore (who was a utilitarian) perhaps exaggerates when he says that we should *never* break principles which we know to be in general sound (1903: 162 ff.); but a utilitarian who takes his utilitarianism seriously is likely to recommend that we form in ourselves, and continue in all our actions to foster, a firm disposition to abide by the principles whose general inculcation will have, all in all, the best consequences.

The inculcation of these general principles has always been a prime concern of churches and other moral 'authorities'; but

---

[2] This phrase is used in a slightly different context by Professor G. E. M. Anscombe (1958: 17).

in the present context it is more relevant to point out that this
is equally true of armies. In the case of the typical military
virtues this is obvious. Courage in attack and stubbornness in
defence are strenuously cultivated; and the duty to obey
orders and not to run away in battle is the centre of all
military training. These are not moral duties in the narrow
sense (though their cultivation is instrumental to the perform-
ance of our moral duty when we are fighting in just wars, if
any). If armies were to say to soldiers when training them,
'On the battlefield, always do what is most conducive to the
general good of mankind', or even 'of your countrymen',
nearly all the soldiers would easily convince themselves
(battles being what they are) that the course most conducive
to these desirable ends was headlong flight. Instead they say,
'Leave those calculations to your superiors; they are probably
in some bunker somewhere out of immediate personal danger,
and therefore can consider more rationally and dispassionately,
and with better information than you have, the question of
whether to withdraw. Your job is to get on with the fighting.'
Only in this way can wars be won; and *if* the wars are just, the
training was for the best. It is beyond the scope of this paper
to discuss whether there are any just wars; I am inclined to
think that there have been such in the past, though whether
there could be just wars under modern conditions (except
perhaps minor ones) is a hard question into which I shall not
enter (see H 1966 and p. 74 below).

The same is true of the more narrowly moral virtues. Let us
assume for the sake of argument that it is for the greatest good
that marital fidelity should be generally practised. I could
produce good arguments, concerned especially with the
welfare of children, to show that this is so; but this is not the
place for them. To say this is consistent with admitting that
there may be cases in which adultery would be for the greatest
good—for I said 'generally' and not 'universally'. But fidelity
will not be even generally practised if people who are
contemplating adultery ask themselves on each occasion
whether their own might not be one of these cases; they will
persuade themselves all too often that it is, when it is not. It is
for the greatest good that statesmen should in general not tell
lies in their public utterances—we have recently had an

example of the troubles that ensue when they do, and Suez was another. It is true, admittedly, that situations can arise (say, when a currency is in trouble) in which it is quite obvious to a statesman that he ought to tell a lie; and this sort of thing can happen in private life too (which is why the ordinary man does not, for the most part, accept the duty of truth-telling as one without exceptions). But if statesmen and other men too do not cultivate the firm disposition to tell the truth and to hate lying, they will, both in this failure itself and in their particular acts, be most probably not acting for the best.

For the same reasons, as Brandt has indicated, military training should (and in all civilized armies does) include instruction in the laws and usages of war; and this training should be backed up by legal enforcement where possible. It looks as if the failure adequately to do this, and not any particular massacres and atrocities, ought to be the main target of critics of the United States Army in the present war (though it must be said in fairness that wars against guerrillas present peculiarly difficult problems). Even when armies are fighting wars which can be morally justified (if any), the individual soldier ought to be enabled to have as clear an idea of what he can legitimately do to the enemy as he has of when he can legitimately turn his back on the enemy. Neither kind of instruction is easy, but both are possible.

The crucial question remains of what principles are to be the basis of this training. Brandt has sketched in a most illuminating way the kind of method by which this can be rationally determined; it amounts to an application of the five methods of moral reasoning which I was trying to merge at the beginning of this paper. He has also reached some provisional conclusions by this method; with these in the main I agree, though much more discussion is obviously needed.

A stumbling block to the understanding of the method may possibly be removed if I point out that there are in play here, in different parts of the reasoning, two quite distinct things which might both be called rule-utilitarianism. The failure to distinguish between them, and to see that they are quite compatible with each other provided that their spheres are kept separate, has caused havoc in this part of moral philosophy. There is first of all what may be called *general* rule-utilitarianism. This is the doctrine, supported in the last section, which says that we ought to inculcate and foster in ourselves and others, and in our actions cleave to, general principles whose cultivation is for the greatest good. In terms of a distinction which has been used in discussions of this subject, the utility appealed to by general rule-utilitarianism is an *acceptance*-utility—i.e. the utility of the general acceptance of certain principles, even if it falls short of universal observance. Such an insistence on having good general, fairly simple, teachable principles is essential to any view which takes the task of moral education (including self-education) seriously.

Secondly, there is what I have called *specific* rule-utilitarianism, one of the five mergeable theories which I listed at the beginning. This provides a kind of microscope wherewith we can, when we are in doubt about the general principles, examine particular cases in as minute specificity as we require, though always ending up with universal judgements, however specific. When using specific rule-utilitarianism we judge the morality of a particular act by assessing the utility of universal *observance* of the highly specific principle which requires acts of just this sort in just this sort of circumstances. By thus assessing particular acts in terms of the *observance*-utility of the highly specific universal principles enjoining them, we can assess the *acceptance*-utility of the general principles to be used in moral education. Once general principles are questioned, they can only be examined thus in the light of the particular results of their general adoption (of whether the policy of inculcating these principles is conducive *in general* to actions which can be thus minutely justified). Specific rule-utilitarianism thus has its place in higher-level discussions as to what the 'good general principles' ought to be, and what should be done in cases where they conflict, or where there is a strong indication that the situation is so peculiar that the application of the general principle is unlikely to be for the best.

How are we to decide which cases these are? This is a matter for practical judgement rather than for theoretical reasoning (for the question is 'Ought we to reason theoretically? Have we time? Are we likely to indulge in special pleading if we do?'). It might be objected to what I have said that although I have in theory allotted separate spheres to these two kinds of utilitarian reasoning, so that in principle they do not conflict, I have failed to say how we are to determine into which sphere any particular piece of reasoning is to fall. But the objection is not a real one. When faced with a choice between sticking to one of the simple general principles we have learnt and engaging in more specific reasoning, we have to ask ourselves which procedure is likely to approximate to the result which would be achieved by a reasoner not hampered by our human frailties. On the one side, there is the danger that a too rigid adherence to the standard general principles will lead us to disregard special features of the situation which ought to make a difference to our appraisal of it. On the other side, there is the danger that, if we once allow ourselves to question the general principle, our lack of knowledge and our partiality to our own interests may distort our reasoning. Which of these dangers is likely to be greater in a particular case for a particular person is not a philosophical question, and it is therefore no objection to a philosophical position that it does not answer it. My own inclination, in the light of my assessment of my own limitations, is to think that the occasions on which I should be safe in departing from my firm general principles (which are not of *extreme* generality) are very rare.

It is worth pointing out that when, by the employment of specific rule-utilitarianism at the higher level, we are seeking to select the best general principles for our general rule-utilitarianism of the lower level, we ought to consider those cases which are likely to occur. The use of hypothetical examples in philosophy, even fanciful ones, is perfectly legitimate; but in this particular field it can lead us astray. For we are seeking to discover principles which will be the most reliable in cases which are likely to preponderate in our actual experience; it would be out of place, therefore, to base our selection of the principles on a consideration of fanciful cases.

My aim has been to convince the reader that a sound

theoretical foundation can in principle be provided for moral thinking about war, and that this foundation is available to Brandt and to those who seek to put his conclusions into practice. They are much more likely on this basis than on an 'absolutist' one to secure an improvement in our present customs, either by new international conventions or simply by the preservation and spread of right attitudes in soldiers and their commanders and governments. A great deal has been achieved in the past along these lines (do Nagel and those who write like him about the present war ever read what the wars of earlier centuries were like?). Although the invention of new weapons brings with it new temptations, which are often succumbed to, especially by those who have a temporary monopoly of these weapons, it is not impossible to bring their use under control, provided that their potential users are willing to adopt rational procedures in discussing the matter with one another. This is asking a lot; but the history of such negotiations is not exclusively a history of failure. In World War II poison gas was not, after all, used, though many expected that it would be. In both the world wars the Red Cross was for the most part respected. Without some background of written or unwritten international convention, neither of these restraints might have been exercised; and the conventions owed more to rational thought than to emotion, even if the reasoning had more of prudence in it than of morality.

Against these modest gains, I do not think that Nagel has much to offer. He is trying to justify the very same kind of rules as Brandt has, in my view, succeeded in justifying. But whereas Brandt is able to fit these rules into a rational system which also provides means for their selection and justification, Nagel, who is confined to one level of moral thinking, predictably finds himself torn between utilitarian arguments and absolutist ones, and thinks that in difficult cases he may be in 'a moral blind alley', in which 'there is no honorable or moral course for a man to take, no course free of guilt and responsibility for evil'. It is dangerous to talk like this, because many people will think that, if there is no way of escaping guilt, only the neurotic will worry about it.

Is 'guilt', in any case, the most appropriate concept in terms of which to discuss these problems? A man with good moral principles will be very likely to *feel* guilty whatever he does in cases such as Nagel is speaking of. If he did not, he would not be such a good man. For a person, on the other hand, who is mainly concerned to avoid feelings of guilt, the best advice is to grow a thick skin. If he finds this impossible, a *pis aller* would be to get himself a set of not too exacting principles of an absolutist sort, and think that he has done all that is required of him if he has not broken any of them—no matter how disastrous the consequences of his actions for other people. Though Nagel is perfectly right in saying that it is incoherent to suggest that one might 'sacrifice one's moral integrity justifiably, in the service of a sufficiently worthy end', it is not incoherent to suggest that one might so sacrifice one's peace of mind. And moral integrity and peace of mind are easily confused if one equates having sinned with having a sense of having sinned. If, say, we are theists and can convince ourselves that God has laid down some relatively simple rules and that by observing these we can keep ourselves unspotted and safe from hell-fire, this may seem a good way of avoiding the agony of mind which comes, in difficult cases, from calculation of the consequences of alternative actions. This may explain the undoubted attractions of absolutism.

The real Nagel, to his credit, avoids this kind of Pharisaism; for he remains enough of a utilitarian to see that the implications of consistent absolutism are unacceptable. That is how he gets into his 'moral blind alley'; but there is an obvious way out of it: to treat the general principles of the absolutist as indispensable practical guides, but not as epistemologically sacrosanct, and to admit a level of thought at which they can be criticized, justified, or even on occasion rejected in their particular applications when conflicts arise or when a case is sufficiently out of the ordinary to call for special consideration.

But even if there were not this defect in Nagel's absolutism—that of trying to give his principles a higher status than they can have, and thus locking them in irresoluble conflict, on the same level, with the utilitarian principle in which he also believes—it would be defective for another reason: indeterminacy. He attempts to systematize and justify his intuitions by subsuming them under a more general principle: 'whatever one does to another person intentionally must be aimed at him as a subject, with the intention that he receive it as a subject. It should manifest an attitude to *him* rather than just to the situation, and he should be able to recognize it and identify himself as its object.' It is difficult to think that a principle as vague and obscure as this could be of much use in practical dilemmas. One would be likely to find rival parties justifying opposite courses of action on the basis of this same principle. We have grown accustomed to moral philosophers telling us that we can ascertain our duties to other people by appeal to an a priori principle that we ought to treat people as people (see *FR* 211–3). But Nagel's is an unexpected use of the method, which displays how accommodating it can be. He has done nothing to show that one could not treat people as people just as well by hating them as by loving them. The simplest way, in dealing with the enemy and his friends and relations, of 'manifesting an attitude to *them*', would be to learn to hate them. Then we can manifest this attitude by any barbarity that takes our fancy, in the assurance that we are not doing what Nagel's principle forbids. This would seem as good a way as any of avoiding being 'bureaucratic', and of securing the 'maintenance of a direct interpersonal response to the people one deals with'.

In the days before wars became even as humane as they *sometimes* are now, this was an almost universal attitude. Anyone who reads the Bible, or Herodotus and Thucydides, can find massacres of *already defeated* peoples accepted as normal; and Priam in the *Iliad* (22.60 ff.), when he describes the horrors that await him at the 'kill', when Troy is sacked, does not imply that the actions of the victors will be wicked— only unpleasant.

I have probably got Nagel all wrong. Brandt interprets him more charitably; and maybe all he is saying is that moral judgements have to be universalizable. That is to say, we are to think of those affected by our actions, including the enemy, as people like ourselves, and do to them only what is permitted by a set of universal principles that we are prepared to see adopted for cases in which we are at the receiving end.

If this is what he is saying, his position is not so very different from my own. The difference is that I would include more people in the class of those whose sufferings are relevant to our moral decisions (for example, in the Hiroshima case, those that will die if the war is not ended quickly, as well as those actually killed by the bombing). I cannot find in Nagel's argument any justification for leaving the former class out; but if they are included, this version of the method he advocates will join the list of mergeable positions set out at the beginning of this paper. Only further clarification will reveal whether our views can be reconciled in this way.

6
Philosophy and Practice: Some Issues about War and Peace

I CAN honestly say that Professor Ayer is more responsible than anybody else for putting me on the right track in moral philosophy. He did this by convincing me, when young, that the ways people were doing it at that time had no future. In the famous chapter on ethics in his marvellously readable and exciting book, *Language, Truth and Logic*, Ayer was thought to be trying to show that moral philosophy itself, and perhaps even ordinary first-order moral thinking, was a waste of time. From later work of his, and from his occasional pronouncements about moral and political questions, it is evident that the second of these slanders was false. But even on the theoretical side the lessons I learnt from his book were positive as well as negative. That is not to say that the negative lessons were unimportant. Some people have still not absorbed them, and continue to waste our time. But here are two positive points in Ayer's book, which for me were crucial.

The first also occurs in Carnap and some other emotivists. Ayer says, 'It is worth mentioning that ethical terms do not serve only to express feeling. They are calculated also to arouse feeling, and so to stimulate action. Indeed, some of them are used in such a way to give the sentences in which they occur the effect of commands' (1936: 108). This made me think that, even if moral judgements (or ethical sentences, as it was then the fashion to call them) do not *state* anything, as Ayer maintained, because they are not in the strict sense statements, it is going much too far to say, as he slips into saying, that they do not *say* anything (ibid.). When I tell someone to do something (for example to mind the step), I am saying something to him—something which he has to

From *Philosophy and Practice*, ed. A. P. Griffiths (Royal Inst. of Ph. Lectures 19, suppl. to *Philosophy* 59, Cambridge UP, 1985). Professor Ayer took the chair at the lecture.

understand if my communication is to be successful; and there is
no more reason for philosophers to neglect this kind of saying
than any other. That this was only a slip is clear from the fact
that Ayer himself, like Carnap, has his own account to give of
what 'ethical sentences' do say. Though I have never agreed
with this emotivist account, and always resented it when
people who did not understand the issue called me an
emotivist (perhaps because they adopted a quite untenable
emotivist account of the meaning of imperatives, as Ayer does
in the passage I have quoted) I took the point that there were
other things that moral judgements might be besides statements of empirical fact, or statements, in the narrow
descriptive sense, of any kind. This set me thinking what
could be their role in language; and of course the idea that
there are many different language games, many different
kinds of speech act, was already becoming familiar through
the work of Wittgenstein and Austin—the latter, in particular, being impelled to attack what he called 'the descriptive fallacy' by the work of the emotivists (1961: 234; 1962:
3).

In looking for a non-emotivist account of moral judgements
which could still survive the criticisms brought by the
emotivists, I was helped by the second positive point I got
from *Language, Truth and Logic*. When he is discussing the
objection that it must be possible to argue seriously about
moral questions because undoubtedly the discipline called
'casuistry' exists, Ayer says, 'Casuistry is not a science. It is a
purely analytical investigation of the structure of a given
moral system. In other words it is an exercise in formal logic'
(1936: 112). The ideas that moral judgements might be in
some ways like imperatives, and that, nevertheless, they can
be constituents in logical inferences and can therefore,
presumably, enter into logical relations, set me thinking. I was
determined to do moral philosophy, because I wanted to have
some help with practical moral questions which troubled me,
like the one I am going to talk about later, when I have
finished reminiscing. Could it be that the task of the moral
philosopher was to explore these logical relations, and on
them base an account of moral reasoning?

It was clear to me from the start that moral judgements

were not in all respects like the imperatives of ordinary speech. In my first book I pointed out the main differences, and said that it was 'no part of my purpose to "reduce" moral language to imperatives' (*LM* 2). Could it be, however, that they shared some of their characteristics, notably that of action-guidingness or prescriptivity? This would already make it impossible to treat them just like ordinary statements of fact. These can, indeed, in a sense guide actions; but not in the sense in which imperatives or, as I thought, moral judgements do. So in his negative contentions Ayer was right. All this might be true, although they shared *other* characteristics with descriptive statements, in particular the characteristic known as universalizability: the feature that two acts, etc., cannot differ in their possession or non-possession of some moral property P if they have all their descriptive properties in common (H 1984). As I pointed out in my second book (*FR* 11), an analogous feature holds trivially of descriptive statements too; but its possession by moral judgements is so far from being trivial as to be the foundation of any satisfactory theory of moral reasoning.

A lot of other features go with this feature of universalizability, among them the element in the meaning of moral judgements which since Stevenson's book *Ethics and Language* (1944) has been called 'descriptive meaning', and their undoubted possession of which still misleads people who ought to know better into thinking that they are *in all respects* like purely descriptive statements.

The idea that in moral thinking we are trying to find prescriptions which we are prepared to universalize to all exactly similar cases, even those in which we would be the victims, is of course a highly Kantian one. But it also led me in a utilitarian direction. For if you are trying to find such prescriptions when you are deciding what moral judgements to make, you will have to treat other people as if they were yourself. If you are not prepared to say that it ought to be done to you, you must not say that you ought to do it to somebody else. And so we have to love our neighbour as ourselves, which means treating his or her preferences as of equal weight to our own. And since the weight we give to our own preferences is positive, we shall be seeking the satisfactions of the preferences of all equally; and we shall have done our best if we maximize those satisfactions over all those affected considered impartially, which is exactly what the utilitarians are recommending. So Bentham's slogan 'Everybody to count for one, nobody for more than one' (Mill 1861: ch. 5) takes its place, along with Kant's other formulations of his categorical imperative, as an equivalent expression to his first and main formulation in terms of willing the maxim of one's action to be a universal law.

There are well-canvassed objections to utilitarianism. After I had satisfied myself, guided by Kant, that it had a firm basis in the logic of the moral concepts, I naturally returned to these objections, to see what force they had. I very soon realized that they were nearly all the result of failing to recognize that our moral thinking takes place at more than one level. This is an old idea. It is to be found already in Socrates, who started moral philosophy. He distinguished between what he called knowledge and what he called right opinion (*Meno* 98b). In this he was followed by Plato and by Aristotle. Although the idea is overlaid in these writers by descriptivist ideas, the essential point can be taken over into a non-descriptivist system. The idea is that for much, indeed most, of the time when we think morally it is all right—indeed desirable and necessary—that we should not stop to give reasons for what we think, or work out all the pros and cons. The 'right opinion' of the morally well-educated person will guide him as well as any sophisticated reasoning process (ibid. 97b). If one were clear enough about the 'that' there will be no need to have the 'why' as well (Aristotle 1095b 6). This is true of the everyday level of moral thinking (what I call in *MT* 25 ff. the 'intuitive' level).

But this level is not self-sustaining (as Plato and Aristotle well recognized, although many of Aristotle's self-styled followers have not). This is because we do need to know why the intuitions we have are the right ones (people sometimes have wrong intuitions); and so we need a higher level of thinking which will determine this. Aristotle is quite clear that for virtue, properly so called, practical wisdom (*phronēsis*) is required as well as the moral virtues (1144b 31). Also, we often get into situations in which our intuitions conflict (I am going to illustrate this in a moment). Not only do the intuitions of different people conflict, but a single person's different intuitions may conflict with one another, so that whatever he does, he will be erring against deep moral convictions that he has. Only a higher level of moral thinking (I call it the 'critical' level) can then resolve the conflict.

The classical utilitarians Bentham and John Stuart Mill (1861: ch. 5) adopted this division of moral thinking into two levels in order to answer their critics. Whether they got it from Socrates I do not know. It provides an answer, because nearly all the standard objections to utilitarianism rely on an appeal to our common moral convictions: utilitarians are supposed to have to outrage these by requiring us to do things which either infringe people's 'manifest' rights or are in some other way 'obviously' wrong. The utilitarian can answer that of course we have these intuitions, and should have them, because it is highly desirable from the utilitarian point of view that people should be brought up in this way. Having been so brought up, they will have the intuitions, and these will lead them to do the right things nearly all the time, if they follow them. If this were not so, the intuitions would not be the best intuitions to have; their upbringing would not have been sound. But if you want to determine what *are* the best intuitions, or the best upbringing, it is no use appealing to the intuitions you have been brought up with. They are what is in question, and they may not have been for the best. You have to do some critical thinking, and this is utilitarian. The best intuitions to have are those which, in general, will lead people to act for the best; and these are the ones which a sound upbringing will inculcate, and which wise moral thinkers will cultivate and respect. If they disregard them in the supposed interests of utility, they will most likely get it wrong and not act for the best, and therefore will not have been showing themselves good utilitarians. For it is almost impossible for us to calculate exactly the consequences of our actions, and there are many other dangers which attend the pursuit of expediency—dangers which a utilitarian who knows the moves in this argument can easily recognize. Once the levels of moral thinking are distinguished, nearly all these standard objections to utilitarianism collapse. For it turns out that a utilitarian also (even what is called an act-utilitarian) would bid us follow our intuitions in all clear cases, because that gives us the highest expectation of utility.

As I said, I took over this defence of utilitarianism from earlier thinkers. What came as a pleasant surprise to me was that the same manœuvre also enables one to understand why people find it so hard to accept the kind of non-descriptivism which I had come to see as the only viable way of applying philosophical thought to practical problems. If you have had a stable moral education, as most of us have, you will think that you *know* that certain things are wrong. You *cannot doubt* that they are wrong. This is because you have been taught that they are wrong, and the teaching has stuck. If it was sound teaching, that is all for the best. So you will naturally give to these deliverances of conscience the status of *facts*, and will think that any philosopher like Professor Ayer who calls in question their factual status is morally subversive. Actually Ayer and his fellow emotivists were the saviours of morality from the dead end into which descriptivists of various breeds were, and still are, trying to lead it. But people did not understand this; and his book was thrown into the fire or out of the window by the good and great.

In *MT* I have been into all this in some detail, and it would be inappropriate in a paper about philosophy and practice to go into the arguments and counter-arguments at length. This has therefore been only a sketch. I am going to content myself with merely affirming that a rational non-descriptivism can, and descriptivism of all kinds cannot, provide the person who is troubled about practical moral problems with a way of sorting them out. The reason why no kind of descriptivism can do this is that the essentially practical nature of morality is ignored by it. We need a way of reasoning about what we should *do*, and this no kind of descriptivism can provide.

I am going to illustrate the way that I advocate by discussing one of the most troubling sets of problems of all (and the one that made me myself into a moral philosopher in the first place), namely problems about war. I am going to explain first of all why people become pacifists, and why they would not become pacifists if they did some more careful

critical thinking. I shall then try to say in what sense
patriotism is a virtue, and in what sense it is a vice. And I will
leave a little time at the end to say something (not much,
because I am no expert) about nuclear disarmament. A
philosopher as such cannot hope to decide that issue, because
it requires knowledge that philosophy by itself does not yield.
But he can at least say clearly what the issue is; and that I
shall try to do.

The two-level structure of moral thinking that I have been
advocating puts us in a position to explain how a great many
people now become pacifists. We are most of us nowadays
brought up to abhor violence. This was not always the case,
nor is it so in all cultures. But I take it for granted that critical
thinking would justify this upbringing in our present circumstances. That people think like this leads to there being less
violence in our life, and that is a very good thing. More harm
than good would come if people stopped condemning violence,
and instead cultivated the virtues admired by some football
supporters (not, I am sure, including Professor Ayer, in spite
of his love of the game). The very strong feelings which
support this principle of non-violence readily extend themselves to cover all violence which is similar in its effects on the
victim, no matter what its motives or justification.

But this is only an intuition, and might (indeed does)
conflict with other intuitions which, again, most of us have
acquired from our upbringing. I may mention especially ones
which require us to protect the weak, and in particular those,
such as our own families, to whom we are commonly thought
to have special duties. These special duties too we recognize
intuitively; and these intuitions can be defended in the same
way by critical thinking, because it is a very good thing, in
general, that we have them. A wise utilitarian educator would
seek to inculcate into his charges both these kinds of
intuitions: that is, both that which condemns violence, and
that which bids us protect the weak, especially our own
dependants. And it is very easy, and probably to a limited
extent right, for this latter set of duties too to get extended into
a general duty of loyalty to the group in which we find
ourselves living, often our country. This is probably the best
way for most people of protecting their dependants and

themselves, namely belonging to a stable community with the power to enforce law and resist external aggression.

Thus it is that there builds up a conflict between the two principles of non-violence and loyalty, and pacifists and patriots come into confrontation. Some more unworthy motives commonly reinforce the feelings of both: the patriot often appeals to sentiments of national pride of the '*über alles*' or 'wider still and wider' variety; and the pacifist is often (I speak from experience of my own feelings when I was attracted by pacifism) moved by fear of himself being involved in violence at the dirty end. This is, indeed, a sign of grace; for it at least shows that we have a lively sympathy for the victims of violence, and understanding of their situation. Sympathy is a vital ingredient in moral thinking, because only if we have it can we be sure that in universalizing our moral judgements we are doing so with an understanding of what their acceptance in cases where we were the victims would mean for us, i.e. what it is like to be at the receiving end.

What I have to suggest is that critical thinking *can* sort out these conflicts, as it can others. That is what it is for. We ought to be aiming at a resolution of them which will allow us to retain modified forms of the principle of non-violence and the principle of loyalty, and to be clear about which should override which in particular cases. It will then be possible to be at the same time a patriot of the right kind, and, without being an extreme pacifist of the Tolstoyan sort, to go on abhorring violence in nearly all cases. At any rate, that is my own position, and I think it yields defensible answers to particular questions about war.

I am going first of all to discuss the justification for having a principle requiring loyalty. A superficial thinker might suppose that, by founding my account of moral thinking on the thesis of the universalizability of moral judgements, I have ruled out particular loyalties. If I have to universalize all my moral judgements, how can I say that there are duties to particular people or groups who are related to *me* in certain ways (duties to *my* children or *my* country). This is really a rather elementary mistake, but it is so common even among professional philosophers that I am going to spend a few minutes explaining it.

To put it formally, the principle

For all *x* and *y*, if *y* is the child (or country) of *x*, then *x* has certain particular duties to *y*

is universal in the sense required by the thesis of the universalizability of moral judgements. It starts with a universal quantifier, or pair of them, 'For all *x* and *y* . . .', and contains no individual constants (references to individuals).

The idea that universalizability forbids particular loyalties is due to a confusion of this universal proposition with another which is not universal in the required sense:

a (some individual, say George) has certain particular duties to *a*'s child (or country).

Here there is an individual constant, '*a*' (standing in this case for a proper name). This second proposition *could* involve its holder in a breach of the thesis of universalizability; but only if he held it while refusing to universalize it. But he would not be breaking the thesis if he held it, but was prepared to universalize it by extending it to ascribe the duty to *anybody* in just the same situation. 'The same situation' must of course be taken as meaning that it is the same in all respects, including all the characteristics of people affected, and in particular their preferences—for otherwise we should find ourselves having to say that because *a* ought to do such and such to his child, who likes it (e.g. tickle his toes), *b* ought to do the same to his child, who detests it.

If the patriot is prepared to universalize the principle of his patriotism, he is in the clear so far as the thesis of universaliz-ability goes. This does not mean (and about this too there has been much confusion) that, just because a certain judgement passes the test of universalizability, in the formal sense that a universal judgement can be *framed* which it exemplifies, it must be acceptable. If someone is prepared to universalize his judgement, it *qualifies* as a moral judgement (provided of course that it satisfies the other formal qualifications). But that in itself is not a sufficient reason for accepting it (it might be eligible as a candidate, but be rejected by all the rest of us in favour of other candidates by critical thinking). The general form of the solution to the problem of what moral principles to accept, among those that qualify, is this: we are to accept those which we can approve by critical thinking for general adoption; and we shall approve those whose general adoption will do the best for all those affected considered impartially, not giving any special weight to any interest because it is ours, and not giving priority *in the critical thinking* (though we may at the intuitive level, for reasons explained below) to those related to us in particular ways, who cannot be identified without reference to ourselves as those individuals.

This complete impartiality at the critical level can justify the selection of principles requiring partiality at the intuitive level, if those are the principles whose general acceptance will most conduce to the good of all, considered impartially (H 1979). The question, therefore, that we have to ask is, what these principles are, in the field of people's attitudes to their countries. The answer will depend on a question of empirical fact: what are likely to be the consequences of the general acceptance of such principles by those who are likely to be got to accept them? Of course there will always be rogue elephants, and the calculation of consequences must allow for their existence; but what we are talking about are the principles whose general acceptance by peoples of good will— and I am optimistic enough to believe that these will be in the great majority—will be for the best. The problem of what to do about the rogues is especially difficult when we are discussing nuclear weapons.

I will start my discussion of patriotism with the premiss that government is necessary. I could by critical thinking justify the rejection of anarchism (see papers 2 to 4). Next, it does seem that the preservation of the political liberty of individuals and their meaningful participation in decisions of government by a democratic process requires the division of the world into territories of manageable size, in each of which its inhabitants have the responsibility for setting up and maintaining their own government. This is impossible if the inhabitants are for one reason or another (e.g. communal divisions) not able to share a common loyalty. That liberty and democracy are themselves good things I could show by a similar exercise of critical thinking, but there is not time for that (see pp. 124, 164). I would say that the United States and India have reached something near the limit of size at which, by present techniques, democratic government can be carried on—the latter perhaps straining at the limit. And even for non-democratic systems like Russia and China there is a size-limit. Certainly world government is at present impracticable, if by that is meant a world body which is responsible for all the functions of government. There is nothing, however, to stop smaller 'states', as they are usually called, grouping themselves into larger units to which they assign some of these functions; the European Community is an example.

If some such territorial division of responsibility exists, as it does, and as it is best that it should, the question arises of the duties of the inhabitants of each territory (the citizens of each state) to each other and to the state itself. It seems to me (as a matter of empirical fact) that there are certain ways of carrying on by the citizens which will greatly increase the preference-satisfactions in aggregate of all the citizens considered impartially, and that these would be, by a sound critical thinker, included in a set of principles laying down (to use an old-fashioned phrase) the 'duties of a citizen'. To give examples: such duties would include the duty not to evade taxes, and in general the duty to obey the law and assist in its enforcement (which does not exclude *some* law-breaking in exceptional circumstances when good moral reasons can be given for it; see pp. 21, 25). They include a duty to secure and preserve good laws, in particular by giving an informed vote in elections and by taking a part in the political process; the duty to resist encroachment on liberty by government agencies; to be willing to undertake service to the community, and in general to display what is known, in another old-fashioned phrase, as 'public spirit'. All these duties could be justified by the same kind of critical thinking as I am advocating; but I am going to confine myself to the duty, if there is one, to bear arms in defence of the state.

That brings us to the area of conflict *between* states, and to the question of the extent to which patriotism, the support of one's own state to the possible detriment of others, or at any rate the giving of priority to loyalty to one's own state, is a duty or a virtue. The application of our method to this question is in principle simple and is the same as before. In critical thinking we are not allowed to give priority to the interests of any state, or its inhabitants, just because it is our state. But critical thinking may, all the same, recommend to us certain *universal* principles laying down duties which *any* citizen has to *his* state. Or we could specify these principles further, without making them less universal, by saying that certain duties exist only in certain kinds of states (for example in a tyranny the citizen might have a duty to rebel).

If any principle is a candidate, formally speaking, for inclusion in the list, it will be accepted or rejected according to whether its general acceptance is likely to advance the preference-satisfactions of all the inhabitants of all the countries considered impartially. Even some quite partial principles will pass this test. For example, it is for the good of everybody in all nations, on the whole, that people should be politically active in relation to the governments of their own countries, but not in relation to the governments of other countries. One reason is that we do not know enough about the consequences of our interventions in the politics of other countries to be sure that we are acting for the best (see p. 170). I say 'on the whole', because there are exceptions to this rule; but they are few.

When it comes to bearing arms, the situation is more difficult. But at least in times when weapons were not so frightful, we can find good arguments for saying that people did right to defend their own territories against aggressors; and in default of a probably impracticable system of 'collective security' (as it used to be called in the days of the League of Nations), I do not see how else international order could be preserved even to the limited extent that it has been. The effect of forgoing the organized use of force to repel aggression would be a rapid growth of disorganized and probably much more damaging use of force, which would result in the weak going to the wall and a relapse into anarchy.

What this brings us to is a kind of patriotism which is morally acceptable, because we are prepared to prescribe it universally to the citizens of all countries and not just of our own. It is forbidden, however, to support their governments, either by bearing arms or in any other way, in the pursuit of aggressive policies. If there were room I could show how such utilitarian critical thinking can develop what I have just said into something like a version of the traditional doctrine of the just war. The difference between me and most just-war theorists is that they commonly base the doctrine on intuition, or on natural law (which is nothing but an appeal to intuition), or on supposed revelation. They are unable to give any reasons for their views, but a utilitarian can do this. Also, the principles of the just war are only intuitive prima facie principles; they are not necessarily applicable outside the range of situations for which they were developed. The views, however, may be the same in their content and practical implications—which is not to say that an absolutely clear and concrete formulation of these is yet available.

I should like to mention in passing that, if one looks at the patriotic attitudes that were widespread in most European countries before the First World War—patriotisms of the 'wider still and wider' sort—one notices (and perhaps some of my anti-utilitarian colleagues should be surprised at this) that a change to different attitudes has been brought about by what I can only call critical thinking on the part of the public. This is a confirmation of my theory about the two levels of moral thinking. People used to have those intuitions and those attitudes that led directly to the Great War (that was how the ruling classes in Britain and France and Germany and Austria were brought up). I am old enough to remember a generation in which such attitudes were dominant even in Britain. The appalling carnage of the war, floodlit by a succession of poets and novelists, convinced people that those attitudes had a very low acceptance-utility, and they were abandoned except in Germany and Italy. Their abandonment, after the Second World War, became almost universal in the West. This was real moral progress, and it was the result of critical thinking, albeit largely inarticulate.

The task for the critical thinker now is to determine what should replace those attitudes. I am arguing that it should not be pacifism, as many people think, but rather a non-aggressive kind of patriotism which all can share, and which permits the use of force in self-defence. My reason is that this is the only attitude that will preserve international order and stability (which is a dominant element in the preferences of anybody who thinks seriously about it) from the countries that

I called rogue elephants—I mean those whose governments do not share the same attitudes.

I should like to mention also that I wrote an earlier version of this paper to use as a lecture before the outbreak of the Falklands War, for delivery in the coming term to my class at Oxford. When the war started I began to wonder whether I should have to alter my views and my lecture as a result of it. But actually, by the time the war was over and I came to deliver my lecture, I did not see any reason to alter any of it except to refer to what had happened as an illustration of my thesis about patriotism. One thing I had done was to set myself a test to determine whether my opinion that we did right to resist the Argentinians was one that I would be prepared to universalize. I asked myself whether I thought that the Iranians were similarly justified in resisting the equally unlawful aggression of the Iraqis in the Gulf War. This was a good test, because I could not possibly accuse myself of bias in favour of the Iranian government, which is a regime as detestable as any. But I unhesitatingly answered that they were right to defend themselves; for unless those who are able to repel aggression do so, there will be no limit to aggressions in the world. The fact that on critical reflection I found that I could prescribe this universally made me think that my initial intuitions about the Falklands were the right ones. One can argue a lot about expediency and costs and benefits, and it is right to do so; but most good comes in the long run by having the kind of intuitions which made us resist the aggression of Argentina and the Iranians that of Iraq. In default of them any country that thinks it can grab anything will do so. I am not, of course, arguing that the *subsequent*, and the *present*, conduct of the Iranians is justified. Having resisted the aggression, they should have been ready to negotiate a peaceful settlement; and so should we be if the Argentinians would reciprocate.

So I am happy with this kind of defensive patriotism as it applies to wars with conventional weapons. But of course the situation is altered when we come to consider nuclear weapons. For there the notion of defence fades, and we have nothing left but the threat of retaliation. I am not going to have room to go in detail into the question of nuclear disarmament, unilateral or multilateral. But perhaps I can say some things which will help to get the issue clearer.

The first is that, as I hope to have shown, pacifism in general is not acceptable (it has, in fact, a very low acceptance-utility in the world as it is, given the existence of rogues). People become pacifists only because they overemphasize one of the intuitions with which they have been brought up at the expense of all the rest. Now the leaders of the CND have a way of saying that they are not pacifists, and I am sure that this is true of some of them. The fact remains that without the spread of pacifist sentiment, and without the considerable stiffening given to the movement by a very solid core of pacifists in it, it would not have had nearly the following that it has. To give just one example, would the Bishop of Salisbury's working party, which produced the report *The Church and the Bomb*, have come to just the conclusions that it did but for the presence on it of Canon Oestreicher, a committed and extremely persuasive pacifist? If we are to take seriously the arguments of CND supporters, we have to subtract from them everything which appeals to pacifism as a premiss, for this premiss will not stand up; and we have to see what is left.

The second thing I wish to say is that, as we all recognize, nuclear war would be so frightful that the avoidance of it must be the preponderant aim of anybody who is thinking critically and trying to maximize the satisfaction of people's preferences considered impartially. But this is very far from establishing the unilateralist case, because it could well be that the weakening of the West's power to retaliate would make a nuclear attack more, and not less, likely. I have to testify that there have been three occasions since the Second World War on which I have been really frightened that somebody might start a nuclear war. The first was during the Korean War. The second was during the Cuban missile crisis. Both of these dangers passed, and I am persuaded that the possession by the United States of nuclear weapons was a stabilizing factor in those crises; and so, perhaps, was their possession by the Russians. The third is now; and what frightens me now, more than anything before except those two crises, is the growth of the 'Peace' Movement. If the resolve of the Western alliance is called in question, anything can happen. These are only my inexpert opinions; but the question certainly needs to be argued, whether unilateral disarmament would make nuclear war more or less likely.

The third thing I wish to say is that the very novelty of our present situation—the fact that nuclear weapons are so many orders of magnitude more frightful than weapons were even in the recent past—makes moral intuitions (of all sorts) an insecure guide; for they were formed as a result of past experience, and our present situation is so different. This of course applies to various patriotic sentiments that people have—for example people, like some in this country, and more, apparently, in France, who insist that we must have an independent nuclear armament because otherwise we shall be admitting that we are second-rate. *La gloire* is not now a sensible object of policy. But it also applies to some sentiments on the other side. I am by no means as certain as the Bishop of Salisbury's group was that intuitive principles about the just war can be applied without further thought to our present situation.

I should also like to mention in particular the argument that what it would be wrong to do, it would be wrong to threaten to do. This seems to me to be a mere intuition, and one which cannot be sustained in all situations. It is a question of balancing the utilities and disutilities of possible alternative principles; and it seems to me that there could be, and well may be now, situations in which the expectation of utility, that is, of preference-satisfaction, would be maximized by making threats the carrying out of which would not maximize utility. If so, then a principle forbidding one to make such threats can at most be a prima facie principle; it can have exceptions. If it is claimed that the threat would not be believed because we are moral and will not carry it out, this shows insufficient understanding of human motivation. In face of the appalling disaster of nuclear war, deterrence is achieved by even a quite small possibility that the threat will be acted on.

Though I am not certain, I do think that, even with Hitler in 1939, who was a bit crazy, war would not have broken out if both sides had had nuclear weapons. And I also believe that if, or when, India and Pakistan have them, war on that subcontinent will be less, not more, likely, because they will then be afraid to indulge in the kind of more or less gentlemanly wars they have had in the recent past, for fear of starting something worse. I must add that the thought of Hitler, or even Mrs Gandhi and General Zia, having the bomb appalls me; but nevertheless what I have just said could be true.

Although intuitions are not a secure guide in this unfamiliar labyrinth, they are at least some guide, inasmuch as our present situation is not *totally* different from those which people have faced in the past, and formed their moral convictions accordingly. Though the technical situation is quite novel, the human reactions of the various parties are depressingly much the same as before. Since the difficulties in deciding what to do arise not so much from technical and games-theoretical complexities as from the unpredictability of the human agents involved, intuitions about what they will do may be all we have to go on. And perhaps these factual intuitions are more reliable than any moral intuitions. If you ask me what Mr Reagan or Mr Andropov is likely to do in a certain situation, I at least have some idea. Moral judgements, which are what we are trying to make, must depend on our assessment of the probable consequences of alternative actions (those philosophers who pretend otherwise are irresponsible as well as confused). And in assessing them the philosopher is no expert. That is why I am not now going to say more about nuclear disarmament, except this: what we all have to decide is what attitudes to it, and to war in general, give us the best chance of survival.

7

Rights, Utility, and Universalization: Reply to J. L. Mackie

MR MACKIE (1984) starts with a contrast between utilitarianism and what he calls 'right-based' views or theories such as he has himself advocated. I must therefore first ask some questions about this supposed distinction. My trouble is partly that some of the tenets which are said to distinguish right-based theories from utilitarianism are ones which I, a utilitarian, have no difficulty in assenting to; and partly that the basic distinction which is supposed to divide the two kinds of theory is one which entirely eludes me, although, to judge by the widespread use made of it, everybody else understands it perfectly well. Or can it be that what everybody else is doing is parroting a slogan with which John Rawls ends his otherwise more or less fair statement of his disagreements with utilitarianism? He says, 'Utilitarianism does not take seriously the distinction between persons' (1971: 27). This might suggest to a careless reader that utilitarians do not realize that there are distinct people in the world, with separate interests which have to be considered. But what utilitarian has ever denied this?

Mackie, at any rate, guards against this misinterpretation. But the question remains of what, if not this obvious truth, he is accusing the utilitarians of denying. What is it to 'insist, to the end, on the separateness of persons' (1984: 86)? What the utilitarian is doing is not denying this, but trying to give meaning to the requirement, on which Mackie himself lays stress, 'that everyone should have a fair go'. It is hard to see what this could mean, except, in Bentham's words, to 'count everybody for one and nobody for more than one' (Mill 1861: ch. 5 s.f.). But Mackie attacks the utilitarians for doing this. It is indeed rather mysterious that critics of utilitarianism, some of whom lay great weight on the 'right to equal concern

From *Utility and Rights*, ed. R. Frey (Minnesota UP, 1984).

and respect' which all people have, should object when utilitarians show this equal concern by giving equal weight to the equal interests of everybody, a precept which leads straight to Bentham's formula and to utilitarianism itself.

It should hardly be necessary to spell this out. To have concern for someone is to seek his good, or to seek to promote his interests; and to have equal concern for all people is to seek equally their good, or to give equal weight to their interests, which is exactly what utilitarianism requires. To do this is to treat others' interests in the same way as a prudent person treats his own interests, present and future. It is thus inevitable that having equal concern for everybody will lead us, as Mackie puts it, to weigh together the interests of different individuals 'in the way in which a single thoroughly rational egoist would weigh together all his own desires or satisfactions'. To do this is not to fail to 'insist on the separateness of persons'.

We can perhaps begin to understand why advocates of right-based theories get into the paradoxical position of advocating equal concern but dismissing the theory (utilitarianism) which secures precisely this, if we notice that certain rights, or the principles of safeguarding them, initially demand *un*equal concern for people. Suppose that Tom (the lecher!) is consumed with a desire for the favours of Ann, but that she resists his advances because of a preference, though only a marginal one, not to indulge him just now. We say that she has a right to refuse, and indeed to be protected in her refusal by the law. But this is to show *more* concern for her than for him: we are frustrating a consuming desire of his in order to meet what may be a mere whim of hers to accommodate him later rather than now.

It is true that we should secure *formal* equality between them by adopting a universal principle forbidding rape by *anybody*. But the right-based theorist is very reasonably not likely to be satisfied by that. A principle universally *permitting* rape, or universally requiring females to yield to the advances of males, would pass this formal test just as well. Why then do we, in spite of our belief in the right to equal concern and respect, adopt, out of these principles, all of which are formally universal, one in particular—one which in this case requires inequality of concern?

Mackie has the answer, but does not explain how it is inconsistent with utilitarianism. He says (1984: 87),

[A right-based theory's] formal structure will be something like this. Having started with the assignment to all persons alike of the rather vague right to a fair go, we first try to make this somewhat more explicit, in the light of ordinary human needs and purposes, by an assignment of some basic abstract *prima facie* rights. These, I suggest, will include the traditional rights to life, health, liberty, and the pursuit of happiness.

The right which stands in the lecher's way is presumably a particular case of the right to liberty: the liberty in question is the freedom not to have one's body interfered with contrary to one's wishes. As we have seen, the right demands *un*equal concern in this case.

These two stages in Mackie's account correspond closely to the two levels, critical and intuitive, in my own (*MT* 25–64). The explanation of how equal concern at the critical level can lead to unequal concern at the intuitive is that an impartial critical thinker equally concerned to give everybody 'the right to a fair go' would see that the right-assigning principles whose general acceptance would be most likely to achieve this aim would assign rights whose detailed observance in particular cases would sometimes require unequal concern. A two-level utilitarian theory makes this transition clear; whereas Mackie's phrase 'make more explicit, in the light of ordinary human needs and purposes' conceals the nature of the process of getting from 'the rather vague right to a fair go' to more substantial principles governing our actions in the concrete world among real people.

Is Mackie's 'formal structure' in fact different from my own utilitarian theory? The *content* of both theories might well be the same. Both, having set before themselves the aim of giving everybody a fair go, or having equal concern for all, find that the best way 'in the light of ordinary human needs and purposes' of achieving this aim is to devise a set of prima facie principles, some of them entrenching prima facie rights, for use in our moral thinking. My list of these could well be the same as Mackie's. But is the *structure* of the two theories different? I am inclined to think not.

I will not enquire what Mackie means by calling his rights 'abstract' (perhaps the point he is making is the same point as I commonly express by calling the principles used in intuitive thinking 'simple' and 'general'). But by calling them 'prima facie' rights he seems at first sight to be accepting (as he does later accept) my division of moral thinking into two levels, and to be putting the moral judgements based on these rights into the intuitive level. This certainly seems to be their natural habitat; and that, as I have repeatedly stressed in my book, does not entail any diminution of the sanctity of the rights in question. I have given reasons why we should be extremely reluctant to let them be overridden, and even if we do, should feel bad about it (*MT* 28). Mackie himself sums up these reasons (1984: 91). But he also agrees with me that the rights have to be 'defeasible' (another word, we might almost say, for 'prima facie'), because they can conflict in particular cases. This lays on the right-based theorist the task of giving a method for the resolution of these conflicts, as I try, in my book, to do in terms of my own theory. My account, though not entirely simple, does seem to me to yield a passably true-to-life model of the moral thinking that wise people actually do in such situations.

I am left somewhat in the dark as to the differences which he finds between a right-based theory and my own—or, which comes to the same thing, as to the sense in which his theory could be said to be 'based' on rights and mine not. For in so far as the rights are only prima facie and defeasible, it surely cannot be based on them; and the only right he produces which is more than prima facie is the right to equal concern and respect, which is preserved, at the highest level, and indeed really used as a basis, by my own theory.

This unclarity, it seems to me, infects the first of the new objections that Mackie makes against my theory. He puts it forward only after a very fair account of my suggested division of moral thought into two levels, which, he agrees, enables me to deal with the vulgar objections to utilitarianism based on counter-intuitiveness. He also recognizes the close relation between my version of even-handed utilitarianism and the quasi-Kantian universality of moral prescriptions on which I seek to base it. He goes on to attribute to me the view, in summary, that 'what is morally right is, ultimately, what would be chosen from a point of view that combines or amalgamates all points of view'.

We must notice that it is Mackie, and not I, who introduces the word 'amalgamate', with its suggestion, which he draws out, that 'all are blurred together into a mere aggregate of purposes', leaving the boundaries between persons no longer visible. What I actually say is rather different. In an article I published a long time ago (H 1969: *s.f.*) I quoted the lines

> Momentous to himself as I to me
> Is every man that ever woman bore.

My *MT* is full of the idea that we have in critical moral thought to think ourselves into the shoes of each of the persons affected, one by one—which is why, as we shall see when we come to Mackie's third objection, critical moral thought is so difficult for human beings. So far individual distinctions are preserved.

The question which then arises is how, when we think morally and therefore universally, we are to balance the preferences of these separate people against one another so as to be fair to them all. My answer is that we have to give equal weight to equal preferences, counting everybody for one. This is no more to *amalgamate*, let alone *blur*, the separate persons than it is when a judge, having heard what each of the parties to a suit has to say, tries to be fair to them all. As Mackie himself says, thinking this to be a point against me, 'Harean universalization might' (he implies that in my hands it does not) 'generate a persisting concern for each separate individual'. But in fact I do not in my critical thinking depart from this concern; I only seek a way in which concern for different individuals can be fairly balanced, and find it by treating their equal preferences as of equal weight.

As we have seen, this impartiality or equal concern at the critical level can yield principles which, in particular cases at the intuitive level, may require partiality or *un*equal concern, as when somebody's right has to be preserved at greater expense to somebody else. It is not clear how a right-based theory would justify this, since it purports to treat rights as 'basic'. I justify it on the ground that the general acceptance of such principles would on balance best serve the interests of all considered impartially (*MT* 135–40). That is to say, there is no other set of principles which would do more for their interests in sum, when interests are counted equally in proportion to their strength.

It is the 'in sum' that Mackie is principally attacking. In the course of his attack he appeals to an analogy, which I also use, between adjudication of *inter*personal conflicts of interest and adjudication of *intra*personal but inter*temporal* conflicts. If I am now trying to decide between courses of action, of which one will in total maximally satisfy the preferences which I have at all times as to what should happen *at those times*, and the other distributes preference-satisfactions in some different way, I shall be forced into an adjudication between the interests of different phases of my own person which is analogous to that between the interests of different people. Mackie suggests that, contrary to the utilitarian solution of this prudential problem, someone in this position might 'try to ensure that no substantial phase of his life was too miserable, even if very great satisfactions at other times were to compensate for this'. How miserable is 'too miserable', and what 'compensates' for what? If we ask these questions, we see that even such a way of thinking requires us to place values on the preferences that we are going to have at the various times.

I say 'place values' and not 'assign strengths'. I shall not in this paper go into the problem of the 'interpersonal commensurability of utilities' which is discussed briefly in *MT* ch. 7. But, given that we can assess the strengths of the preferences, we still have to decide how much each of these preferences, present or future, our own or other people's, is to count for us, at the time when we are making the decision. My own answer is that, if we are prudent, they will count for us equally, strength for strength, irrespective of the times at which they are felt; and that, if we are thinking morally, other people's will count equally with each other and with our own.

The first of these theses holds because that is what we mean by 'prudent'. It has to be asked whether the person who follows the suggestion just quoted from Mackie is being prudent. On the face of it he is not; but it is perhaps possible to interpret what Mackie says in such a way that he is. All we have to say is that *by following the suggested policy*, he is showing that he places a greater negative value on the misery than the positive value he places on the sum of the spread-out satisfactions at other times that the misery makes possible. This involves taking 'compensate' in a Pickwickian sense. They do not really and fully compensate for the misery, in his present estimation, or he would not follow the policy. And he *is* being prudent in following it, if the actual values to him, at the times when they occur, of the various experiences will be the same as he now places on them (as manifested by his following the policy). If, however, they are not, he is being imprudent, most probably because he does not fully represent to himself now the values he will place upon them. Such imprudence is of course extremely common, but does not support Mackie's argument; on the other hand if, to support it, he were to allege that a *prudent* person could follow the policy in question, this, as I have just explained, will be because the satisfactions will *not* in fact compensate for the miseries; so the intrapersonal prudent calculation is, after all, analogous to the interpersonal utilitarian calculation, and the support for Mackie's argument collapses.

The second thesis, that, if we are thinking morally, other people's preferences will count equally with each other and with our own, holds because, when we make a moral judgement, we are prescribing universally for all situations of a given identical kind, irrespective of what individuals occupy the different roles in those situations (the preferences had by the individuals being part of the roles; they do not travel round with the individuals). But if we fully know what it is like to be a certain individual in a certain situation (and if we did *not* fully know, our moral thinking could be faulted for incompleteness of information) then we shall have the same preferences with regard to what should happen to us were we in that situation as the person who is actually in it and therefore actually has the preferences. For example, if I fully know what it is like to be burnt at the stake, I shall want not myself to be burnt at the stake just as much as does the person who is actually being burnt. Put these two premisses together, and it becomes inescapable that we prescribe, if we are prescribing morally, for all situations as if we were going to be in them forthwith, and therefore giving the same weight to the preferences of the people in them as *they* actually give to them. I have summarized the argument, and there is a lot more to be said about it; but it is not this part of my argument that Mackie challenges in his paper.

This, then, is my answer to Mackie's first, 'internal', objection: the objection that, even if my universal prescriptivist theory be accepted for the sake of argument, it does not lead inevitably to utilitarianism, but is consistent with his right-based theory. The answer is that, first of all, it does so lead, for the reason I have given; and that, secondly, if it is consistent with his right-based theory, then so is utilitarianism itself (as, indeed, I think it is, if 'based' is not taken too narrowly).

The first part of this answer, however, leads us directly to Mackie's second objection, which he calls 'external', because it takes issue with my underlying theory, universal prescriptivism. I myself base this theory on conceptual analysis or philosophical logic. The moral words do, as a matter of linguistic fact, have the logical properties of prescriptivity and universalizability on which my argument for utilitarianism is based. This is to be established by appeal to *linguistic* (not *moral*) intuitions: in our ordinary use of the words we do, as part of the meaning we give to them, assign to them these logical properties. We know that somebody who says, 'He is in just the same situation as I am, including all his personal psychological characteristics, both occurrent and dispositional, and yet he ought to do it but I ought not' is offending against the logical rules which give 'ought' its meaning, in just the same sort of way as we know that somebody who says, 'All the books on the shelf are blue, yet there is one which isn't' is offending against the logical rules which give 'all', 'not', 'is', etc., their meanings. It is open to anybody to adopt a different meaning for the word 'ought' (provided that he advertises the fact in order to avoid misunderstandings); but if he does so, when he asks 'Ought I?', he will, because he has changed the meaning and the logical properties which are linked with it, no longer be asking the same question as we were asking when we used the same words; it would therefore not be surprising if he were able to give a different answer. Compare the person who says 'All the books on the shelf are blue', but means what most of us would express by 'Some of the books on the shelf are blue', or by 'All but one (the one written by me) are blue.'

This position can be, and has been, attacked in two different ways. First of all, it might be alleged that we do *not* use the words consistently in that way; my linguistic intuitions are at fault. But secondly, it might be alleged that although what I say about ordinary language may be true, (or may be admitted for the sake of argument to be true), we do not want to be tied and bound, in our practical reasoning, by contingent facts about ordinary language. So somebody might say, 'If the ordinary uses of words commit me, if I use them in my moral thinking, to being a utilitarian, to hell with the ordinary uses of the words!'

Mr Blackburn, who was kind enough to comment on an earlier draft of *MT*, advised me, in view of these possible objections, to take a course whose availability I had, indeed, already seen; and I was respectful enough to add a paragraph pointing out the alternative course (*MT* 20). Mackie quotes this passage as 'conceding' the basis of his second objection Actually, it concedes at most one (the third) of the three grounds[1] that he adduces (1984: 94); and even concerning this one I make it clear in my book that this is not my preferred way of handling the matter. It is a long stop, in case anybody is so imperceptive as not to see the force of the arguments on which, in the main, I rely. The first and second of Mackie's three grounds I would reject, because I appeal to only one kind of universalization (*MT* 108), and that has a logical and

---

[1] In full the three grounds are: 'First, even if analysis of established moral concepts shows that they involve some sort of universalizability, it is far from clear that they involve the precise sort that Hare is now using. His present method embraces all three of the stages of universalization that I have distinguished, but our ordinary concepts may well involve only the first, or perhaps the first and second, without the third. Secondly, since there are these complications, opting out of the moral game and ceasing to ask recognizably moral questions is not the only alternative to using Hare's method. Thirdly, even if we accepted his conceptual analysis, we might well ask why that should matter, what power the analysis of existing concepts has to constrain our thinking, if there are other coherently possible ways of thinking about choices and patterns of behavior.'

linguistic basis which I have just reiterated. For this reason his first premiss, which requires there to be different kinds of universalization, misses the target, and so, therefore, does the second, which depends on it.

The 'alternative course' into which Blackburn wished to draw me was to say, 'All right, let us admit for the sake of argument either that my linguistic intuitions about ordinary language are wrong, or that it simply does not matter what logical properties ordinary language assigns to the words. Let us rather tell ordinary language to go to hell, and devise an *artificial* language whose words do have, by stipulation, the required properties. Then any user of this artificial language will have to be a utilitarian in his moral thinking. It remains open to anybody, provided that he makes his use clear, to use those words in some different way from that laid down in the rules of this artificial language, just as he could escape in the same way from the rules of our natural language. He will then not be asking the same questions as we are. But he may not want to ask those questions. What we have to show him is that there is some reason why he should use that language and ask those questions, or, contrariwise, why we should not give up using our language and ask instead the questions that he is asking.'

In *MT* ch. 11 I address myself to the task of justifying the asking of moral questions (which is the same task, whether following Mr Blackburn's advice I treat them as questions in an artificial language, or whether, following my own inclinations, I claim that our natural language already serves to ask them). After admitting the possibility of there being a character whom I call 'the consistent amoralist', who has abandoned the moral language and its rules (whether natural or artificial), I try to show what reasons there are for us not to become amoralists, and, still more importantly, what reasons there are for not bringing up our children to be amoralists, even if we have only their interests at heart. This part of my book amounts to a prudential defence of the institution of morality. As such it will raise eyebrows, but it is not my task in this paper to lower them.

Let me make it clear, as Mackie does, that I am not merely

giving a utilitarian justification of utilitarian morality; that would be trivial and easy. I am not, that is to say, only maintaining that an archangelic utilitarian thinker would come out with excellent moral reasons for inculcating the moral language with its rules. I am maintaining something much more substantial: that even a person who had nothing at heart but his own interest would do well to adopt this language and this way of thinking as a matter of ingrained habit. This, I maintain, holds for the world as it is and for people as they are; it does not hold for all logically possible worlds. The discussion, as Mackie says, is a long one, and my summary here will have to be even briefer than his. Note that I am not saying that the morally right *act* is always in the agent's interest; such a claim would be extravagant. I am maintaining that the interests of all ordinary humans (as opposed to impossibly clever devils) are likely to be furthered *in general* if they inculcate into themselves moral habits of thought—habits tenacious enough to make them actually suffer in mind if they transgress their morality, thereby giving them an added prudential reason for not doing so. The main reason, however, is that in the world as it is, and as we have helped, for reasons of self-interest, to make it, the easiest way of seeming to be upright is to be upright (an opinion which Xenophon attributed to Socrates in *Mem*, I, 7).

If anybody thinks that even this is an extravagant claim, I ask him to notice that the more thoughtful of us, when we have to think about the education of our children, and probably think much more about their good than about the good of the general public or about morality, in fact try, with varying degrees of success, to inculcate into them moral habits of thought. And it would go worse with the children if we did not.

There is, it goes without saying, room here for empirical differences of opinion as to whether this is so; for it is an empirical question what kind of education is most likely to lead to the maximal satisfaction of the children's preferences in the course of their lives. All I can say is that I believe that most thoughtful and experienced people, to judge by their practice, think it is so. The arguments which are brought against this position, like a lot of bad arguments against utilitarianism itself, rest largely on contrived examples, or too simple treatment of real ones. It is in this light that we should regard Mackie's example of the child brought up in a slave-owning aristocracy (1984: 96). He suggests that critical moral thinking, such as I advocate, might lead such a fortunately endowed child 'to support some tendency to reform this unequal social structure, rather than merely to accept it and flourish within it, if there were any real possibility of successful reform'. But if there were any such real possibility, it could only be because there were factors at work, as there have been in many slave-societies before their reform, which made the foundations of the society shaky; and these same factors would very probably make it in the interest of its more fortunate members (especially if they had regard to the interests of their posterity) to contemplate and work for a change to a more stable, because more equal, society. To substitute a more up-to-date example: does Mackie's argument commit him to saying that in present-day South Africa it is in the interest of a child to be brought up on diehard *verkrampte* rather than on more liberal *verligte* lines?

Although near the end of my book I do confront the question 'Why should I be moral?', I am not staking my reputation on the success of my answer to it. I should be content with something more modest: to have shown that the moral questions we are posing all the time are posed in terms whose meaning and logic generate a way of answering them which constrains us, once we ask the questions. If an amoralist refuses the questions themselves, that is another issue. However, I do believe that as a matter of fact there *is* a pre-established harmony between morality and prudence, to this limited extent, that if we were to bring up a child (or ourselves) to ask moral questions and answer them by means of the two-level structure of moral thinking which I say our language imposes on us, we should be acting in the child's (or in the second case our own) best interests.

Mackie's paper contains an illuminating digression about recent sociobiological theories and Peter Singer's first-rate appraisal of them (1981). I shall not go into the question in detail, as I have discussed Singer's book elsewhere (H 1981*b*).

I agree with his contention that the limited altruisms which 'the selfish gene' can produce (kin-altruism, group altruism, and, more generally, reciprocal altruism) tend to escalate into a more universal kind of altruism, even though genetic factors might not by themselves *directly* produce this. The explanation he gives is that the power of reason evolves because it helps us to secure, by its more selfish applications, the survival of the genes which produce it; but that, once we have this power, we cannot stop ourselves using it in ways which lead us towards universal impartial benevolence. He compares morality with mathematics: counting and adding are good for our genes; but once we can do them we are on an escalator that carries us up to topology and other pursuits which, even if useful, could not have grown up because they helped our genes to reproduce themselves. In the same way, the kinds of thinking which, within a limited kin-group or small reciprocally helpful society, conduce to the reproduction of the genes responsible for them, may tend to escalate into a morality of universal equal concern for all sentient beings. And this, though not genetically produced, might in the end, in the present world-nexus of interlocking interests, prove to be genetically useful. To Singer's invocation of the escalation of reason, I would add a mention of the escalation of the moral *language* in which we reason; but the general lines of his suggestion seem to me promising.

But Mackie could agree, and still be left with his most powerful argument against me. It might be, he concedes, that the adoption of something like the standard system of prima facie moral principles for use in our ordinary thinking would be recommended both by a perfect moral thinker and by a similarly perfect prudential thinker. But if it were merely a contingent empirical fact about the world that this was in general the case, it would not, he thinks, support my prudential defence of morality. For although the prima facie principles would be the same, the route by which a prudential and a moral thinker would arrive at them would be different. And the consequence of this would be that in all difficult cases, especially those in which morality and prudence diverge, as I have admitted that they may, the critical prudential thinker may cease to agree. Though it may be prudent to cultivate a repugnance to lying, there are surely (Mackie could argue) cases in which, once the question has been raised whether I ought to tell a lie in my own interest although it would be morally wrong, the perfect prudential thinker will say that I ought, and the perfect moral thinker will say that I ought not.

As I have already suggested, the most promising way of answering this objection is by an appeal to contingent facts about human nature and about the world in which we actually live. First, I do not think it practically possible to bring people up so that they follow the prima facie moral principles with the consistency which even their own interest demands, without implanting in them quite strong feelings of aversion to breaking them. But if they have these feelings, it will become to that extent contrary to their interest to break them, because it makes them feel bad. So, when the perfect prudential critical thinker takes this additional factor into account, he too will recommend telling the truth. The original aversion therapy was in our own interest, and, once we have undergone it, it makes it in our interest to avoid the aversive events (e.g. lie-telling by us) even in those cases (which for my argument will have to be rare) in which it is otherwise in our interest that they should occur.

Secondly, even if the coincidence between morality and prudence in general were purely fortuitous (which it is not, though it is not logically necessary either), it would be sufficient for my argument (which is designed to show why we should not bring up our children and ourselves as amoralists) if there were this contingent correlation. For when we are bringing them up (at a stage when they certainly cannot *distinguish* clearly between morality and prudence) we shall cultivate in them the sound moral principles in their own interest. So there is prudential justification for the original aversion therapy. But what shall we, if we have their interests at heart, include in our education on the question of what to do when in difficult cases morality and prudence conflict? The time will come when they will be able to distinguish between moral and prudential critical thinking, even if, being humans, they cannot manage either at all well. My guess is that we shall warn them against supposing too easily that they can win the prudential game by abandoning the moral one. Critical thinking of any sort is extremely difficult, and, for my part, I think it both easier and wiser to do it in the moral way, by appealing to truly universal principles, than to attempt self-interested cost–benefit analyses. I know of so many people who have erred, even prudentially speaking, by supposing otherwise.

This leads me to a discussion of Mackie's third and last main objection, which will have to be brief. It relates to what he calls the inaccessibility of critical thinking to human beings. I do not find so much difference on this point between him and myself as he does. I stress repeatedly in my book that only a perfect being (God, or the character I call the archangel) could do it perfectly. Bishop Butler therefore, as Mackie says and as I have said in the past, leaves the whole thing to God, to find out the best prima-facie principles and reveal them to our consciences. But, as Hobbes says, 'Though God Almighty can speak to a man, by Dreams, Visions, Voice, and Inspiration; yet he obliges no man to beleeve he hath so done to him that pretends it; who (being a man) may erre, and (which is more) may lie' (1651: ch. 32). If we either do not believe in God, or believe in him but also think that the line of communication between him and us is fallible, what are we to do? Intuitive thinking, as I hope to have shown in my book and as Mackie agrees, cannot be self-supporting, because we cannot without circularity appeal to intuitions to justify intuitions. So critical thinking has somehow or other to be done.

The question therefore turns into one about whether Mackie's or my suggestions about the best method of critical thinking are more promising. He first considers a method which, he says, could be put forward as an amendment to my own which on reflection I might accept. But no reflection is necessary, because the suggestion is entirely consistent with my views from the beginning and is no amendment. This is that my

thoroughgoing prescriptive universalization might amalgamate the points of view of all the individuals concerned in a way that took serious account of the separateness of persons, by assigning such basic abstract rights as I have suggested to each person. That is, we could have a right-based method of critical thinking (1984: 98).

As I have already said, this is how my own method proceeds: the abstract right in question is that to equal concern and respect (which is a mere rephrasing of universalizability). All the other rights which Mackie wants he calls prima facie, and therefore cannot think them to be the basis of critical thinking; and anything else he wants to put in as a basis of critical thinking could, I am pretty sure, be shown to be derivative from this right to equal concern.

But Mackie rejects this approach because he wants us not to base ourselves on conceptual analysis: 'Right and wrong have to be invented . . . morality is not to be discovered but to be made' (ibid.). This is surely not a bone of contention between us. For if he is here speaking about the concepts, of course I can agree that they had to be invented (or at least, to allow for a Chomskian innate grammar, that they had to develop somehow among men); and if he is speaking about the *content* of morality, it is in accord with my prescriptivist views, which have often been attacked on this very ground, to say that we have to come to our own moral principles and cannot look them up in any encyclopaedia.

However, for whatever reason, Mackie rejects this approach, and suggests instead that

critical thinking might itself be a process of interaction, negotiation, and debate between diverse groups with different starting points, different traditions of thought. Rather than proceeding *de haut en bas*, being pursued by one or more detached thinkers who try to stand above the whole conflict of interests and ideals, it would work up from below, from those conflicting views and claims themselves (1984: 100).

This gets me quite wrong, if it was intended to suggest that on my view moral thinking can be done without discussing other people's interests, ideals, claims, views, etc., with them. Why should it be thought that I wish to dispense with such discussion and negotiation? But the question is, 'When we have finished stating our claims and views, what do we do then?' Some people, perhaps, are content to leave the issue thereafter to a power struggle. Mackie, with proper caution, goes on

The details of this process would be contingent upon the input to it and are therefore not open to any precise description *a priori*. But it is reasonable to expect that any such process of interaction, negotiation, and debate would be roughly equivalent to some distribution of entitlements that are not merged into a pure collectivity—in other words, that this too would be, in effect, a right-based approach.

I find this suggestion somewhat obscure; but in so far as I can understand it, it seems not too different from my own. The main difference is that I, unlike any right-based theory so far produced, provide a clear basis for the negotiation: the prescriptions they come to in the end have to be such as they can all accept for universal application whatever individual role anybody plays. This is a method often in effect used in negotiations, and it works. The use of this rule in critical thinking will lead the negotiators to assign to each other at least one 'entitlement' at the critical level, namely the right to equal concern. It will also lead them to give each other a lot of prima facie 'abstract' (as Mackie calls them) entitlements for use at the intuitive level. In fact the whole thing will go just as I say it does, given this ground rule. If this is not to be the ground rule, what other way is there of disciplining the negotiations?

I will end with a suggestion. My own ideas were developed *pari passu* with fairly engaged and involved thought about a lot of practical moral issues such as often divide the negotiatiors in such disputes. I would be willing to let my method and a right-based method (when one has been fully worked out) be tried out on such issues, to see how well they serve to resolve them. I think it would turn out that the methods, in so far as they served, were not all that different.

8

Utility and Rights:
Comment on David Lyons's Paper

I MUST confess to a certain difficulty in handling Professor
Lyons's objections to utilitarianism (1984). He is a thoughtful,
sophisticated, and well-read philosopher (much better read
than I am). He shows himself, not only in other writings of
his, but in this very paper, to be conversant with some
possible replies to his objections. Neither the objections, nor
the replies to them, nor Lyons's replies to the replies, are
new—only restated in a somewhat more involved way. The
argument is in its essentials an old one, going back at least to
Mill and Bentham. What puzzles me is why Lyons should
think his objections damaging to a careful utilitarian. And it
puzzles me still more that so many people—perhaps the
majority of moral and legal philosophers at the present time—
should think that utilitarianism can be defeated by arguments
about rights which, once the position is fully understood, have
little power. The only explanation must be that they have *not*
fully understood the position; so I am going to have another
try at explaining it. In doing so I shall introduce only one
move that is not to be found in Lyons's paper, and this move is
not new either (it could be argued, but not here, that it goes
back to Plato). I myself have explained it in H 1972*a*, 1976,
and *MT* pt. 1. This move is the distinction between different
levels of moral thought, the intuitive and the critical. It is just
possible that not seeing this distinction is what has led people
to rely on such weak arguments; but I am not sure.

Sometimes, in our moral thinking, we simply apply moral
principles, intuitions, feelings, reactions, dispositions (it makes
no difference to the argument which of these terms we use)
which we have learnt or acquired in the course of our moral

From *Nomos* 24, 'Ethics, Economics and the Law' (1984).

development. The principles in question have, for their purposes, to be fairly, but not extremely, general; that is to say, the reactions are attached to relatively broad, and perhaps not very exact, characterizations of actions and circumstances. The reason for this is that a highly specific response to highly specific situations could not be learnt, and, even if it could, would not be useful. Moral upbringing and development consists, in part, in the acquisition and building into our characters of responses of a fairly general sort (e.g. a repugnance towards lying or cruelty) which will be activated by situations resembling one another in certain broad features, though not necessarily features which are easily captured by a verbal description.

It is important to notice that these dispositions, though if they could be expressed they would be expressed by moral principles or universal prescriptions, are by no means the same thing as dispositions to verbalize such prescriptions. If all that someone is disposed to do is to *say*, 'I ought not to tell this lie' when faced with an opportunity for telling a lie, then he just does not *have* the principle (he is not a truthful person; he lacks the virtue of truthfulness).

Nor is it enough to have, for some extrinsic reason (e.g. to keep out of trouble) a constant *practice* of not lying. What is needed in addition is a firm disposition, backed up by quite strong feelings and deeply embedded in his character, to pursue truthfulness for its own sake. That is why I was sorry to see Lyons using the expression 'rules of thumb'. I regret having myself used this phrase, even in a different connection (*LM* 66), and it is certainly out of place here. Rules of thumb are used by engineers and others to save time and effort and get approximations to the right answers to questions of fact or practice. They do not represent the true *motivations* of those who for convenience follow them; they are not deeply ingrained in their characters, do not excite compunction or remorse if broken by themselves or indignation if broken by others; they have little in common with what I am speaking of and would much better be left out of this discussion.

In most of our moral decisions we think intuitively in this way; and it is highly desirable, at least from a utilitarian point of view, that we should. It would be, not only impossible for

lack of time, but dangerous because of our notorious tendency
to special pleading in situations of stress and temptation, to
proceed in any other way. A wise act-utilitarian educator,
seeking in his educative acts to promote utility (however
defined) will do his best to inculcate in himself and others
sound general dispositions and the feelings that go with them.
If he is successful, the people so brought up will count as well
brought up and will be much more likely in the course of their
lives to promote utility than somebody who takes a lot of time
off to do felicific calculations. But nearly all of our acts are to
some degree educative, in that they have an effect on the
moral attitudes of ourselves and others. So a consistent act-
utilitarian will reason that there is a very high probability that
any act of his in relation to lying will have quite far-reaching
effects on people's attitudes, including his own. It is an
empirical assumption that this is likely; I believe it, but am
not called upon as a philosopher to justify it. The fact that
most of us believe it amply accounts for our fostering, even if
we are utilitarians, of the disposition not to depart from the
principle without the strongest grounds.

Some people, though I am sure that they do not include
Lyons, have been superficial enough in their thinking to try to
erect on this basis an argument *against* utilitarianism. It is
obvious that if an act-utilitarian could justify, in terms of his
own theory, acts of following and fostering the disposition, it is
an argument *for* the theory to point out that we tend to do and
approve of such acts—that is, it is an argument *against* those
who claim that utilitarianism is at variance with our common
moral notions. It would be a very inept utilitarian who was
put out of his stride by the thought that his utilitarianism
could often require him to follow his intuitions, as the most
likely way of hitting off the optimific act, rather than do a
cost–benefit analysis on the spot.

The account which intuitionists (which is what nearly all
anti-utilitarians are) give of the intuitive level of moral
thinking is for the most part correct: we do have intuitions,
and it is right in general to follow them nearly all the time.
Where the intuitionists go wrong is in neglecting the *other* level
of moral thinking, which I call the critical. The intuitive level
cannot in principle be self-supporting. The somewhat general

principles which are the content or basis of our intuitions frequently conflict in particular cases (an inevitable consequence of their generality and the extreme variability of the world). But even if another level of thinking were not required to deal with such conflicts, it would be required in order to satisfy us that the principles embodied in our intuitions are the best ones so to embody. How are we to be sure that the people who brought us up were wise? Some people, after all, have very pernicious intuitions—that it is, for example, quite all right to discriminate against blacks. How are we to be sure that any one of our intuitions is not like that one? Those who have challenged our intuitions about what it is all right to do to dumb animals should at least have taught us to ask such questions.

I have written in the places referred to above of what goes on in critical thinking when rationally done, and tried to show that its rationality is founded on the logical properties of the moral concepts. Here I need only to put the question: *Suppose* that the rational method of critical thinking, which appraises our moral intuitions and adjudicates between them when they conflict, is utilitarian, as I think it is, what then must we say of Lyons's arguments and others like them? I hope to show that they become very weak.

These arguments consist essentially in appeals to received opinion. The answer to them all is to point out that the opinions in question may indeed be received ones, but that a utilitarian can easily explain both the fact that they are received, and, in the case of most but not all of them, the advantages of their being received. If, as I think, the intuitive principles that nearly all of us employ are, for the most part, sound ones from the utilitarian point of view (i.e. good utilitarian reasons can be given why we should cultivate them), then critical thinking, if utilitarian, will give our intuitions a fairly clean bill of health, but will pin-point a few that we ought to think again about (for example about the place of women in the home).

But before we can understand the application of all this to Lyons's argument, we shall have to make clear some distinctions which might be obscured to readers by his use of expressions like 'the moral force of legal rights'. This could be taken, in the writings of some natural-law theorist, as meaning that no distinction can be drawn between the legal and the moral spheres; but obviously Lyons does not so intend it. It could, secondly, be taken as meaning that the according by courts and legislatures of certain legal rights is morally a good thing, can be morally justified, etc. Clearly Lyons does not mean this by it, because he says that utilitarians cannot account for the moral force of legal rights, and yet allows that a utilitarian could, consistently with his theory, provide reasons why these legal rights morally ought to be accorded. Thirdly, it might be taken as meaning that, given that, (as a matter of historical fact, which he is prepared to grant may be of itself morally neutral) legislatures and courts have accorded certain legal rights, individuals (including policemen and other officials) have a prima facie moral duty to preserve these rights to other individuals by respecting and enforcing the law (see pp. 13 ff.). It seems to be this third thing that Lyons means.

If so, then this restatement enables us to clarify, but also to undermine, his thesis that utilitarians cannot give an account of the moral force of legal rights. We are then to take him as granting that utilitarians *can* give an account of why legislatures and courts *do*, and even of why they *ought* (morally) to accord certain legal rights (and therefore that in *that* sense what he calls the *Inclusion of Legal Rights Thesis* is immune to the arguments in his paper); but as maintaining that in a historical situation in which they have done so, it could still be the case, according to utilitarians, that officials, policemen, and others ought to disobey the laws.

Let us, with this interpretation of his argument in mind, address ourselves to his example of Mary and her driveway, in which I am tempted to park without permission. What he is then saying is that, although utilitarians can perhaps give a moral reason why Mary should be *accorded* her right to the unobstructed use of it, they cannot give any moral reason why other people, including policemen, should *respect* and *enforce* this right in cases where utility might be marginally increased by not doing so. Since we all have moral intuitions to the effect that they should, he hopes thereby to display utilitarianism as having counter-intuitive consequences.

This position is, however, undermined by the separation of levels of moral thinking. At the intuitive level most of what anti-utilitarians say is correct; and at that level we do not need to, and shall often be wise not to, use utilitarian considerations, even if we are act-utilitarians. For we shall know that in all but the most extraordinary cases (and Lyons's own intuitions, which incorporate a 'threshold', allow him to make an exception of these) the most *likely* way of getting the optimific act is to follow our intuitions. If this is not so, then our upbringing has not been as good as it should be; for its object ought to have been to give us those intuitions, to follow which would be most likely to have this effect. If I am asked how I know that most of our existing intuitions are such as to lead us to do optimific acts on the whole, I answer that I do not know, but think it to be so. I think this' because I have some experience, supplemented by that of others going back through the centuries, of how the world actually goes. I appeal neither to philosophy nor to sociology but to common knowledge (though this is open to correction by sociologists if they are to be trusted).

If anybody doubts that in the case of Mary's driveway a sensible act-utilitarian would follow these intuitions, I ask him to say what else he would do. Perhaps the policeman, instead of enforcing Mary's legal right without further ado, ought to sit down on the sidewalk in the posture depicted by Rodin, and do an hour or two's deep critical thinking; perhaps he should call up headquarters from time to time on his radio to get all the information he would require about the consequences of alternative actions, which his magical colleagues have somehow obtained?

It would be obvious to an act-utilitarian that this would not, from the viewpoint of his own theory, be the best way of proceeding, though of course policemen should be encouraged to do some critical thinking about the moral principles applicable to their vocation when there is leisure for it. And it would also be obvious to an act-utilitarian that the best moral equipment for a policeman who has to face such embarrassing situations is a firm grasp of people's rights and of the right ways to set about enforcing them. 'Rights' here could mean 'legal rights' or 'moral rights'; the well-instructed policeman will have a good practical grasp of both (within the limits to which any man of action is subject), and of the distinction between them. And there is nothing to stop act-utilitarians from applauding well-instructed, conscientious, and in other ways virtuous policemen, and holding them up as examples to the rest of us. We too, even if we are act-utilitarians, will do right to cultivate sound intuitions and traits of character. But some policemen and others (e.g. in racist societies) have *bad* intuitions; and when we ask which are the sound ones, we shall have, in order to answer, to do some critical thinking.

I might have argued on different, but related, lines that if Lyons grants, as he does grant, to the utilitarian that he can account for the moral justification of the *institution* of legal rights, then he must at the same time grant that there is a moral duty in general to respect and enforce the rights. For to have a morally justified system of legal rights but no moral duty to enforce or respect them in particular cases would be self-defeating. In other words, the moral duty to enforce and respect is part and parcel of the 'moral force' of the system itself. Suppose we were to say to the legislators, 'You have a moral duty to establish a system of legal rights, but *we*, the people, shall then have no moral duty to respect and enforce them', the legislators will reasonably reply, 'In that case, what is the point of our establishing the system? For if people do not acknowledge a moral duty to respect and enforce the rights, no mere legal sanctions are going to make the system work. There aren't enough policemen; and those that there are will not do their job very conscientiously if all they are thinking about is what penalties they will incur if they take it easy.'

I have not used this argument, because it is effectively covered by what I have said already. According to utilitarians, a moral justification can be given, in terms of the benefits secured, for having a system of legal rights. But the benefits will evaporate if in particular cases people do not have, and except in unusual cases follow, the moral intuition that the law ought in general to be obeyed. In nearly all ordinary cases an act-utilitarian, well brought up by other act-utilitarians, can say to himself, 'I have a strong moral intuition that I ought to respect this legal right; it is most probable that to go against the intuition would have effects, including the most important side-effect of impairing respect for law, which would make it less than optimific; so my best bet as an act-utilitarian is to follow my intuition.'

I do not think I have said anything unfamiliar in this comment. But in case I have, let me summarize my defence of utilitarianism against objections based on appeals to our intuitions about the moral force of legal rights. The moral duties to which this moral force gives rise are always founded on intuitive principles (above all, on the principle that we ought, in general, to obey the law). At the intuitive level it is a sufficient justification for an act that our moral intuitions require it. But if they conflict, or if a justification is asked for having and following *those* intuitions, we have to ascend to a higher level and employ critical thinking, which is based on the logical properties of the moral concepts, and, if I am right about those properties, is utilitarian in its method. This explains why legal rights have a moral force, not only in the sense, which seems not to be Lyons's, that the according of them can be morally justified, but in the sense that there is a prima facie duty to respect and enforce them in particular cases. That there is this prima facie duty is a consequence of the facts, if they are facts, (1) that the according of the rights by legislatures and courts could be morally justified by critical thinking; (2) that the cultivation of the intuitive principle that we morally ought in cases like this to obey the law could be likewise justified; and (3) that in the case as described the probability is that to follow such intuitive principles would yield the optimific act. Lyons has not given, and I should be surprised if he could give, any reason to suppose that all these are not facts in the case he adduces. But if they were not, then what (for Lyons as much as for a utilitarian) would have become of the legal right's moral force? Might he not have to question it, if (1) the law according the right were a bad one, or (2) the intuitive principle that we morally ought to obey the law were one which morally ought not to be cultivated, or (3) the case were such that one would obviously do best not to respect or enforce the right (Lyons himself provides some cases of this sort)?

As a parting shot (but not at Lyons, because he does not

here employ that kind of argument) let me insist that nobody be allowed to doctor the example, by introducing bizarre features into it, so that it becomes clearly the case that the optimific act (namely what it is best to do) is one that infringes Mary's rights. For, first of all, it is conceivable that bizarre problems require bizarre solutions, and Lyons rightly allows that there may be a threshold beyond which we are allowed to disregard rights for utility's sake. And, secondly, the fact (if it really is a fact) that in such bizarre cases our intuitions come down in favour of respecting legal rights proves nothing; a sound moral upbringing is designed to cater for cases which are likely to occur, and a well-brought-up man will be in some perplexity if confronted in real life (not in philosophy books) with bizarre cases.

There are, on the other hand, as Lyons realizes, other perfectly ordinary cases, not bizarre at all, in which most of us would find it in accordance with our moral intuitions to infringe somebody's legal right. Lyons mentions emergency vehicles; but since these have in many jurisdictions a legal right to park where they need to, a better example is provided by my taking a short cut between two right-of-way footpaths across my neighbour's field when out for a walk. I am infringing his legal right in so doing, but I know it will do him no harm and that he will not object. These same factors which remove the disutility of infringing the right make most of us think that I do no moral wrong in infringing it. Here too our intuitions have a threshold built into them.

If I were in a case in which it would obviously be for the best, counting in all the side-effects which are often considerable, to infringe somebody's legal rights, but in which my intuitions told me clearly and unambiguously that I ought not to do it, I might be led to question the applicability of my intuitions about rights to that case, which would have to be a very unusual one. But to anyone with a proper awareness of human fallibility it would have to be very obvious indeed (for our intuitions are on the whole reliable); and I do not expect to find myself in such a case often. I think it will be hard to find a case which does not admit of one of these two ways out: either to say 'In spite of appearances, if you count in the side-effects it probably will be for the best to follow your intuitions', or to say 'The case really is so out of the way that it does not come within the scope of your intuitions about rights.' But in a difficult case it will take a wise man (a man with very good judgement about what is actually likely to ensue) to say which of these ways out is the appropriate one.

9

Arguing about Rights

THE word 'argue' is used in at least two senses. When parents say to their children, 'Don't argue', they mean 'Don't dispute what I say.' In this sense there are plenty of arguments (i.e. disputes) about rights going on all the time, some of them violent and most of them confused. That is not the sense in which I shall be using the word, but rather that in which it means 'reason'. This is more like its primitive sense; it comes from a Latin word meaning 'prove' or 'try to prove'. Since few of the arguments about rights in the first sense contain much by way of attempts by the disputants to reason with each other, I think it would be useful if philosophers asked, more than many of them do, how such reasoning is to be done.

Some of the worst offenders, indeed, are philosophers. It has come to be accepted in many philosophical circles that one does not reason about rights; one appeals instead to one's own or one's readers' intuitions either about particular cases, or about the principles involved. It is not surprising, therefore, that philosophers of this sort have not helped very much in resolving the disputes about rights which rack the world, since they are only following a method which is already being employed by the disputants. Thus John Rawls (1971) appeals to one lot of intuitions in order to support a system of justice and rights which, we have been told by Sir Stuart Hampshire (1972: 37), is to be commended for expressing so well the ideals of the British Labour Party; and Robert Nozick (1974) appeals to another set of intuitions in order to support a wildly different set of political attitudes, which I suppose would be more congenial to Mrs Thatcher or Mr Reagan. Nowhere in either of their two books can one find any convincing answer to the question: 'If your intuitions conflict, how are you going to set about settling the conflict in a rational way?' When even philosophers carry on like this, what hope is there that

First published in *Emory Law Journal* 33 (1984) with additional references.

ordinary politicians and statesmen will learn to settle their disputes without violence? Professor Brandt has amply shown the futility of such a procedure (1979: 16–23; see H 1973*a* and *MT* 10 ff.)

I shall not spend time stressing the importance of the distinction between moral rights and legal rights, nor of that, made current by Wesley Hohfeld (1923: 36–8), of the various kinds of rights (liberties, claim-rights, etc.) which people still mix up. Nearly all of what I shall say will apply to rights in all of these senses. In spite of my disagreements with Rawls, there is one point at which I think he shows a marked superiority over Nozick. He has got hold of an important truth, that we have to attack questions like these in two or more stages, or, as I prefer to put it, at two levels. This is an old idea; it could be argued that it goes back to Plato (*Meno* 98b). If we are to settle, at the first of these levels, questions of what particular acts are just or, in general, right, or of what would be an infringement of somebody's rights—or, in general, what rights people have—then we have to have what Rawls calls 'principles of justice' (1971: 4), including principles determining people's rights. And the question of how these principles are to be selected is a *further* question, to be tackled at a different level of moral thinking. Rawls does it by supposing that we have a set of people in what he calls the original position, who select principles of justice and rights ignorant as to how their own personal interests will be affected by the choice. This extremely promising suggestion, however, does not produce in Rawls's own work a satisfactory answer to the challenge, for reasons which I have given elsewhere in detail and shall not repeat (H 1973*a*). The basic reason is that he is content in his argument to rely on his own moral intuitions in order to save him from being a utilitarian—a fate in his opinion worse than death. The crucial point is that Rawls's denial that his contracting parties would treat their occupation of any one of the affected roles as equiprobable is based on no rational ground and is insisted on simply in order to make his system conform to his anti-utilitarian intuitions. His method if consistently carried through without appeals to moral intuitions, *would* yield utilitarian conclusions (see further Harsanyi 1975).

He would have done better to accept those conclusions. The prejudice against utilitarianism which seems to have affected most of the philosophical world has a number of causes, which I shall not be able to go into; but it can be quite easily dispelled if we realize that once the two levels of moral thinking are distinguished (that at which we adjudicate particular cases in accordance with principles which we have learnt, and that at which we ask whether the principles themselves are the right ones to hold) a place can be given to the intuitions, moral convictions, and even prejudices on which many famous anti-utilitarian arguments are based; and in spite of that utilitarianism, as a way of selecting moral principles, can be left unscathed.

This is how it is done. At what I shall call the *intuitive* level of moral thinking, we are allowed to use our moral intuitions (and indeed our deeply ingrained moral and other feelings, if intuitions are different from those) in just the way that intuitionists say. They give what is for most purposes an adequate account of this level of thinking, and utilitarians do not need to quarrel with it, *at that level*. However, even at that level, questions will arise which cannot be answered by appeal to moral intuitions. They arise principally in two kinds of cases. The first is when two of our intuitive convictions, sometimes deeply held, conflict in a particular case, i.e. cannot both be acted on. The second is when we ask whether the intuitive principles which we have ourselves acquired through our upbringing are the ones which we ought to pass on to our children.

Either of these kinds of cases makes us call in question our intuitive principles themselves; and since most of the really agonizing moral problems are of one of these two kinds, it is no accident that all moral philosophers who can see even a little below the surface of their subject have been occupied in the main with such cases, and have sought, whether or not they distinguish the two levels of moral thinking, to say how questions at the second or, as I shall call it, the *critical* level are to be answered. How, since we are supposed to be talking about human rights, are we to decide what *are* the 'Rights of Man'? A clearer way of putting this question is, 'What rational way is there of deciding what intuitive principles about rights we ought to teach to our children (and ourselves) and, in general cleave to with the kind of ingrained conviction that is appropriate to moral principles?'

In a moment I will give my answer to this question; but first I ask the reader just to assume for the sake of argument that there is such a way. By choosing moral principles, and in particular principles which determine rights, in accordance with it, we shall equip ourselves with a set of principles which we can cultivate, so that they become second nature and have for us the force of intuitions. In the sphere of rights, there will be certain rights which we are *sure* that we and other people have, and we shall treat these rights, in Ronald Dworkin's word (1977: xv), as 'trumps'; have, in Sir Stuart Hampshire's words (1978), feelings of 'outrage or shock' when we see them infringed; and in general behave at this intuitive level just as intuitionists say we behave. So nothing I am going to say is in the least inconsistent with this part of the intuitionist position, and therefore any complaints against what I say based on these phenomena of the moral life will entirely miss the target. However, we do need to question the assumption, made by all such thinkers, that the particular set of principles or rights to which they appeal is self-evidently correct. It cannot be, because the principles appealed to by different intuitionists are in conflict with one another. Each needs to be argued for. It is no use appealing to the intuitions themselves, as they all do, to justify those intuitions.

A related difficulty arises even if we confine ourselves to *our own* moral convictions, and disregard those of people who think differently. Since the principles which are enshrined in our intuitions are, and have to be, rather general, there will inevitably be cases in which they conflict—in which, for example, we cannot preserve one person's well-established right without contravening some well-established right of another person. And what are we going to do then? If the child in the womb has a right to life, and the mother has the right to dispose of her own body, what are we going to say? Both of these rights may seem very important ones *in general*. Such conflicts can be resolved only by ascending to the critical level and asking what principles about rights we ought to have, and which of them ought to override the other in this particular case. So let me now give my account of this level of moral thinking.

There is one purely formal right which it must be agreed everybody has, and that is what has been called the right to equal concern and respect (see p. 79). I say 'purely formal' for two reasons. The first is that this right to equal concern and respect does, by itself, nothing to determine what, in particular, anybody has a right to do or to have. We must not commit the common mistake of supposing that this formal right will take us further in argument than it actually will, establishing, for example, some kind of substantial right of equality in wealth or power or status or whatever. All it does is to establish that the equal interests of different individuals (including ourselves) are to have equal weight in our moral thinking. The merely numerical[1] difference between individuals is not to count as morally relevant. It is important to notice that this formal equality between individuals does not, by itself, do more than forbid us to discriminate morally between Tom, Dick, and Harry on the ground that Tom is Tom, Dick Dick, and Harry Harry. It does not, by itself, forbid us to discriminate on the ground that Tom is black, Harry yellow, and Dick pink. That requires a further move, which I shall make in a moment.

The second reason why I call this right to equal concern formal is that it can be established on the basis of the formal properties of the moral concepts. If it be granted (and I shall not have room to argue this) that moral judgements are universal or universalizable prescriptions, then in prescribing that such and such ought to be done to someone (say Tom) I am implicitly prescribing that the same be done to any other individual (me for example) in any precisely similar situation, and vice versa. By 'precisely similar' I mean to include the personal characteristics of the participants (I have to imagine that I become black, and react in the same way as Tom does). So it cannot make any difference to my moral thinking whether it is Tom in the situation or myself; and this forces me to treat Tom's interests, in that situation, as if they were my

---

[1] There is a 'numerical' difference between two people if when counting people we have to count them as two, not as one. A merely numerical difference is one unaccompanied by any difference in universal properties.

own. And this, in consequence, makes me treat the equal interests of all individuals, *qua* those individuals, as of equal weight. That, in passing, is why I cannot, if I think it through, discriminate morally on grounds of colour (for example denying to blacks rights which I accord to pinks); for to do so would involve prescribing that were I to change colour I should be denied the right too, and this I shall not be prepared to do.

However, this kind of argumentation will not take us all the way. The 'right to equal concern and respect', which, I say, can be established on the basis of the formal properties of the moral concepts, has a much more powerful employment than this. Suppose that we accept that in our moral thinking equal interests are to be given equal weight, no matter whose interests they are. Then, since these interests include our own interests, the weight accorded to them will be positive, as well as equal. It follows that in my moral thinking I shall be equally trying to secure the satisfaction of everybody's equal interests. By a similar argument, it will follow that where interests are not of equal weight, I shall prefer the satisfaction of the greater interest to that of the less, whosever interests they are; for this is what I would do, were both interests my own, and universality forbids me to treat other people's interests in any different way from my own. Thus I shall accord weight to all the interests, whosever they are, in proportion merely to the strength of the interests. And since, as we have seen, the weight will be positive, my moral thinking, if done in the light of all this, will lead me to prescribe whatever actions, etc., will maximize the expectation of satisfactions of the interests of all individuals, treated impartially. I have abbreviated the argument and jumped several steps; for a full treatment see *MT*.

What we have arrived at is, of course, one kind of utilitarianism; but let us not call it that, because there are a lot of different kinds, and in any case the philosophical world is so prejudiced against utilitarianism that, if I so much as use the word, people will shut their minds and fail to see that the position I am maintaining actually *follows* from the 'right to equal concern and respect' of which anti-utilitarians like Dworkin have made so much (1977: 272 ff.), once one thinks at all deeply about what such a right involves. Let us call it instead 'interest-egalitarianism' or some other such inoffensive name. Or call it plain Kantianism; for it has a certain affinity with several of Kant's formulations of his categorical imperative.

That, then, is an outline of the method. How, when we are talking about human rights, are we going to use it? As I said, principles about rights are one kind of moral principles; so it will do if I say how this method is to be used in selecting moral principles for cultivating ourselves and teaching to our children. Acts of cultivating or teaching have, then, to be judged just like any other acts. When we ask what moral principles to cultivate, we have to decide this on the basis of what principles, if cultivated, will maximally satisfy the interests of all those people whom we are treating with equal concern. And this enables us to confront and settle particular questions about rights. Shall we cultivate respect for a right of everybody who feels so inclined to punch anyone else on the nose? No, because we can be sure that the cultivating of respect for such a right will be very far from maximizing the satisfaction of the interests of all, weighed impartially.

I am coming to more contentious examples in a moment; but this simple one will do to illustrate how, according to this rational method, we decide what rights we ought to cultivate and accept. We ought to accept those which we can accept when we give equal weight, impartially, to the equal interests of all those affected by their acceptance. This means that rights are to be selected in accordance with their acceptance-utility (I ought to have said, 'on interest-egalitarian grounds').

It is important for me, in what follows, to choose examples which will most clearly illustrate the method I am recommending for thinking about rights. Some examples are too simple, like the one I just used. They are simple, because we are all going to agree at once what rights should be preserved and what denied. Other examples will be unhelpful for the opposite reason; they bring up questions about rights which are so complicated or so bitterly debated, or both, that there is no hope in the course of a short paper of even beginning to indicate how one would use the method to settle the questions. It is indeed such questions that I really want to handle by means of the method, and have elsewhere in this volume. So let nobody accuse me of neglecting all the human rights that people get so stirred up about. I too feel deeply about most of these conflicts, on one side or the other, and am fairly well acquainted with some instances of denial of human rights (for example in Czechoslovakia); only I want to find a way of telling which rights *ought* to arouse these feelings, and the actions which they inspire.

Since principles about rights, like other intuitive moral principles, have to be couched in rather general terms, they will inevitably conflict in some unusual cases. Then, as I think Aristotle saw (1137b 19–32), it will be necessary to employ critical thinking to resolve the particular case. But if we are reasonably confident that our intuitive principles are sound ones, it is usually unwise, unless we are forced to do so by a conflict, to question them when under stress in a particular case; the probability of getting by this means an answer that would stand up to critical reflection when we next have the chance to do it is less than that of our indulging in special pleading, helped out by lack of information about the case. How easy it is to convince oneself that to tell a lie is, in these awkward circumstances, for the best!

A manœuvre often used by anti-utilitarians is that of producing unusual or even cooked-up cases in which the solution which critical thinking would yield runs counter to some of our cherished intuitive principles (*MT* 131–42). Since intuitive principles are and should be chosen to cater for the general run of cases, it does nothing to impugn either them, or critical thinking, if in these bizarre cases the two conflict.

Let me now start with an example which some will think silly, but which has given trouble to legislators and courts.[2] One section of the population, appealing to a right of freedom of the individual, thinks it has a right to go on the beach without any clothes on. Another section thinks it has a right to go on the beach without having to look at the genitals of the first lot.

If what I have said is accepted, the way to settle this

[2] For example *Williams* v. *Hathaway*, 400 F. Supp. 122 (D. Mass. 1975) (contest between nude bathers and residents of Cape Cod resort); *Eckl* v. *Davis*, 51 Cal. App. 3d 831, 124 Cal. Rptr. 685 (1975) (suit to enjoin enforcement of ordinance controlling nude bathing); Los Angeles, Cal., Ordinance 146,360 (11 July 1974) (municipal regulation of nudity on beaches and in city parks).

question is to ask what rights we ought to teach our children and ourselves to respect; and this second question is to be answered by asking a third, namely what rights are such that acts of teaching people to respect them will do the best, all in all, for the interests of all those affected, treated impartially. So what is the answer to this third question?

It requires more investigation into the facts than I have room for; but I will base my opinion on what I *think* to be the facts. They are, first of all, that many people who want to go on the beach undoubtedly are shocked by the sight of other people's genitals, and it is therefore a harm to their interest if nudity is allowed. Secondly, there are undoubtedly some people who like disporting themselves with nothing on, and seeing other people do the same. These facts are undoubted; the rest are more tentative. It may be said that the first lot (call them the prudes) would fairly soon get over their feelings of shock if it came to be generally acceptable to wear no clothes on the beach; so, although there would be a transitional period during which shock would be experienced, the result in the end would be that the nudes would get their pleasure without causing any distress to the ex-prudes. This would be an argument for giving the right of the nudes priority over that of the prudes in our moral education.

On the other hand, it might be said that the pleasure to be had by wearing *nothing* on the beach is very little more than that to be had by wearing at least something, and that therefore the transitional distress is not adequately counter-balanced by the additional pleasure. The decision between these two views would have to be made by finding out how strong were the preferences of the two parties, and how rapidly they might change as a result of new ideas on the subject becoming current—and of course also on how numerous the two parties were, and how their numbers would change given certain policies on the part of educationists and legislators. This question is currently being sorted out, both in America and in Europe, by amateur but none the less quite convincing experimental sociology i.e. by seeing how people feel when the old rules are relaxed on certain beaches or in general. It is not my purpose in this paper to speculate on the result, but my guess is that the nudes will win the argument, for the same sort of reason that in England it is no longer forbidden, as it was in many places when I was young, for men to go on the beach without their chests covered or in the company of their wives.

At this point it may be said that I have left out a very important consideration, namely the general effect on public morals of a relaxation of standards in this particular. It will be said that if people make a habit of looking at other naked people of the opposite sex on beaches, then they will tend to become more lascivious or in general immoral. I do not believe it; but I shall not have room to discuss the question now. It comes up in a closely analogous form in my next, not quite so silly, example, to which this first example has been a kind of introduction. This is the example of the suppression of pornography.

Bernard Williams, who is one of the cleverest and most prejudiced critics of utilitarianism, was asked a few years ago to be chairman of a committee set up by our British Home Office to prepare a report on Obscenity and Film Censorship (Williams 1979). There was a report a few years before that of a US Commission on a similar subject, Obscenity and Pornography (1970). Both are good reports (though owing to government inertia and timidity neither has resulted in much in the way of legislation). But I must say that in my view the Williams Report is incomparably better—perhaps in part because the chairman, a philosopher, was able to sort out the issues in a peculiarly clear way. Much of it, one could suspect on stylistic grounds, was written by Williams himself, and it all bears the stamp of his genius. Though I have no wish to disparage his other writings, I think it is the best thing he has done in moral philosophy, because it is the most in touch with real-life issues.

The most striking thing to me about the report, however, was the contrast between Williams's actual practice, when it came to dealing with such real issues, and the philosophical arguments which he marshalls with equal skill against the utilitarians in his own published works. One would expect such a thinker to argue about such questions in terms of the *right* to freedom of expression; or, on the other side, of the *right* not to have to look at obscene matter or the *right* to have one's

children's morals protected. 'Integrity' might also have had a
mention, in the rather eccentric sense in which Williams uses
it (1973: 99 ff.; see H 1976: 120 n.). But actually the Report is
utilitarian through and through. The crucial chapter in it
is called 'Harms?', and in it various arguments, all of a
utilitarian sort, for or against suppressing or not suppressing
different kinds of pornographic matter are set out and assessed
on the basis of whether the alleged harms (or benefits) really
are caused. It is, in fact, a prolonged and brilliantly executed
cost–benefit analysis. That is how the Committee determined
what rights ought to be protected.

Some years before the appointment of the committee,
Ronald Dworkin and I held a seminar on the same subject in
Oxford which was addressed by, besides him and myself, a
number of distinguished people in literature, the arts, and the
law. For this seminar I made a table of reasons for and against
restricting the sale of pornography, all of a utilitarian sort (I
could not think of any other relevant reasons). These were in
fact the kinds of reasons relied on by everybody in the
seminar, including the arch-persecutor of utilitarians, Dworkin.
They led us both, so far as I can remember, to very much the
same conclusions on what ought actually to be done. Of
course people differed about the magnitude of the various
harms and benefits which would result from various proposed
measures; but all talked in terms of harms and benefits—even
those who feared what they thought of as the greatest harm to
society, the corruption of its moral standards.

It is hard after many years to be sure that I am correctly
remembering what anybody said. But the hypothesis that
Dworkin could found his view about pornography on basically
utilitarian arguments is supported by his critical notice of the
Williams Report (1981). Dworkin first claims that the
Report's arguments, which he agrees with me in thinking
essentially utilitarian in character, do not support all its
liberal conclusions. He says that what is required in addition
is the admission of a *right*, which he calls 'the right to moral
independence'. An appeal to this right, he says, will enable us
to justify more liberal laws about pornography than a
utilitarian cost–benefit analysis would support. This accords
with Dworkin's favoured procedure of using extra-utilitarian

rights to 'trump' utilitarian arguments. I did not find this part of Dworkin's attack on Williams entirely persuasive; for whereas Williams sets out in careful detail the facts about our actual situation in that country and that culture which justify his cost–benefit analysis, Dworkin is often content to appeal to sketchy and sometimes contrived hypothetical counter-examples such as ought not to be admitted in this kind of reasoning about practical issues.

Be that as it may, Dworkin then goes on to ask how his 'right to moral independence' could be established. The remarkable thing is that his arguments are again basically utilitarian. Although he does not commit himself to accepting a utilitarian foundation for morality, or even for this part of legislative morality, he argues that a utilitarian system, starting from equality of concern, would need to incorporate such a right in order to achieve its own ends. This is, in effect, to operate a two-level utilitarian system of the kind I have been advocating. Utilitarianism or, as I have euphemistically called it, interest-egalitarianism at the critical level generates certain rights for use at the intuitive level at which most of our practical moral decisions have to be made; and at this lower level they can usefully be entrenched and used to 'trump' the more direct, but also less reliable, application of cost–benefit calculations.

Dworkin himself acknowledges that a two-level theory could escape his main argument against Williams's utilitarian method; but he strangely claims that 'the neutral utilitarian theory we are now considering' would not avail itself of this escape route. In fact, a utilitarian who knew the ropes would say that we should be impartial at the critical level between good and evil preferences, but that this same impartial treatment of preferences at the critical level would lead us to adopt, for use at the intuitive level of everyday practical decisions, principles which are partial towards good preferences, and bid us thwart the bad ones. This is because the disposition to do this is one the cultivation of which, because of its consequences, conduces to the maximal satisfaction of all preferences weighed impartially in proportion merely to their strength (*MT* 140–6).

Dworkin and I therefore seem to be agreed that a two-level

utilitarian system could enable Williams to support his conclusions. The difference is that Dworkin relies, in order to get his 'right to moral independence' from his equal-concern starting-point, on somewhat abstract a priori reasoning based on hypothetical and sometimes improbable examples, whereas I cannot follow him in such reasoning; I would hope rather that Williams, if he were more conscious than he is of the two-level character of moral thinking, could show, by appeal to the contingent facts of our present society, that the entrenchment of such a right is more likely than its denial to conduce, all in all, to the maximal satisfaction of people's preferences, considered impartially. If, instead of speaking of preferences, he thought it more tasteful to use the elusive expression 'human flourishing', I should not object on any but stylistic grounds.

Some time after the Williams Committee had been set up and had asked for evidence from the public, on the instigation of a friend who had been at the seminar, I wrote to Bernard Williams sending him my own material from the seminar and asking if he would like me to put it into a form suitable for submission to his Committee as evidence. He did not reply, and did not, as I heard from another member of the Committee, show it to the Committee as it stood. I think he had good reason for this; not only had I left it rather late, but the deliberations of the Committee had almost certainly, by that advanced stage, reached the conclusions set out in the report, which are, in most particulars, similar to those which Dworkin the anti-utilitarian and I had both reached, and on the same grounds.

I mention all this because I think it striking how three philosophers, one of them a utilitarian and the other two quite the reverse, when they come to discuss a practical issue like this, arrive at the same utilitarian conclusions and give utilitarian reasons, even if not quite the same utilitarian reasons, for them. I will not give the conclusions because there is not room; but they are in the Report, with which I agree in almost every particular.

There are two possible retorts which I think Williams might make. The first is that there is something special about the question of obscenity law which makes utilitarian arguments alone relevant to it; and that in other fields of morality they may be less relevant. Even this would not accord with the tone of his other writings, in which he has hardly a good word for utilitarian arguments of any kind. And it is not easy to see how he is going to confine the scope of utilitarian arguments so narrowly. Will they not also be relevant in all fields of public policy (which were Bentham's and Mill's chief interest)? And will they not have a bearing on all moral questions where the interests of other people are affected, for the same reasons as on questions of public policy? Where others' interests are *not* affected, I myself have no wish to employ utilitarian arguments (*MT* 54).

The second retort is this. He might say that I have left out of my account of the arguments of the Committee a very crucial premiss which is not utilitarian. The basis of the argument, he might say, is this. There is a *right* which we all have, namely the right to freedom of expression. This means that we have a right to say, publish, buy, read, or look at anything that we want to, provided that reasons are not adduced why we should not say, or publish, it, etc. So what he has done is to take for granted this fundamental right, which is not based on utilitarian grounds, and to look for and assess arguments for denying it in particular sorts of cases (e.g. that to publish certain things will be so harmful that the right ought to be overridden). All these secondary arguments may be utilitarian, but the original right is not. So the argument of the Committee is after all based most fundamentally on a right, not on utility.

However, it is easy to demolish this retort. For the alleged fundamental right of freedom of expression turns out to have a utilitarian ground after all. It is one of the most basic tenets of utilitarianism that preferences, likings, or, to use the general word I have been using, interests, are what count in making moral judgements. It follows from this that if someone prefers or likes to do something, he ought to be allowed to do it in default of reasons why he should not. For the utilitarian, these reasons will have to do with conflicts with the preferences or interests of other people. Now the right of freedom of expression is simply a particular case of the right to do what one wants in default of reasons why one should not. It too, therefore, can be established on utilitarian grounds. Williams may have dug it out of his intuitions, but he did not have to. And the reasons or alleged reasons for denying this right in certain cases which were so admirably discussed in the report were avowedly all utilitarian. So if the whole report was not utilitarian, it was only because Williams neglected to give utilitarian reasons for his fundamental premiss (and for one or two other less important contentions), but relied on the intuitions of the Committee. Whether he could have given any *other* reasons I shall not ask; but he did not need to.

I hope I have shown that even anti-utilitarians, when they have a practical job of work to do, tend to argue like utilitarians. This is in support of my general point that there is a utilitarian way (or, as I euphemistically put it, an interest-egalitarian way) of arguing about rights, and that this way can be reconciled with the existence of strong intuitions in all of us. The point is that, valuable as these intuitions are, they are valuable only at the intuitive level. Once we are driven, as we inevitably are, to go above the intuitive to the critical level and question our own intuitions, they lose their cogency.

10
Liberty and Equality: How Politics Masquerades as Philosophy

IT is my intention in this paper to highlight the dangers which arise when people appeal to moral intuitions to settle questions in political, and in general in applied, philosophy. But first I want to ask why all or nearly all of us are in favour both of liberty and of equality—why all our intuitions are on their side.

In the case of liberty it is easy to understand why. Although philosophers have held diverse theories about the concept of liberty—theories which have been drawn together into two main groups in a famous lecture by Sir Isaiah Berlin (1958)—there cannot be much doubt that in the mind of the ordinary man to have liberty (to be free; I shall not distinguish between freedom and liberty) is to be under no constraint in doing what one wants to do. This, at any rate, is a main constituent of the concept of liberty as all of us understand it.

Since, therefore, it seems self-evidently true that we want to be able to do what we want, we are bound to want liberty and, in general, to be in favour of it. We want it for ourselves; if we universalize our prescriptions, this constrains us to be in favour of it for others as well. That explains why, if any politician can claim that he is fighting for liberty, he is likely to win a large following.

In the case of equality the matter is not so clear cut. There have been many societies in which equality was not valued. As the well-known hymn (Alexander 1848) has it:

> The rich man in his castle,
>   The poor man at his gate,
> God made them, high or lowly,
>   And ordered their estate.

From *Social Philosophy and Policy* 2 (1984).

This has been the view of *anciens régimes* throughout the ages, and Plato is echoing an extremely common sentiment when he complains of the Athenian democracy of his day that it 'distributes a sort of equality to equals and unequals alike' (*Rep.* 558c). If, today, it is as easy to get political support by appealing to equality as to liberty, this is because such regimes have become outmoded. I have given reasons elsewhere why equality (at any rate moderate equality) is a good thing, and I shall return to these reasons later.

Thus it has come about that in the mouths of most of us both 'liberty' and 'equality' are hurrah-words. But any well-read political philosopher knows that this is only the beginning of a tangle of problems. Just because they are hurrah-words, the prescription to pursue liberty and equality in our society seems self-evidently right, but it is entirely unclear what in particular it tells us to do. Let me give some examples, not only of conflicts *between* liberty and equality as political aims, but of conflicts between different aims, each of which could claim to be motivated by the desire for liberty; and the same for equality. Of conflicts between liberty and equality we have heard a great deal in recent years. It is notorious that if you start with an equal distribution of wealth in society, and give people the liberty to dispose of their own wealth as they think fit, you will very soon end up with an extremely unequal distribution. Thus in the economic sphere at any rate it has come to be generally accepted that there is no fraternity between liberty and equality: so far from being happy brothers they are natural enemies.

But even within each camp there is a conflict. My wife and I were recently taken by a kind German friend to see the Befreiungshalle, or Hall of the Liberation, built on a magnificent site above the Danube gorge near Regensburg. It is a splendid rotunda in the purest classical style (looking a bit like a gas-holder designed by Phidias), and was put up by King Ludwig of Bavaria to commemorate the liberation of the Germans, and of Bavaria in particular, from Napoleon. To my English eyes it was strange that, among the many military leaders who figure as liberators, the Duke of Wellington is not included (though Blücher is). Although far from being a liberal (were any of them?), the Duke could claim in some sense to be a liberator. But what is more to the point is that the 'tyranny' from which the Germans were thus liberated was that of a man whose political roots lay in the Revolution, and whose armies were inspired by thoughts of liberty. For them, King Ludwig was a tyrant.

There is another example nearer home. When the American ex-colonists expanded into the West, they had the liberty to do so because the French were no longer there; and the French were no longer there because they had been expelled by British arms (assisted of course by vigorous local efforts). But when the Americans rebelled against the British, it was the freedom not to be taxed in order to provide for their own protection that the Revolutionaries above all sought. The French, naturally, were delighted. So here again the winning of one sort of liberty had militated against the preservation of another. Today in many parts of the world peoples have obtained freedom from imperial rulers only to fall under the power of the most odious local tyrannies. Think of Cambodia.

Equality is just as divided against itself. The best general example is the conflict between equality of wealth and equality of power. The principal motive for setting up socialist regimes all over the world has been to promote equality of wealth. Egalitarian sentiments always bulk large in the propaganda of socialist parties. Yet the putting into practice of these ideas has almost always resulted in (indeed required) the concentration of enormous power into the hands of a small number of people, who have seldom followed liberal principles in the exercise of it. This, indeed, is in accord with Marxist theory. It has proved possible in a very few western-style democracies to combine moderate equality of wealth with a moderate spread of power among the governed. But this is a very difficult political art, and the conditions under which it can be practised occur relatively rarely, and are very delicate and easily disturbed by extremist measures either of the left or of the right.

Some philosophers, viewing these conflicts between liberty and equality and within them both, of which I have been able to give only the sketchiest of examples, will try to provide a remedy by seeking better definitions of the two concepts. If we could only find the right kind of concept of liberty or of equality, they seem to be thinking, we should be able to recommend self-consistent policies which would pursue the best sort of liberty and the best sort of equality simultaneously. Some philosophers even think that they can thus reconcile other desirable political ends as well, such as order. Hegel is an outstanding example. But I am inclined to think that the ambition to solve these problems by finding a single definition of either concept is naïve, and does not go to the root of the matter. A single definition there might be of each concept; but it would not help, because it would be too lacking in content (as indeed definitions should be) to provide specific political guidance.

The truth is that the conflicts are inherent. This is because liberty for one person to do one thing may be inconsistent, in the world as it is, with liberty for another person to do something else that he wants; and equality between people in one respect may, as we have seen, militate against equality in other respects. These conflicts, like all moral conflicts, should make us re-examine, in more depth than I have done so far, the reasoning processes which have led us to our conflicting aims and opinions. And the first thing that may then happen is that we shall acquire a healthy distrust of moral intuition.

It is common political form in most western countries to think that liberty must be a good thing, and that equality must be a good thing. It is even held, contrary to all the evidence, that democracy must be a good thing in all circumstances (see p. 173). I am a very strong believer in democracy; but there is a danger in letting our belief in it rest on simple moral conviction. This may weaken our power to argue; and then, when we need to show *why* democracy is, in certain familiar circumstances, preferable to dictatorship, we shall find ourselves at a loss. Having been brought up from our earliest years to think that it is a good form of government, we are convinced that it is so, but cannot for the life of us think why. Only by using our reasoning powers shall we be able to show why the democratic process is, in many societies which can manage it, the most efficient and best way of governing ourselves; and when there are exceptions (when it turns out, for example, that a democratic constitution leads to governmental impotence, corruption, and chaos) to show what peculiarities of the particular society (deep communal divisions, for example) led to the collapse of democracy. In all this reasoning we shall have to have regard, not initially to our moral convictions (they will come later when we have done the reasoning) but to facts about societies. It is a relevant fact, for example, that it was the western democracies that defeated the dictatorships of Germany, Italy, and Japan in the Second World War, and not vice versa; they showed themselves the more efficient form of government in this formidable test. But even there Russia was the exception.

So to argue in defence of democracy, morally or in any other way, demands thought about our principles and about the situations to which they are to be applied. Our conviction that democracy is a good form of government is only secure when it can be defended by sound reasoning on the basis of established historical facts. And the conviction will become, albeit more secure, less extreme in the process: we shall remain convinced that democracy is a good form of government, but ready to admit that it may not be the best form of government in all societies at all times.

This digression about democracy has illustrated why it is a mistake, and weakens our political and moral thought, to rely on intuition. I now want to apply this lesson to liberty and equality. We need to be able to show by clear thinking in the light of the facts, not merely that liberty and equality are on the whole good things, but why they are, and, more importantly, what sorts of liberty and equality are good things, and in what circumstances. And in doing this thinking, we have to have an eye to the actual conditions under which the liberty is going to be exercised and the equality enjoyed.

We must notice how radical a departure this would be from the practice of many philosophers. Both liberty and equality are often referred to as 'rights'. 'The right to be free' occurred in a wartime slogan that I remember; and people are constantly demanding equal treatment in some respect as a right (and in many cases I applaud them for doing this). What I am going now to say about liberty and equality is simply an application of what I have said elsewhere about rights. When philosophers talk about rights, either in general or in arguing about particular rights, they commonly assume that we *know*, really, what rights people have. Our intuitions inform us of this, if only we can get them clear. So we find Judith Jarvis Thomson (1971) naïvely supposing that if only we can think clearly about her case of the lady hooked up to a great violinist, our intuitions will tell us what we ought to say about it, and thus we shall be able to generalize from this particular case and say something secure about abortion (something of course which will support the feminist view). This is an outstanding example of how, as I put it in my title, politics masquerades as philosophy. We start off with intuitions, which we hope will be sufficiently widely shared for us to attract a following, and apply them to particular well-chosen cases. The answers come out as we wish, and we then derive a general conclusion about some important political question. Never, in the whole thought-process, is it asked whether the intuitions are ones which we should have. It is assumed that people (women for example or, if you are on the other side, foetuses) have rights, and that we can intuit what they are, if only we pay close enough attention to our own navels. It is never asked what rights these parties *should be accorded*. But that is the fundamental moral question on the answer to which all our practice should be based.

The same thing happens when Robert Nozick (1974) talks about liberty. In his famous Wilt Chamberlain example, he *assumes* that the snap answers that we shall most of us give are the right ones. We know already, by intuition, that he ought to be free to exchange his services for whatever fee he can get from other willing parties. The fact that the general application of this finding, which Nozick proceeds to make, would lead to the grossest inequalities in distribution, not only of wealth, but also of power derived from wealth, and that this runs counter to *other* intuitions which most of us have, is conveniently played down by Nozick. He is, like all those who use this method, highly selective in the intuitions to which he appeals.

John Rawls (1971) reaches very different conclusions by appeal to *his* intuitions. One is inclined to suspect that both of these writers *start* from a certain political position, just as Professor Thomson starts from a feminist position. This is what determines what intuitions they are going to have, and so, naturally, the arguments based on these intuitions come out as they wish. In fairness to Rawls, he does have, unlike Nozick, a method of moral reasoning. I think it is a good one, and would lead to the right conclusions if it were consistently applied (see H 1973*a*). The method relies on asking what people would say in the original position, ignorant of the role which they were to play in the society governed by the principles of justice they were choosing. The great merit of this method is that it asks initially not 'What social arrangements are just?' but 'What are the principles of justice by which we should determine the justice of social arrangements?'. Applied to questions about rights, this procedure will lead us to ask first, not 'What rights do such and such people have?' but 'How (by what principles) should we determine what rights ought to be accorded to those people?'. Applied to questions about liberty, it will lead us to ask first, not 'What rights to what sorts of liberty do what people have?' but 'How should we decide what things people should be free to do and what things they should not be free to do?' Applied to equality, it would lead us to ask first, not 'What rights to equal treatment do people have in various circumstances?' but 'How should we determine what rights to what kind of equal treatment should be accorded to people under varying conditions?'

Rawls is absolutely right to treat as basic the questions which I say should be asked first. We have to have, first, a method of arguing (his method is that of the original position), and then use the method to establish general principles. Only after that can we apply the principles to particular questions about justice, rights, liberty, and equality. The sad thing is that, although he has a method for settling these questions, Rawls vitiates his procedure by continual appeals to his own moral intuitions, which he hopes his readers will share. He is not content to rely on the method; it has to yield results consistent with his intuitions in reflective equilibrium, or he will tinker with the method. In particular, it has to yield results different from those yielded by utilitarianism; for one of Rawls's firmest intuitions is that utilitarianism is wrong. But if the method is played straight, it does yield utilitarian conclusions (see p. 47 and H 1973*a*). Rawls himself admits that an ideal observer theory will yield such conclusions. But it is only by *ad hoc* tinkering, and by depriving them of the factual information on which sound moral judgement has to be based, that Rawls manages to get his ideal rational contractors out of the position of ideal observers and into a position in which they will make a non-utilitarian contract. In order to ensure their impartiality, which is the only function of his veil of ignorance, he only needed to conceal from them their individual roles, not other more material facts. If he had restricted himself to this 'formal' veil of ignorance, his rational contractors would have been subject effectively to the same restrictions as the ideal observer, and would have reached the same utilitarian conclusions.

My point is that we have to have a method of moral thinking before we start thinking—at least, the method is logically prior; though there may be perfectly good inarticulate intuitive thinking without any prior explicit grasp of method, the method is implicit in any sound thinking that can give reasons for what is thought. Thus, we have to ask how we should determine what liberties and equalities people should have before we address the substantial question. I shall go on now to discuss how I would myself answer the methodological question, and how I think the answer to it puts on a much more hopeful basis all our arguments on practical questions about liberty and equality.

Like Rawls, I think that the first things to look for are principles of justice, determining rights, which are acceptable to rational thought. Unlike Rawls, who is rather contemptuous of appeals to the logic of our concepts, I think that the way to find these principles is first to study our moral language and concepts (which are, so far, neutral between different substantial moral and political standpoints). These concepts and their logic will determine for us certain rules which we have to obey in our thinking, if we are to do it rationally. When we do it in accordance with these rules, we find that, in the light of the facts of the world in which we live, some principles of justice and other moral principles are acceptable and some not. That is how we get our principles of justice.

I have explained the method much more fully in *MT*. Here, I can only summarize: the conceptual points about the logic of moral thinking are that moral statements in their central use express prescriptions, and these have to be universalizable. The recognition of this leads to a method which is at the same time Kantian and utilitarian. If we know that in making a moral judgement we are prescribing universally for all similar cases, we shall not prescribe for others what we are not prepared to prescribe for ourselves were we identically placed. This will lead us to give equal weight to the equal preferences of all, since we shall give equal weight to theirs and to ours, and of course it will be positive. Thus we shall be, as utilitarians do, counting everybody for one and nobody for more than one, and shall be trying to maximize the satisfaction of everybody's preferences, treated impartially. And, as Kantians do, we shall be acting so that we can will the maxim of our action to be a universal law; we shall be treating humanity in ourselves and others as an end; and we shall be acting as if we were legislating members of a kingdom of ends.

If this method were applied directly to acts, it would enjoin us to judge them by their utility, in the sense of preference-satisfaction. However, even an act-utilitarian (which is what I am) must recognize that our ability to predict the consequences of our acts (what we shall be in effect doing if we perform them) is very limited. Even an act-utilitarian, therefore, will only demand of himself that he give himself the best chance that he can: the greatest expectation of utility. And the way to do this, the world and human nature being as they are, is to cultivate and religiously follow sound general principles whose acceptance-utility is highest. There is much more to be said about that, but that will have to suffice.

The posture of the wise Kantian utilitarian will therefore be just like that of an intuitionist brought up on sound lines, except that he can justify his upbringing and the intuitionist cannot. Some of the intuitions he will have will be about justice and rights. He will have come to have those intuitions (acknowledge those principles of justice and those rights) which have the highest acceptance-utility; that is, whose acceptance in society, and in particular by him, is most likely to do the best, all in all, to satisfy the preferences of those affected. This, then, is how we should determine what rights we should acknowledge: in particular, what liberties we should safeguard either by law or by moral sanctions; and how equally we should treat people and in what respects.

Since all that is much too summary and general, I am going to illustrate it by discussing briefly a particular class of cases which seems to me to be an extremely good example of the application of this method in the political field. This is the case of legislation about employment and trade unions (see p. 142).

If we look at the rhetoric used by both sides in this area, it is obvious that appeals to liberty and equality are frequently made. One of the main motives of labour leaders is the desire for equality. But the equality desired may be of different kinds. There is, first, the wish to lessen differences in power and wealth between capitalists, or managers, and workers. But more prominent recently has been a wish to secure equality with other groups of workers. This has revived in miniature an old conflict between different interpretations of 'equality'. One interpretation is used to support higher wages for workers at present at the bottom of the scale, in order to make their pay more equal to that of others. But on another interpretation the others are then being unequally, in the sense of unfairly, treated because the differential has been eroded; it is assumed, on this interpretation, that the old differential yielded *proportionate* equality (in very much the sense supported by Aristotle (1131a 10 ff.), equal pay for work of equal value), and it is therefore claimed that equality demands a return to the old proportionate differential. However, this very same argument is looked on askance if it is applied to the pay of judges, army officers, or Members of Parliament. As is well known, the alternation or leap-frogging of these two arguments is a potent rhetorical weapon in the hands of union leaders. It is a kind of ratchet device whereby pay can be increased indefinitely, provided that the unions who appeal to these conflicting intuitions have enough industrial muscle.

In order to preserve their muscle, union leaders frequently invoke other intuitions about liberty. If they are successfully to prosecute the class war, workers have to have the liberty to combine against their employers and coerce them into giving better terms of employment. 'Liberty to coerce' is of course somewhat of a paradox. The liberty is secured by obtaining for trade unions legal immunities, so that they cannot, like ordinary people, be sued in the courts if, for example, they induce their members to break contracts, or damage third parties not involved in a wage claim. The liberty is even demanded to use violence in the course of strikes, at least by way of barring 'scabs' from a factory by a threat of trouble, in order to avoid which the police, if the government is benign, will, in effect, help to keep the picket line peaceful but secure. But if the police are absent, the scabs know what to expect.

On the other side, employers and Conservative politicians will marshal another lot of intuitions. They will complain that firms are not being treated equally if the laws of contract and tort are not applied to trade unions as they are to everybody else, including the firms in their dealings with one another. And they will complain that employers' liberty is being infringed if they are not allowed to make enforceable contracts (the best they can obtain by free bargaining) with their employees. And the bargaining, they will say, is not free if they are subject to the threat of strike action. Not all those on the two sides would use all these arguments. It is far from my intention to support any of them. I think they are all bad arguments, in so far as they rest on unreasoned intuitions whose sole basis is political. Yet I should not be at all surprised to find arguments having just the same form, and just as little sound basis, in the writings of our philosophical colleagues. They are what their epistemology encourages. I have at any rate shown how deeply intuitions about liberty and equality are embedded in such disputes.

How *should* we decide what rights of liberty and equality should be accorded by the law, and sanctioned by morality, to those engaged in industry? The first part of the answer is relatively easy. The formal properties of the moral concepts require us not to differentiate morally between identical cases: a moral prescription for one case will have to apply to any identically similar case, whoever is at the receiving end. This is what is called formal justice, which comprises both formal equality (identical cases are to be treated equally by the moral law) and formal liberty (each person is to be the judge of what he here and now prefers and therefore prescribes). I am referring to singular prescriptions as to what should happen *to him now.* He is not necessarily the best judge of what he will prefer if things happen to him which he does not now fully represent to himself (for not everybody is prudent); and he is not necessarily the best judge of what prescriptions, if universalized, will maximally satisfy the preferences of all, considered impartially (for not everybody is moral).

As is generally recognized, formal justice does not take us very far. But I have already said how it leads directly to a utilitarian method of moral reasoning which can settle more substantial questions. If, in choosing what principles to cultivate in the field of labour relations, we realize that we are prescribing universally, and subject therefore to the requirement of formal justice, we shall have equal regard to the equal preferences of all those affected. These will include, besides the workers and employers in a particular industry, all who buy its products, and in some degree the whole of society. This, as I have said, will make us choose the principles with the highest general acceptance-utility, in the world of industry as it is. So should we or should we not have combination acts forbidding trade unions? We should not, because the existence of trade unions has, by and large, brought enormous benefits to employees without actually harming industry or the consumer in the long run. But ought trade unions to be given all the legal immunities that they have traditionally in Britain, for example? That is at present being argued; and the way to argue it rationally is to ask, 'What principles covering legislation about trade unions and in general about wage-fixing are likely, if accepted, to result in the greatest preference-satisfaction for all, treated impartially?' If we follow such principles, the laws that we make will do better for the general preference-satisfaction than the present law does, unless it is already optimal. I doubt whether the present state of the law in Britain *is* optimal. It certainly gives in most respects greater liberties to trade unions than those of most other countries.

Will a law made in accordance with such principles be just? It will be formally just, because we shall be treating like cases alike, whoever is affected, as universalizability leads us to do. It will also be formally just as regards the operation of the law itself, in that the law applies to everybody who falls under the conditions specified in it, and is impartially administered by the courts. But the first kind of formal justice (the moral, as contrasted with the legal) is the more fundamental.

Will such a law secure substantial justice? It will, because it will be approved by principles of justice (moral principles) which have the highest acceptance-utility, taking into account the preferences of all those affected, considered impartially. The substance is put in by the preferences themselves (different preferences will justify different laws). If the Chinese *prefer* industry to be ordered differently, a formally just way of legislating about it in China will come out with different laws from those in a country whose inhabitants have different preferences. In either case, the laws will *be* just, because they allot utility impartially; and they will be *seen* to be just, if people have the moral intuitions about justice and rights, in this area, that they should have—i.e. the intuitions whose content is moral principles having the highest acceptance-utility.

In other words, our object should be to get both laws and moral principles adopted in society which do the best, all in all, for the members of society considered impartially. If I may speculate about the outcome, it might be that ideas became current very different from those which now motivate a supposed class war. People would begin to ask themselves whether more good is done to all by co-operation than by conflict. Trade unions would have an important place; but their actions would be governed by principles directed to the good of all members of society, whether in the role of workers, as nearly everybody is, or of consumers, as everybody is, or, as many employees are now in Britain through the operation of pension funds, of capitalists. All this could be effected if people really understood how to think about these matters.

11

The Rights of Employees:

The European Court of Human Rights and the Case of *Young, James, and Webster)*

I AM going in this paper to discuss a class of cases in which very bitter disputes about rights occur, and which offers a peculiarly clear example of how to argue, and how not to argue, in order to settle such disputes. These cases all arise in the area of industrial relations. We hear a great deal about the rights of trade unions, and about the rights of employers and of their own members against trade unions. A great many of the arguments that are current in this area are moral arguments, and I think that the method I have advocated in my books can shed a lot of light upon them.

I will start with the case of *Young, James, and Webster*, which actually came recently before the European Court of Human Rights (1981). It concerns the rights and wrongs of the closed or union shop. This consists in an agreement between unions and employers that the latter will employ only union members. The three applicants were employees of British Rail, and were dismissed in 1976, in pursuance of a closed-shop agreement, because they refused to join one of the railway unions, mainly on grounds of political dissent.

The case was heard by the full Court, not, as is sometimes done in less important cases, by a select Chamber of the Court. The judgement consists of a majority judgement of (on the crucial question) 18 votes to 3 holding that Article 11 of the Human Rights Convention had been breached; 2 different concurring opinions by 6 judges and 1 judge respectively; and a dissenting opinion by the 3 judges of the minority, all Scandinavians. The first clause of Article 11 reads as follows:

1. Everyone has the right to freedom of peaceful assembly and to

Not published before. Privately printed and circulated to participants in a conference at Leiden University, 1985.

freedom of association with others, including the right to form and to join trade unions for the protection of this interest.

The main judgement is not as clear as it should be; but it appears that the chief ground for finding a breach of Article 11 was that a right to join a union logically implies a right *not* to join one if one so desires. The judgement calls this right not to join, a 'negative' right, and the right to join, a 'positive' right. Here are some quotations from the judgement.

The Court recalls, however, that the right to form and to join trade unions is a special aspect of freedom of association; it adds that the notion of a freedom implies some measure of freedom of choice as to its exercise . . .

To construe Article 11 as permitting every kind of compulsion in the field of trade union membership would strike at the very substance of the freedom it is designed to guarantee (52) . . .

Each applicant regarded the membership condition introduced by that agreement, [i.e. the closed-shop agreement] as an interference with the freedom of association to which he considered that he was entitled (54) . . .

The situation facing the applicants clearly runs counter to the concept of freedom of association in its negative sense. Assuming that Article 11 does not guarantee the negative aspect of that freedom on the same footing as the positive aspect, compulsion to join a particular trade union may not always be contrary to the Convention. However, a threat of dismissal involving loss of livelihood is a most serious form of compulsion and, in the present instance, it was directed against persons engaged by British Rail before the introduction of any obligation to join a particular trade union. In the Court's opinion, such a form of compulsion, in the circumstances of the case, strikes at the very substance of the freedom guaranteed by Article 11. For this reason alone, there has been an interference with that freedom as regards each of the three applicants (55) . . .

An individual does not enjoy the right to freedom of association if in reality the freedom of action or choice which remains available to him is either nonexistent or so reduced as to be of no practical value (56) . . .

Accordingly it strikes at the very substance of this Article to exert pressure, of the kind applied to the applicants, in order to compel someone to join an association contrary to his convictions (57).

The dissenting opinion of the minority is very much clearer, and states unambiguously that the issue is whether the positive right or freedom implies the negative.

The issue under Article 11 is whether or not freedom of association as protected by that Article implies a right for the individual not to be constrained to join or belong to any particular association or—in the terminology adopted by the Court—the negative aspect of the freedom of association is covered by Article 11 (1) . . .

In the present case, however, the problem is whether the negative aspect of the freedom of association is part of the substance of the right guaranteed by Article 11 (5) . . .

The minority judges answer unequivocally that it is not:

The so-called positive and negative freedom of association are not simply two sides of the same coin or, as the Court puts it, two aspects of the same freedom. There is no logical link between the two . . . However strongly such protection of the individual may sometimes be needed, it is neither in logic nor by necessary implication part of the positive freedom of association (6).

It is, I think, highly significant that the three dissentient judges were the only Scandinavians in the Court. In the Scandinavian countries, unlike most other European countries except Britain, there has been a very strong tradition of analytical philosophy, stemming from an offshoot of the Vienna Circle. This has given rise to an equally strong tradition of analytical jurisprudence, including the study of deontic logic. I may instance, for example, the well-known work of von Wright, and of the Danish jurist Alf Ross, whose *Directives and Norms* was published in English, and, though I think it contains errors, is still a good introduction to the subject. When I read the dissenting judgement, I thought it very likely that the three dissentient judges had been influenced and that their reasoning was clarified by this tradition; and that therefore, in asking whether they or the majority were right, it would be helpful to do a little elementary deontic logic, which is all I am capable of. After I had written this, my conjecture was fully confirmed by an Icelander, Professor Gylfasson, who visited Oxford. He told me that he had himself been consulted by the Icelandic judge, and had instructed him in the necessary deontic logic, thus directly influencing the dissenting judgement.

The right to freedom of association is, as its name implies, one of the class of rights known generally as 'liberties'. I have a liberty-right if it is not unlawful for me to do something. In the present case, the right of freedom of association is preserved by the law if it is not unlawful to join associations. This class of rights, liberty-rights, is often contrasted with another class, called 'claim-rights', which exists if it is not merely the case that it is not unlawful to a do a certain thing, but that it *is* unlawful for anybody to *stop* someone doing that thing. There is a fuller explanation, with a reference to Wesley Hohfeld, in *MT* 149. I am going to proceed at first on the assumption that the right of freedom of association is a liberty-right, because that is the simpler case. Later I will show that the same argument goes through if it is interpreted as a claim-right.

A liberty-right is a kind of legal permission: I have a liberty-right, if the law permits me to do a certain thing, for example join a union. Notoriously the notion of a permission is ambiguous; but the kind we are concerned with here is clear enough. If the law does not forbid something, that something is legally permitted; if the law requires something, the omission to do that something is not legally permitted, and in both cases the converse holds. In symbols, using the usual Polish notation as in Prior's *Formal Logic* (1955),

$$ENONpPp$$

and

$$EOpNPNp.$$

These two equivalences are usually made a matter of definition. '*Pp*' is defined as meaning the same as '*NONp*', so that 'It is legally permitted that *p*' means the same as 'It is not legally required that not *p*'. Alternatively '*Op*' is defined as meaning the same as '*NPNp*', so that 'It is legally required that *p*' means the same as 'It is not legally permitted that not *p*'. This enables us to restate formally the issue which the Scandinavian judges thought crucial. It is, whether '*Pp*' implies '*PNp*', where '*p*' stands, in our present case, for 'Young, James, and Webster join a railway union'. That is, does the fact that they are permitted by law, or have a legal liberty-right, to join a union, imply that they also have a legal liberty-right not to join a union? As we shall see, the real issue is more complicated than that, but that will do for the moment.

I think it is clear that there is no such implication. The fact that it is lawful to do something or other in no way implies that it is lawful not to do it. It is lawful for me to pay my taxes, but it does not follow that it is lawful for me not to pay my taxes. Before I go on to the complications, I will use this example to expose one possible source of confusion which may have misled the majority judges. It is conversationally misleading, and therefore ruled out by the rules of good conversation, to say something weaker when one is in a position to say something stronger and it is important for one's hearer to have the stronger thing communicated to him (Grice 1961: 132). So, if I say that the candidate for a chair is of at least average ability (which is true), when the candidate is in fact a genius, I mislead the Board of Electors and harm the candidate. Similarly here, it is normally wrong to say that I am permitted to pay my taxes, when in fact I am required to pay them. And in the same way to say merely that someone is permitted to join a union may be misleading if he is in fact required to join one. If, in advertising a job, an employer said merely that the person employed was permitted to join a union, when in fact he was required to join, applicants would rightly complain of being misled.

However, these are conversational implicatures and not logical implications. There is no logical inconsistency between '*Pp*' and '*Op*'. Indeed, according to my linguistic intuitions '*Op*' entails '*Pp*', inasmuch as it is self-contradictory to say 'You are under a legal obligation to do it, but are not legally permitted to.' But '*Op*' and '*NPNp*' are definitionally equivalent. So, on this interpretation of a right, '*Pp*' and '*NPNp*' are consistent. But for *Pp* to entail *PNp* is for *Pp* and *NPNp* to be *in*consistent. '*Pp*' cannot therefore entail '*PNp*' (in our example, 'It is permitted to join a union' cannot entail 'It is permitted not to join a union') as the majority of the court thinks it does, and the Scandinavian minority is right.

But I have over-simplified by taking the interpretation of a right as the absence of a law prohibiting something. Probably this is not what the right not to join a union is. The complaint of the applicants was not that the *law* prohibited them from not joining a union, but that British Rail did as a condition of employment. However, having seen the logic of the simpler case, it will be easier to explain that of the more complicated. Let us take the rights in question as claim-rights. That is to say, let us suppose that 'Young, James, and Webster have a right to join a union' means 'It is unlawful for anybody to stop them joining a union'; and that 'They have a right not to join a union' means 'It is unlawful for anybody to stop them *not* joining a union (i.e. to compel them to join a union).' The contention of the majority judges therefore comes to this, that if it is unlawful for anybody to stop them joining a union, it must be unlawful for anybody to compel them to join one. That this does not follow could be shown, I think, by a similar logical argument; but it can be shown more easily by examples.

We all have a right to go on trains if we can show a ticket or a pass and do not misbehave. This right belongs also to those who take employment as engine-drivers. When they take that employment, they do not *lose* their right to go on trains, but they acquire a new obligation, to go on trains in order to drive them. British Rail can then lawfully compel them, in terms of their contract, to go on trains (barring, of course, industrial disputes, where the law gives strikers special privileges which I shall be discussing in the last part of this paper but shall ignore for the moment). So they have lost the right not to go on trains; it is no longer unlawful for anybody to compel them to go on trains. So, in this case, the right (as we are now interpreting it) to go on trains does not entail a right not to go on trains. If we now substitute 'join a union' for 'go on trains', exactly the same holds. The right to join a union does not entail a right not to join a union.

An even clearer case is the following. We all have a right to remain celibate (i.e. it is unlawful for anybody to compel us to marry). Roman Catholic priests, as a condition of their employment, undertake an obligation to remain celibate (they can lawfully be fired if they marry). This new obligation does not destroy their original right to remain celibate; it is not self-contradictory to say 'It is lawful for your employers to require you to remain celibate, *and* it is unlawful for them to stop you remaining celibate.' Again, for 'remain celibate' read 'join a union', and we have 'It is lawful for your employers to require you to join a union, *and* it is unlawful for them to stop you joining a union.' But the majority judges say, or at least imply, that this is self-contradictory; for they say that if it is unlawful for your employers to stop you joining a union it must be unlawful for them to require you to join one. If '*p* and not *q*' is not self-contradictory, then '*p*' cannot entail '*q*'.

Let us now leave these logical points and ask a very general question. Why did the European Court of Human Rights argue the case on this very narrow logical basis (thereby landing itself in a fallacy because its logic was not good enough)? It was because of something about the whole human rights set-up in Europe, which has its counterparts elsewhere (for example in the practices of the US Supreme Court). The procedure has been this: there has been a Convention on Human Rights, signed by various European states, which forms a body of law that the Court then has to interpret. This is treated as analogous to the interpretation of the domestic statutes of one of these states by its own internal courts. I can see nothing wrong so far. But the trouble is that the Convention is framed in terms which are extremely vague (and have had to be because of the nature of the subject and the difficulty of getting any sort of agreement). Exactly the same sort of thing will happen if we have a domestic Bill of Rights in Britain, as some people want. Enormous strain is put thereby on the Court's role of 'interpreting' the Convention. The Court is subject to political pressures and to its desire to make its decision reflect, not just the Convention, but enlightened public opinion and its own moral convictions. So in the present case it was trying very hard to find against the principle of the closed shop (and even the minority seems to think that the closed shop, at least in the form, since abolished, in which Young, James, and Webster suffered from its effects, is a bad thing). But the minority rightly says in its dissenting opinion,

Objectionable as the treatment suffered by the applicants may be on grounds of reason and equity, the adequate solution lies, not in any extensive interpretation of that Article but in safeguards against dismissal because of refusal to join a union, that is in safeguarding the right to security of employment in such circumstances. But this right is not among those recognised by the Convention which—as stated in the preamble—is only a first step for the collective enforcement of human rights. At present, it is therefore a matter for regulation by the national law of each state (7).

The majority, however, consciously or unconsciously decided to fudge the logic in the interests of keeping up with morality.

I have chosen this particular example to discuss, because my own views about the morality of the question are in line with those of the majority: I do think that injustice was suffered by the applicants, and will be suffered by others if closed-shop agreements of that sort are allowed in law. I am glad that British domestic law now bans them, though allowing some perhaps less objectionable kinds. Therefore I cannot be accused of twisting the logical discussion to suit my own moral views; and neither can the Scandinavian dissentients. This is just what the majority did, however, and it is a great danger when laws about human rights are couched in very vague terms and courts are left to interpret them according to their own or the public's moral convictions. I and the dissentient judges *want* restrictions put on closed-shop agreements to preserve rights of employees not to be dismissed as Young, James, and Webster were. But the means taken by the majority judges to this good end strike me as extremely dangerous. In another case they might fudge their logic in pursuit of their own prejudices, with which I, and other right-thinking people, might not agree. The decision on such matters as whether to allow closed shops and with what restrictions is a political one. It is usual, and I hope will remain so, to leave such decisions to the democratically elected governments of states and agreements between them. Only in places like the US, where the democratic legislative machinery is hopelessly clogged up, is it necessary, though still undesirable, for the judiciary to usurp its functions. I hope it will not happen to Britain.

Let us now ask in more detail *how* (i.e. in the light of what considerations) democratic legislators should decide such questions as 'Should there be a legal right not to join a union?'

So far in this paper I have not appealed to my general ethical theory, but have argued on rather narrower logical grounds. But really we have to bring in the general theory if we are to answer our present question. Nobody who has read my *MT* will be surprised at the solution I am going to offer. It is, in my sense, a utilitarian one. The legislators have to consider what legal provision about rights will, if adopted, maximize the satisfactions of the preferences of the affected parties. Who are the affected parties? Obviously the employees concerned, and other employees; the employers, including their shareholders if any; and, most of all, the general public which consumes the products and services they provide. This same public has an interest not only in continuity of production and service, and in avoiding price rises, but also in the preservation of public order and a smoothly working economy.

In Britain, as elsewhere, the abolition of the Combination Acts, which forbade the formation of unions, together with other permissive trade union legislation, starting in the early nineteenth century, has, I am convinced, had on the whole great utility. They have perhaps been, along with the factory acts, the main factor in bringing about improvements in conditions of work and greater equality of wealth, power, and status. Since these improvements and this greater equality can be justified on utilitarian grounds, utilitarians should, and did, support the legalization of trade unions and the conferring on them of certain privileges (especially freedom from liability to be sued for actions which would render anybody else liable for damages). Present disputes about labour laws are largely concerned with the question of whether the process has gone too far—whether the immunities (which are a kind of legal rights) given to trade unions are now greater than utility can justify. I think that the method of reasoning which I have advocated can shed a lot of light on this question.

From the beginning the question has frequently been discussed in terms of rights, legal or moral; and I see no harm in that, provided that we keep a good grip of the argument. The permissive legislation I have been speaking of conferred certain *legal* rights on trade unions. The conferring of them could be justified in two ways, but it is important to see that they come in effect to the same. The first way is directly utilitarian. We can say that the introduction of a certain legal right (for example to combine against an employer) will, all in all, maximize the preference-satisfactions of all those affected, considered impartially. As I have said, I think the earlier legislation can be justified in this way.

But we can, alternatively, seek to justify it in terms of *moral* rights, or of *justice* used as a term of moral approval. It may be said (speaking morally) that the workers have a right to try to improve their conditions and wages by such and such means. Or it may be said that it would be unjust to prevent them. The means may be held to include the coercion of 'free riders' who get the benefits of union action without supporting it. People who say this are usually appealing to their own intuitions, and to those of people who they hope will share them. That is why appeals to rights and to justice are such a powerful rhetorical weapon if the intuitions, or even the prejudices, are there to be appealed to. Again, I see no harm in this, provided that we keep a grip of the argument. The method of moral thinking which I am advocating has an honourable place for intuitions and even prejudices. But the crucial question is, '*What* intuitions and prejudices, in particular, ought to be allowed this honourable place?' There were, after all, those who insisted with equal vehemence on the right of employers to manage their own business on their own property and employ whom they would, on whatever terms they could negotiate. Robert Nozick still says this sort of thing. How are we to argue about what moral rights people have, and what legal rights they morally ought to be given?

This, on my method, brings us back again to utilitarianism at the first remove. Both the moral rights and the legal rights which we morally ought to accord to people will depend on the acceptance-utility of according them. By using this criterion we are being *fair* to all those whose interests are affected by the according or the withholding of the rights. It is reasonable to ask anybody who rejects this way of arguing about rights, what other way he is going to suggest. I cannot see any promise in the way which is commonly followed, and which I have already described: the appeal to intuitions unsupported by any argument about what are the best intuitions to have and to cultivate. This, as we have seen, is mere rhetoric and leads to no firm conclusion because intuitions, when not criticized and amended in the light of argument, will conflict.

Let me then say a little about the utility of various labour laws, or of repealing them (see also p. 130). To understand this, we have to inquire into the consequences, in the actual state of society and of the economy, of having or repealing them. This is a field in which I, a philosopher, am not competent. Here, as in other cases, my policy will be this. I shall try to make clear, in as unbiased a way as I can, what the facts *would* have to be in order, by my critical method, to justify the views of the various parties. I shall make no firm claims, though for illustration I shall have to make suggestions, about what the facts *are*. But without doing this I think I can fulfil the philosophical part of the task.

May I say first that things have altered a great deal since the beginnings of permissive trade union legislation? In the nineteenth century when it started firms were small and numerous, and the public was not greatly incommoded if the employees of one firm went on strike; they could always buy from another firm. In cases where there was a public or private monopoly or near-monopoly, attempts were often made, and still are, to put restrictions on strike action, for the sake of the convenience or even the safety of the public. It was such restrictions, for example, that enabled Mr Reagan to defeat the air controllers' strike. The European Convention on Human Rights says, in Clause 2 of the same article about the right to freedom of association that we have been discussing,

No restrictions shall be placed on the exercise of these rights other than such as are prescribed by law and are necessary in a democratic society in the interests of national security or public safety, for the prevention of disorder or crime, for the protection of health or morals or for the protection of the rights and freedoms of others. This Article shall not prevent the imposition of lawful restrictions on the exercise of these rights by members of the armed forces, of the police or of the administration of the State (50).

The vague wording obviously gives frightening scope for judicial 'interpretation'. However, such attempts to protect the public by restrictions on strike action by certain classes of employees have been largely ineffective in Britain. It is not unknown for nurses, doctors, firemen, gas workers, air controllers, and others to strike or threaten to strike to the prejudice of public health or safety, and for it to be said, in a typical appeal to our intuitions about fairness, without argument, that the same right extends morally, and should legally, to the police and the armed forces. The effects of strike action on the public are therefore much greater than they were, and more damaging, inasmuch as they can affect whole industries, and indeed, because of the highly interconnected industrial and economic system that we have, many industries at once. There are threats to shut down the entire economy.

There has also been a growing tendency, along with extended immunities for strikers, to strike or threaten to strike for avowedly political purposes, in order to influence the decisions of Parliament or of the electorate. These actions too are justified by appeals to various intuitions without argument. Strike action can thus be much more effective, and can be used or threatened for much wider purposes, than when it was first legalized. Attempts to ban striking have not been uniformly successful; there were strikes even before they were made legal, and legal restrictions on striking (for example even in wartime) are often ineffective. This too is partly an effect of the powerful intuitions which workers have about their rights; they are prepared to fight for them.

I have said what good consequences have resulted from permissive trade union legislation, and I have also drawn attention to certain changes in conditions which make some people claim that permissiveness has gone too far. I will now try to strike a balance and ask what each side has to show, in the way of supporting facts, in order to justify its position. I shall be able to speak only in rather general terms, because it is a highly complicated subject.

Looking, therefore, at the consequences for the preference-satisfactions of all the affected parties, we have to say that those who want to maintain or increase the legal rights and immunities of trade unions have to show that the advantages secured by trade union action (which I have said are very great) are not now more than counterbalanced by the damage done to the public and even to the members of unions, either directly by depriving them of goods and services, or indirectly by harming and hampering the economy. This is a very difficult balance to strike, and outside my competence, as I said.

There is also the question of what legislation can be made to stick. The supposed advantages of a piece of legislation putting restrictions on industrial action will not be realized if it remains a dead letter. And one of the things which may cause it to remain a dead letter is the insistence, backed up perhaps by illegal action and even violence, on what people call *moral* rights. The fact that people appeal to their intuitions in this way is politically very important. Just because intuitions are on the whole such a good thing, and keep us in the path of moral virtue most of the time, it is possible for people, by an unthinking appeal to them, sometimes to convince themselves and others that they are acting rightly, when they are not, and would not even think that they were if they looked at the whole picture in a critical way. Here, as so often, legislation cannot go too far in advance of public opinion. One of the tasks of the philosopher ought to be to help the public, and trade unionists themselves, to think more clearly and critically about the consequences of their actions, and thus determine what moral rights they morally *ought* to claim. Only when this process has gone some way (and it has gone some way in the past few years) will it become possible to have effective legislation.

Let us call the two parties the *Right* and the *Left*. For the Right to make out its case for the removal of immunities and the imposition of restrictions, it has to show that the admitted good consequences in the past of trade union activity would not thereby be endangered or lost; it has to show that in the present state of public opinion the legislation it is proposing will stick and be enforceable; and it has to show that the advantages to the public and the economy will be great enough to compensate for any losses there may be. This is quite a tall order. What the Left, on the other hand, has to show is that the continuation and extension of trade union immunities and the consequent preservation and enhancement of their power will not do more damage to the public and even to their members than the good achieved in the way of increased money wages (usually overtaken by inflation) and the liberty of workers to work in ways that they like (which may mean not as hard or as efficiently as the Japanese with whom they are competing). This is perhaps an even taller order. I am convinced, however, that if the dispute is conducted on these lines, and not on the basis of unthinking appeals to rights, it is *possible* for legislators and the public to arrive at a reasonable compromise on what *legal* rights should be accorded to trade unions, and what *moral* rights their members should be allowed to claim.

On the question of the closed shop, with which we started, the central issue is this. The closed shop, in various forms, strengthens the power of unions by making strike-breaking more difficult. The closed shop also improves their finances. The extent to which these are advantages depends on how good a thing it is that unions should have this power, and how wisely they are going to exercise it; and this varies from one time and place to another and from one union to another. It also, in the view of some employers, makes labour relations smoother by enabling them to negotiate with a single union for all their work-force; but doubt has been cast on this contention by the frequency of inter-union disputes even where there is a closed shop requiring employees to join *some* union. These are the claimed advantages. The question is whether they are outweighed by the *dis*advantages coming from increased union power and, above all, by the very great harms suffered by individuals like Young, James, and Webster through being faced with a choice between losing their livelihood and joining a union of whose actions they disapprove. I am not going to adjudicate this question; but that is what the question is. And I hope it will be settled not by courts but by democratic legislators and electors.

12
What Is Wrong with Slavery

NEARLY everybody would agree that slavery is wrong; and I can say this perhaps with greater feeling than most, having in a manner of speaking *been* a slave. However, there are dangers in just taking for granted that something is wrong; for we may then assume that it is obvious that it is wrong and indeed obvious why it is wrong; and this leads to a prevalence of very bad arguments with quite silly conclusions, all based on the so-called absolute value of human freedom. If we could see more clearly what *is* valuable about freedom, and why it is valuable, then we might be protected against the rhetoric of those who, the moment anything happens that is disadvantageous or distasteful to them, start complaining loudly about some supposed infringement of their liberty, without telling us why it is wrong that they should be prevented from doing what they would like to do. It may well *be* wrong in many such cases; but until we have some way of judging when it is and when it is not, we shall be at the mercy of every kind of demagogy.

This is but one example of the widespread abuse of the appeal to human rights. We may even be tempted to think that our politics would be more healthy if rights had never been heard of; but that would be going too far. It is the unthinking appeal to ill-defined rights, unsupported by argument, that does the harm. There is no doubt that arguments justifying some of these appeals are possible; but since the forms of such arguments are seldom understood even by philosophers, it is not surprising that many quite unjustified claims of this sort go unquestioned, and thus in the end bring any sort of appeal to human rights into disrepute. It is a tragedy that this happens, because there really are rights that ought to be defended with all the devotion we can command. Things are being done the world over which can properly be

From *Philosophy and Public Affairs* 8 (1979).

condemned as infringements of human rights; but so long as rights are used so loosely as an all-purpose political weapon, often in support of very questionable causes, our protests against such infringements will be deprived of most of their force.

Another hazard of the appeal to rights is that it is seldom that such an appeal by one side cannot be countered with an appeal to some conflicting right by the opposite side. The controversies which led finally to the abolition of slavery provide an excellent example of this, with one side appealing to rights of liberty and the other to rights of property. But we do not have to go so far back in history to find examples of this sort of thing. We have only to think of the disputes about distributive justice between the defenders of equality and of individual liberty; or of similar arguments about education. I have written about both these disputes elsewhere, in the attempt to substitute for intuitions some more solid basis for argument (see p. 122 and H 1977). I have the same general motive in raising the topic of slavery, and also a more particular motive. Being a utilitarian, I need to be able to answer the following attack frequently advanced by opponents of utilitarianism. It is often said that utilitarianism must be an objectionable creed because it could in certain circumstances condone or even commend slavery, given that circumstances can be envisaged in which utility would be maximized by preserving a slave-owning society and not abolishing slavery. The objectors thus seek to smear utilitarians with the taint of all the atrocious things that were done by slave-traders and slave-owners. The objection, as I hope to show, does not stand up; but in order to see through this rhetoric we shall have to achieve a quite deep understanding of some rather difficult issues in moral philosophy; and this, too, adds up to the importance and interest of the topic.

First, we have to ask what this thing, slavery, is, about whose wrongness we are arguing. As soon as we ask this question we see at once, if we have any knowledge of history, that it is, in common use, an extremely ill-defined concept. Even if we leave out of account such admittedly extended uses as 'wage-slave' in the writings of Marxists, it is clear that the word 'slave' and its near-equivalents such as *'servus'* and *'doulos'* have meant slightly different things in different cultures; for slavery is, primarily, a *legal* status, defined by the disabilities or the liabilities which are imposed by the law on those called slaves; and obviously these may vary from one jurisdiction to another. Familiar logical difficulties arise about how we are to decide, of a word in a foreign language, that it means the same as the English word 'slave'. Do the relevant laws in the country where the language is spoken have to be identical with those which held in English-speaking countries before slavery was abolished? Obviously not; because it would be impossible for them to be identical with the laws of all such countries at all periods, since these did not remain the same. Probably we have a rough idea of the kind of laws which have to hold in a country before we can say that that country has an institution properly called 'slavery'; but it is pretty rough.

It would be possible to pursue at some length, with the aid of legal, historical, and anthropological books on slavery in different cultures and jurisdictions, the different shades of meaning of the word 'slave'. But since my purpose is philosophical, I shall limit myself to asking what is essential to the notion of slavery in common use. The essential features are, I think, to be divided under two heads: slavery is, first, a *status* in society, and secondly, a *relation* to a master. The slave is so called first of all because he occupies a certain place in society, lacking certain rights and privileges secured by the law to others, and subject to certain liabilities from which others are free. And secondly, he is the slave *of* another person or body (which might be the state itself). The first head is not enough to distinguish slavery from other legal disabilities; for example the lowest castes in some societies are as lacking in legal rights as slaves in some others, or more so, but are not called slaves because they are not the slaves *of* anybody.

The *status* of a slave was defined quite early by the Greeks in terms of four freedoms which the slave lacks. These are: a legally recognized position in the community, conferring a right of access to the courts; protection from illegal seizure and detention and other personal violence; the privilege of going where he wants to go; and that of working as he pleases. The first three of these features are present in a manumission document from Macedonia dated about 235 BC; the last is added in the series of manumission documents from Delphi which begins about thirty years later (Westermann 1955: 35). The state could to some extent regulate by law the treatment of slaves without making us want to stop calling them slaves, so that the last three features are a bit wobbly at the edges. But we are seeking only a rough characterization of slavery, and shall have to put up with this indefiniteness of the concept.

The *relation* of the slave to a master is also to some extent indefinite. It might seem that we could tie it up tight by saying that a slave has to be the *property* of an *owner*; but a moment's reflection will show what unsafe ground this is. So-called property-owners do not need to be reminded that legal restrictions upon the use and enjoyment of property can become so onerous as to make it almost a joke to call it property at all. I am referring not only to such recent inventions as zoning and other planning laws (though actually they are not so recent, having been anticipated even in ancient times), and to rent acts, building regulations, clean air acts, and the like, but also to the ancient restrictions placed by the common law on uses of one's property which might be offensive to one's neighbours. In relation to slavery, it is also instructive to think of the cruelty-to-animals legislation which now rightly forbids one to do what one likes to one's own dog or cow which one has legally purchased. Legislation of just this kind was passed in the days before abolition, and was even to some extent enforced, though not always effectively. The laws forbidding the slave trade were, of course, the outstanding example of such legislation preventing people from doing what they wanted with their own property.

However, as before, we are seeking only a general and rough characterization of slavery, and shall therefore have to put up with the open texture of the concept of property. This, like slavery itself, is defined by the particular rights and obligations which are conferred or imposed by a particular legal system, and these may vary from one such system to another. It will be enough to have a general idea of what would stop us calling a person the slave of another—how far the law would have to go in assigning rights to slaves before we stopped using that word of them. I have gone into these difficulties in such detail as space has allowed only because I am now going on to describe, for the purposes of our moral discussion, certain conditions of life about which I shall invite the reader's judgement, and I do not want anybody to say that what I am describing *is* not really slavery. The case I shall sketch is admittedly to some extent fantastic; and this, as we shall later see, is very important when we come to assess the philosophical arguments that have been based on similar cases. But although it is extremely unlikely that what I describe should actually occur, I wish to maintain that *if* it occurred, we should still call it slavery, so that *if* imaginary cases are allowed to be brought into the arguments, this case will have to be admitted.

It may be helpful if, before leaving the question of what slavery is, I list a few conditions of life which have to be *distinguished* from slavery proper. The first of these is *serfdom* (a term which, like 'slavery' itself, has a wide range of meaning). A serf is normally tied, not directly to a master, but to a certain area of land; the rights to his services pass with the land if it changes hands. This very distinction, however, separates the English villein in gross, who approximates to a slave although enjoying certain legal rights, from the villein regardant, whose serfdom arises through his feudal tenure of land. Those who unsuccessfully tried to persuade Lord Mansfield in Sommersett's case that slavery could exist in England attempted to show that the defendant was a villein in gross (Mansfield 1772). Secondly, one is not a slave merely because one belongs to a *caste* which has an inferior legal status, even if it has pretty well no rights; as I have said, the slave has to be the slave *of* some owner. Thirdly, slavery has to be distinguished from *indenture*, which is a form of contract. Apprentices in former times, and football players even now, are bound by contract, entered into by themselves or, in the case of children, by their parents, to serve employers for a fixed term under fixed conditions, which were in some cases extremely harsh (so that the actual sufferings of indentured people could be as bad as those of slaves) (Patterson 1967: 74; Sampson 1956: ch. 3). The difference lies in the voluntariness of the contract and in its fixed term. We must note however that in some societies (Athens before Solon for example) one could *choose* to become a slave by selling one's person to escape debt (Westermann 1955: 4); and it might be possible to sell one's children as well, as the Greeks sometimes did, so that even the heritability of the slave status does not serve to make definite the rather fuzzy boundary between slavery and indenture.

We ought perhaps to notice two other conditions which approximate to slavery but are not called slavery. The first is compulsory *military* or *naval service* and, indeed, other forced labour. The impressed sailors of Nelson's navy no doubt endured conditions as bad as many slaves; Dr Johnson remarked that nobody would choose to be a sailor if he had the alternative of being put in prison (Boswell 1759: 348). But they were not called slaves, because their status as free men was only in abeyance and returned to them on discharge. By contrast, the galley slaves of the Mediterranean powers in earlier times really were slaves. Secondly, although the term 'penal servitude' was once in use, *imprisonment* for crime is not usually called slavery. This is another fuzzy boundary, because in ancient times it was possible for a person to lose his rights as a citizen and became a slave by sentence of a court for some crime (Westermann 1955: 81), and in pre-revolutionary France one could be sentenced to the galleys; though when something very like this happened recently in South Africa, it was not *called* slavery, officially (Sampson 1956: 241). Again, prisoners of war and other captives and bondsmen are not always called slaves, however grim their conditions, although in ancient times capture in war was a way of becoming a slave, if one was not fortunate enough to be ransomed (Westermann 1955: 2, 5–7, 29). I have myself, as a prisoner of war, worked on the Burma railway in conditions not *at the time* distinguishable from slavery; but because my status was temporary I can claim to have been a slave only 'in a manner of speaking'.

I shall put my philosophical argument, to which we have now come, in terms of an imaginary example, to which I shall give as much verisimilitude as I can. It will be seen, however, that quite unreal assumptions have to be made in order to get the example going—and this is very important for the argument between the utilitarians and their opponents. It must also be noted that to play its role in the argument the example will have to meet certain requirements. It is intended as a fleshed-out substitute for the rather jejune examples often to be found in anti-utilitarian writers. To serve its purpose it will have to be a case in which to abolish slavery really and clearly would diminish utility. This means, first, that the slavery to be abolished must really be slavery, and, secondly, that it must have a total utility clearly, but not enormously, greater than the total utility of the kind of regime which would be, in that situation, a practical alternative to slavery.

If it were not *clearly* greater, utilitarians could argue that, since all judgements of this sort are only probable, caution would require them to stick to a well-tried principle favouring liberty, the principle itself being justified on utilitarian grounds (see below); and thus the example would cease to divide them from their opponents, and would become inapposite.

If, on the other hand, the utility of slavery were *enormously* greater, anti-utilitarians might complain that their own view was being made too strong; for many anti-utilitarians are pluralists and hold that among the principles of morality a principle requiring beneficence is to be included. Therefore, if the advantages of retaining slavery are made sufficiently great, a non-utilitarian with a principle of beneficence in his repertory could agree that it ought to be retained—that is, that *in this case* the principle of beneficence has greater weight than that favouring liberty. Thus there would again be no difference, in this case, between the verdicts of the utilitarians and their opponents, and the example would be inapposite.

There is also another dimension in which the example has to be carefully placed. An anti-utilitarian might claim that the example I shall give makes the difference between the conditions of the slaves and those of the free in the supposed society too small, and the number of slaves too great. If, he might claim, I had made the number of slaves small and the difference between the miseries of the slaves and the pleasures of the slave-owners much greater, then the society might have the some total utility as mine (that is, greater than that of the free society with which I compare it), but it would be less plausible for me to maintain that if such a comparison had to be made in real life, we ought to follow the utilitarians and prefer the slave society. I deal with this objection only so far as it concerns slavery such as might occur in the world as we know it. Brave New World situations, in which people are conditioned from birth to be obedient slaves and given disagreeable or dangerous tasks, require separate treatment which is beyond the scope of this paper, though anti-utilitarian arguments based on them meet the same defence, namely the requirement to assess realistically what the consequences of such practices would actually be.

I cannot yet answer this objection without anticipating my argument; I shall merely indicate briefly how I would answer it. The answer is that the objection rests on an appeal to our ordinary intuitions; but that these are designed to deal with ordinary cases. They give no reliable guide to what we ought to say in highly unusual cases. But, further, the case desiderated is never likely to occur. How could it come about that the existence of a small number of slaves was necessary in order to preserve the happiness of the rest? I find it impossible to think of any technological factors (say, in agriculture or in transport by land or sea) which would make the preservation of slavery for a small class necessary to satisfy the interests of the majority. It is quite true that in the past there have been *large* slave populations supporting the higher standard of living of *small* minorities. But in that case it is hard to argue that slavery has more utility than its abolition, if the difference in happiness between slaves and slave-owners is great. Yet if, in order to produce a case in which the retention of slavery really would be optimal, we reduce the number of slaves relative to slave-owners, it becomes hard to say how the existence of this relatively small number of slaves is necessary for the happiness of the large number of free men. What on earth are the slaves doing that could not be more efficiently done by paid labour? And is not the abolition (perhaps not too abrupt) of slavery likely to promote those very technical changes which are necessary to enable the society to do without it?

The crux of the matter, as we shall see, is that in order to use an appeal to our ordinary intuitions as an argument, the opponents of utilitarianism have to produce cases which are not too far removed from the sort of cases with which our intuitions are designed to deal, namely the ordinary run of cases. If the cases they use fall outside this class, then the fact that our common intuitions give a different verdict from utilitarianism has no bearing on the argument; our intuitions could well be wrong about such cases, and be none the worse for that, because they will never have to deal with them in practice.

We may also notice, while we are sifting possible examples, that cases of *individual* slave-owners who are kind to their slaves will not do. The issue is one of whether slavery as an institution protected by law should be preserved; and if it is preserved, though there may be individuals who do not take advantage of it to maltreat their slaves, there will no doubt be many others who do.

Let us imagine, then, that the battle of Waterloo, that 'damned nice thing, the nearest run thing you ever saw in your life' (Longford 1969: 489), as Wellington called it, went differently from the way it actually did go, in two respects. The first was that the British and Prussians lost the battle; the last attack of the French Guard proved too much for them, the Guard's morale having been restored by Napoleon who in person led the advance instead of handing it over to Ney. But secondly, having exposed himself to fire as Wellington habitually did, but lacking Wellington's amazing good fortune, Napoleon was struck by a cannon ball and killed instantly. This so disorganized the French, who had no other commanders of such ability, that Wellington was able to rally his forces and conduct one of those holding operations at which he was so adept, basing himself on the Channel ports and their intricate surrounding waterways; the result was a cross between the Lines of Torres Vedras and the trench warfare of the First World War. After a year or two of this, with Napoleon out of the way and the war party discredited in England, liberal (that is, neither revolutionary nor reactionary) regimes came into power in both countries, and the Congress of Vienna reconvened in a very different spirit, with the French represented on equal terms.

We have to consider these events only as they affected two adjacent islands in the Caribbean which I am going to call Juba and Camaica. I need not relate what happened in the rest of the world, because the combined European powers could at that time command absolute supremacy at sea, and the Caribbean could therefore be effectively isolated from world politics by the agreement which they reached to take that area out of the imperial war game. All naval and other forces were withdrawn from it except for a couple of bases on small islands for the suppression of the slave trade, which, in keeping with their liberal principles, the parties agreed to prohibit (those that had not already done so). The islands were declared independent and their white inhabitants, very naturally, all departed in a hurry, leaving the government in the hands of local black leaders, some of whom were of the calibre of Toussaint l'Ouverture and others of whom were very much the reverse.

On Juba, a former Spanish colony, at the end of the colonial period there had been formed, under pressure of military need, a militia composed of slaves under white officers, with conditions of service much preferable to those of the plantation slaves, and forming a kind of elite. The senior serjeant-major of this force found himself, after the white officers fled, in a position of unassailable power, and, being a man of great political intelligence and ability, shaped the new regime in a way that made Juba the envy of its neighbours.

What he did was to retain the institution of slavery but to remedy its evils. The plantations were split up into smaller units, still under overseers, responsible to the state instead of to the former owners. The slaves were given rights to improved conditions of work; the wage they had already received as a concession in colonial times was secured to them and increased; all cruel punishments were prohibited. However, it is still right to call them slaves, because the state retained the power to direct their labour and their place of residence and to enforce these directions by sanctions no more severe than are customary in countries without slavery, such as fines and imprisonment. The Juban government, influenced by early communist ideas (though Marx had not yet come on the scene) kept the plantations in its own hands; but private persons were also allowed to own a limited number of slaves under conditions at least as protective to the slaves as on the state-owned plantations.

The island became very prosperous, and the slaves in it enjoyed a life far preferable in every way to that of the free inhabitants of the neighbouring island of Camaica. In Camaica there had been no such focus of power in the early days. The slaves threw off their bonds and each seized what land he could get hold of. Though law and order were restored after a fashion, and democracy of a sort prevailed, the economy was chaotic, and this, coupled with a population explosion, led to widespread starvation and misery. Camaica lacked what Juba had: a government with the will *and the instrument, in the shape of the institution of slavery*, to control the economy and the population, and so make its slave-citizens, as I said, the envy of their neighbours. The flood of people in fishing boats seeking to emigrate from free Camaica and insinuate themselves as slaves into the plantations of Juba became so great that the Juban government had to employ large numbers of coastguards (slaves of course) to stop it.

That, perhaps, will do for our imaginary example. Now for the philosophical argument. It is commonly alleged that utilitarianism could condone or commend slavery. In the situation described, utility would have been lessened and not increased if the Juban government had abolished slavery and if as a result the economy of Juba had deteriorated to the level of that of Camaica. So, it might be argued, a utilitarian would have had to oppose the abolition. But everyone agrees, it might be held, that slavery is wrong; so the utilitarians are convicted of maintaining a thesis which has consequences repugnant to universally accepted moral convictions.

What could they reply to this attack? There are, basically, two lines they could take. These lines are not incompatible but complementary; indeed, the defence of utilitarianism could be put in the form of a dilemma. Either the defender of utilitarianism is allowed to question the imagined facts of the example, or he is not. First let us suppose that he is not. He might then try, as a first move, saying that in the situation *as portrayed* it would indeed be wrong to abolish slavery. If the argument descends to details, the anti-utilitarians may be permitted to insert any amount of extra details (barring the actual abolition of slavery itself) in order to make sure that its retention really does maximize utility. But then the utilitarian sticks to his guns and maintains that in that case it *would* be wrong to abolish slavery, and that, further, most ordinary people, if they could be got to consider the case on its merits and not allow their judgement to be confused by association with more detestable forms of slavery, would agree with this verdict. The principle of liberty which forbids slavery is a prima facie principle admitting of exceptions, and this imaginary case is one of the exceptions. If the utilitarians could sustain this line of defence, they would win the case; but perhaps not everyone would agree that it is sustainable.

So let us allow the utilitarian another slightly more sophisticated move, still staying, however, perched on the first horn of the dilemma. He might admit that not everyone would agree on the merits of this case, but explain this by pointing to the fantastic and unusual nature of the case, which, he might claim, would be unlikely to occur in real life. *If* he is not allowed to question the facts of the case, he has to admit that abolition would be wrong; but ordinary people, he might say, cannot see this because the principles of political and social morality which we have all of us *now* absorbed (as contrasted with our eighteenth-century ancestors), and with which we are deeply imbued, prevent us from considering the case on its merits. The principles are framed to cope with the cases of slavery which actually occur (all of which are to a greater or lesser degree harmful). Though they are the best principles for us to have when confronting the actual world, they give the wrong answer when presented with this fantastic case. But all the same, the world being as it is, we should be morally worse people if we did not have these principles; for then we might be tempted, whether through ignorance or by self-interest, to condone slavery in cases in which, though actually harmful, it could be colourably represented as being beneficial. Suppose, it might be argued, that an example of this sort had been used in anti-abolitionist writings in, say, 1830 or thereabouts.

Might it not have persuaded many people that slavery *could* be an admirable thing, and thus have secured their votes against abolition; and would this not have been very harmful? For the miseries caused by the *actual* institution of slavery in the Caribbean and elsewhere were so great that it was desirable from a utilitarian point of view that people should hold and act on moral convictions which condemned slavery as such and without qualification, because this would lead them to vote for its abolition.

If utilitarians take this slightly more sophisticated line, they are left saying at one and the same time that it would have been wrong to abolish slavery in the imagined circumstances, *and* that it is a good thing that nearly everyone, if asked about it, would say that it was right. Is this paradoxical? Not, I think, to anybody who understands the realities of the human situation. What resolves the paradox is that the example *is* imaginary and that therefore people are not going to have to pronounce, as a practical issue, on what the laws of Juba are to be. In deciding what principles it is good that people have, it is not necessary or even desirable to take into account such imaginary cases. It does not really matter, from a practical point of view, what judgements people reach about imaginary cases, provided that this does not have an adverse effect upon their judgements about real cases. From a practical point of view, the principles which it is best for them to have are those which will lead them to make the highest proportion of right decisions in actual cases where their decisions make a difference to what happens—weighted, of course, for the importance of the cases, that is, the amount of difference the decisions make to the resulting good or harm.

It is therefore perfectly acceptable that we should at one and the same time feel a strong moral conviction that even the Juban slave system, however beneficial, is wrong, *and* confess, when we reflect on the features of this imagined system, that we cannot see anything specifically wrong about it, but rather a great deal to commend. This is bound to be the experience of anybody who has acquired the sort of moral convictions that one ought to acquire, and at the same time is able to reflect rationally on the features of some unusual imagined situation. I have myself constantly had this experience when confronted with the sort of anti-utilitarian examples which are the stock-in-trade of philosophers like Bernard Williams. One is led to think, on reflection, that *if* such cases were to occur, one ought to do what is for the best in the circumstances, as even Williams himself appears to contemplate in one of his cases (Williams 1973: 99); but one is bound also to find this conclusion repugnant to one's deepest convictions; if it is not, one's convictions are not the best convictions one could have.

Against this, it might be objected that if one's deep moral convictions yield the wrong answer even in imaginary or unusual cases, they are *not* the best one could have. Could we not succeed, it might be asked, in inculcating into ourselves convictions of a more accommodating sort? Could we not, that is to say, absorb principles which had written into them either exceptions to deal with awkward cases like that in my example, or even provision for writing in exceptions *ad hoc* when the awkward case arose? Up to a point this is a sensible suggestion; but beyond that point (a point which will vary with the temperament of the person whose principles they are to be) it becomes psychologically unsound. There are some simple souls, no doubt, who really cannot keep themselves in the straight and narrow way unless they cling fanatically and in the face of what most of us would call reason to extremely simple and narrow principles. And there are others who manage to have very complicated principles with many exceptions written into them (only 'written' is the wrong word, because the principles of such people defy formulation). Most of us come somewhere in between. It is also possible to have fairly simple principles but to attach to them a rubric which allows us to depart from them, either when one conflicts with another in a particular case, or where the case is such an unusual one that we find ourselves doubting whether the principles were designed to deal with it. In these cases we may apply utilitarian reasoning directly; but it is most unwise to do this in more normal cases, for those are precisely the cases (the great majority) which our principles *are* designed to deal with, since they were chosen to give the best results in the general run of cases. In normal cases, therefore, we are more likely to achieve the right decision (even from the utilitarian point of view) by sticking to these principles than by engaging in utilitarian reasoning about the particular case, with all its temptations to special pleading.

I have dealt with these issues at length elsewhere (H 1976, *MT*). Here all I need to say is that there is a psychological limit to the complexity and to the flexibility of the moral principles that we can wisely seek to build deeply, as moral convictions, into our character; and the person who tries to go beyond this limit will end up as (what he will be called) an unprincipled person, and will not in fact do the best he could with his life, even by the test of utility. This may explain why I would always vote for the abolition of slavery, even though I can admit that cases could be *imagined* in which slavery would do more good than harm, and even though I am a utilitarian.

So much, then, for the first horn of the dilemma. Before we come to the second horn, on which the utilitarian is allowed to object to his opponents' argument on the ground that their example would not in the actual world be realized, I wish to make a methodological remark which may help us to find our bearings in this rather complex dispute. Utilitarianism, like any other theory of moral reasoning that gets anywhere near adequacy, consists of two parts, one formal and one substantial. The formal part is no more than a rephrasing of the requirement that moral prescriptions be universalizable; this has the consequence that equal interests of all are to be given equal weight in our reasoning: everybody to count for one and nobody for more than one. One should not expect such a formal requirement to generate, by itself, any substantial conclusions even about the actual world, let alone about all logically possible worlds. But there is also a substantial element in the theory. This is contributed by factual beliefs about what interests people in the real world actually have (which depends on what they actually want or like or dislike, and on what they would want or like or dislike under given conditions); and also about the actual effects on these interests of different actions in the real world. Given the truth of these beliefs, we can reason morally and shall come to certain moral conclusions. But the conclusions are not generated by the formal part of the theory alone.

Utilitarianism therefore, unlike some other theories, is

exposed to the facts. The utilitarian cannot reason a priori that *whatever* the facts about the world and human nature, slavery is wrong. He has to show that it is wrong by showing, through a study of history and other factual observation, that slavery does have the effects (namely the production of misery) which makes it wrong. This, though it may at first sight appear a weakness in the doctrine, is in fact its strength. A doctrine, like some kinds of intuitionism, according to which we can think up examples as fantastic as we please and the doctrine will still come up with the same old answers, is really showing that it has lost contact with the actual world with which the intuitions it relies on were designed to cope. Intuitionists think they can face the world armed with nothing but their inbred intuitions; utilitarians know that they have to look at what actually goes on in the world and see if the intuitions are really the best ones to have in that sort of world.

I come now to the second horn of the dilemma, on which the utilitarian is allowed to say, 'Your example won't do: it would never happen that way.' He may admit that Waterloo and the Congress of Vienna could have turned out differently—after all it was a damned nice thing, and high commanders were in those days often killed on the battlefield (it was really a miracle that Wellington was not), and there were liberal movements in both countries. But when we come to the Caribbean, things begin to look shakier. Is it really likely that there would have been such a contrast between the economies of Juba and Camaica? I do not believe that the influence of particular national leaders is ever so powerful, or that such perfectly wise leaders are ever forthcoming. And I do not believe that in the Caribbean or anywhere else a system of nationalized slavery could be made to run so smoothly. I should, rather, expect the system to deteriorate very rapidly. I base these expectations on general beliefs about human nature, and in particular upon the belief that people in the power of other people will be exploited, whatever the good intentions of those who founded the system.

Alternatively, if there really had been leaders of such amazing statesmanship, could they not have done better by abolishing slavery and substituting a free but disciplined society? In the example, they gave the slaves some legal rights; what was to prevent them giving others, such as the right to change residences and jobs, subject of course to an overall system of land-use and economic planning such as exists in many free countries? Did the retention of *slavery* in particular contribute very much to the prosperity of Juba that could not have been achieved by other means? And likewise, need the government of Camaica have been so incompetent? Could it not, without reintroducing slavery, have kept the economy on the rails by such controls as are compatible with a free society? In short, did not the optimum solution lie somewhere *between* the systems adopted in Juba and Camaica, but on the free side of the boundary between slavery and liberty?

These factual speculations, however, are rather more superficial than I can be content with. The facts that it is really important to draw attention to are rather deep facts about human nature which must always, or nearly always, make slavery an intolerable condition (Patterson 1967; Elkins 1959). I have mentioned already a fact about slave ownership: that ordinary, even good, human beings will nearly always exploit those over whom they have absolute power. We have only to read the actual history of slavery in all centuries and cultures to see that. There is also the effect on the characters of the exploiters themselves. I had this brought home to me recently when, staying in Jamaica, I happened to pick up a history book (Dallas 1803) written there at the very beginning of the nineteenth century, before abolition, whose writer had added at the end an appendix giving his views on the abolition controversy, which was then at its height. Although obviously a kindly man with liberal leanings, he argues against abolition; and one of his arguments struck me very forcibly. He argues that although slavery can be a cruel fate, things are much better in Jamaica now: there is actually a law that a slave on a plantation may not be given more than thirty-six lashes by the foreman without running him up in front of the overseer. The contrast between the niceness of the man and what he says here does perhaps more than any philosophical argument to make the point that our moral principles have to be designed for human nature as it is.

The most fundamental point is one about the human nature

Slavery

of the slave which makes ownership by another more intolerable for him than for, say, a horse (not that we should condone cruelty to horses). Men are different from other animals in that they can look a long way ahead, and therefore can become an object of deterrent punishment. Other animals, we may suppose, can only be the object of Skinnerian reinforcement and Pavlovian conditioning. These methods carry with them, no doubt, their own possibilities of cruelty; but they fall short of the peculiar cruelty of human slavery. One can utter to a man threats of punishment in the quite distant future which he can understand. A piece of human property, therefore, unlike a piece of inanimate property or even a brute animal in a man's possession, can be subjected to a sort of terror from which other kinds of property are immune; and, human owners being what they are, many will inevitably take advantage of this fact. That is the reason for the atrocious punishments that have usually been inflicted on slaves; there would have been no point in inflicting them on animals. A slave is the only being that is *both* able to be held responsible in this way, *and* has no escape from, or even redress against, the power that this ability to threaten confers upon his oppressor. If he were a free citizen, he would have rights which would restrain the exercise of the threat; if he were a horse or a piece of furniture, the threat would be valueless to his owner because it would not be understood. By being subjected to the threat of legal and other punishment, but at the same time deprived of legal defences against its abuse (since he has no say in what the laws are to be, nor much ability to avail himself of such laws as there are) the slave becomes, or is likely to become if his master is an ordinary human, the most miserable of all creatures.

No doubt there are other facts I could have adduced. But I will end by reiterating the general point I have been trying to illustrate. The wrongness of slavery, like the wrongness of anything else, has to be shown in the world as it actually is. We can do this by first reaching an understanding of the meaning of this and the other moral words, which brings with it certain rules of moral reasoning, as I have tried to show in other places (H 1976, *MT*). One of the most important of these rules is a formal requirement reflected in the Golden

Rule: the requirement that what we say we ought to do to others we have to be able to say ought to be done to ourselves were we in precisely their situation with their interests. And this leads to a way of moral reasoning (utilitarianism) which treats the equal interests of all as having equal weight. Then we have to apply this reasoning to the world as it actually is, which will mean ascertaining what will actually be the result of adopting certain principles and policies, and how this will actually impinge upon the interests of ourselves and others. Only so can we achieve a morality suited for use in real life; and nobody who goes through this reasoning in real life will adopt principles which permit slavery, because of the miseries which in real life it causes. Utilitarianism can thus show what is wrong with slavery; and so far as I can see it is the kind of moral reasoning best able to show this, as opposed to merely *protesting* that slavery is wrong.

13

Liberty, Equality, and Fraternity
in South Africa?

THIS article was written in Pretoria as the conclusion of a
series of talks I gave at the University of South Africa in
August 1985, the rest of which had been on ethical theory and
its applications in general. I also wrote another paper for
delivery when I got back to the US, giving my more detailed
and factual impressions of the situation in South Africa. But
because they were only impressions, and I am still not sure of
my facts, and in any case there is no room, I shall not try to
include them here. Since then events have moved fast in South
Africa and, as even this revised version will not be published
till several months after it is written, I cannot hope to keep up
with them. However, I am confident that the philosophical
points with which I shall be mainly concerned will remain
valid and important, since they have been borne in on me by
the study, for many years, of troubled situations not only in
South Africa but in other equally unfortunate countries. I
hoped then, and hope now, that a deeper understanding of
these points might help a little, though whether they will be
absorbed by those who have the power to influence the
outcome is another matter.

After only a month's visit, during which I tried to see as
wide a variety of people, black and white, as possible, I do not
feel qualified to reach any firm conclusions about what should
be done. I have read some history books, and followed events
in the newspapers for forty years or so. But that does not give
me the authority which would be needed for me to tell South
Africans how they should improve matters, although obviously
they could do with some improvement. All I can offer is a
method of thinking which, if applied by somebody better
acquainted with the facts about the situation than I am, might
perhaps help. My earlier lectures had been about this method.

From *South African Journal of Philosophy* 5 (1986) and *Philosophical Forum* 18 (1986).

Its main feature, explained more fully in *MT*, is a separation of moral thinking into two levels, the critical and the intuitive. We use, and should use, the intuitive level of thinking in most of our daily lives; in it, we simply apply to the moral questions that confront us the habits of mind that we have learnt. If we have learnt good habits of mind, then by and large they will give us the right answers to our moral problems.

But situations will arise in which this intuitive level of thinking does not yield clear answers. This may be because two principles to which we have learnt to attach great importance come into conflict in a particular situation. Or it may be because the situation has changed from that in which we learnt our moral dispositions—changed so much that we are driven to call them in question. In either case a higher level of thinking is needed: a level at which we ask, of these habits of mind themselves, whether we ought to retain them unchanged, or seek to modify them in some respect; or, even if we retain them, what we should do when they give conflicting answers. Most of the deep problems of moral philosophy are about the nature of this higher, critical level of thinking.

I suggested in my book and my lectures an account of critical moral thinking which, although it is utilitarian in method, can be defended against the standard objections to utilitarianism. I wish to emphasize that this is not intended to supplant the use of the habits of mind which we rightly use all the time at the intuitive level; it is simply that the intuitive level is not, and cannot be, self-supporting, but needs the higher level to sustain it when problems arise which the intuitive level by itself cannot solve. It is always difficult and dangerous to think critically about moral questions, and therefore it is wise to do it with diffidence; but sometimes we have to. The South African situation seems to me to illustrate this only too clearly.

We cannot give a blanket and unthinking endorsement to all our intuitions. Let me give some examples. A friend in Pretoria told me that (although she had now come to accept it) she had intuitively thought it wrong for a black child to swim in the same pool (even a private pool) as white children. I also know that in Britain there are people who have an intuition that it is right to persecute Zola Budd because she was once (albeit too young to vote) a national of a country with a racist government. For myself, I do not believe that critical thinking would support either of these intuitions. However, let us come to some more contentious ones. Many people have an intuition (that is, they are convinced without question and without asking for reasons) that no form of government is ever acceptable anywhere unless it ensures complete one-person-one-vote democracy. On the other hand, many other people have the more Platonic intuition that political power should be entrusted to those who are likely to exercise it for the greatest benefit of the governed. Later, I shall be examining the first of these two intuitions; but before that I want to say a little more about method.

It is instructive to compare the situation in South Africa with that which obtained in the United States before, during, and after their Civil War in the middle of the nineteenth century. More, perhaps, than any other war in history, it was fought on questions of principle. Of these, the abolition or retention of slavery was the most important, followed closely by the right of the several States to leave the Union if they wished. People had intuitions about such questions of principle, and though certainly they were often prepared to question them, they seem seldom to have thought about them in a way that I would count as critical thinking. The impact of philosophy of any rational sort on the thinking of Americans at this time seems to have been very small.

I read recently an excellent book on this historical period (Brock 1977), in the hope of getting some insights which would help me to understand the South African situation. Again, I have not studied the facts of history in the way a scholar would have to. Brock spends a lot of time discussing the intellectual and ideological disputes that went on; but I notice that philosophers are mentioned very little as having influence on them. John Stuart Mill appears once in the index, but the reference is not to the substance of the disputes or of his views; his is merely one of a list of names of British writers (others are Macaulay, Tennyson, Dickens, and Thackeray) whose prestige gave some reflected glory to American intellectuals. There is no evidence in the book that utilitarianism of Mill's sort was seriously invoked as a help in sorting out the arguments. The only other philosopher who is mentioned in the book is the romantic Emerson, who came down against slavery but was not very strong on arguments.

If the Americans had to have a very bloody civil war in order to sort out the questions that confronted them, it may have been because they did not make enough use of rational argument; and in this, philosophy could perhaps have helped them. The situation in South Africa is not the same as that in America before the Civil War. In some respects it is more hopeful, in some more dangerous. For one thing, the problem is not slavery—only great inequality, economic, social, and political. Those are problems which Americans have begun to solve in the last half of the twentieth century. For another, in America there were two fairly equally matched sides; that was one reason why they had to have a war. In South Africa there is a white minority holding nearly all the economic and political cards, and a black majority with really only one card, that it has in the end to be lived with in terms acceptable to it. Thirdly, in the American Civil War foreign powers did not intervene much (I think wisely); but in South Africa world opinion and possible intervention have to be reckoned with. So I do not think that direct comparisons are possible, except one: that in both cases what was and is needed is serious thought and rational argument on both sides, based on the facts and possibilities. This means that they have to listen to and understand each other's arguments. And in this, philosophy, which is the understanding and assessment of arguments, ought to be able to help.

I want to look at some of the arguments that are used and try to assess them, though I do so without a full enough knowledge of the facts. I am going to divide up the arguments into three, according to that hoary old slogan 'Liberty, Equality, and Fraternity'. It was one of the idiocies of the French revolutionaries to suppose that liberty and equality are congenial to each other, whereas nearly everybody who has studied the subject now realizes that they are mutually antagonistic in many ways. And it is worse than that: one kind of liberty militates against another kind, the liberty of one person or group against that of another, equality in one respect against equality in another. Often we have to choose. But as a way of dividing up the subject it will do (see also pp. 122 ff.).

I will start with equality. Let us think first about economic equality. It is evident that there is great economic inequality in South Africa, which is in a way a microcosm of the world. The well-to-do South Africans enjoy an affluence which compares with that of well-to-do Americans, and nearly all of both are white. They work just as hard for it, and use it just about as well. There is also poverty in South Africa to compare, not with that to be found in Ethiopia or the Sahel, but at least with a great many countries which we regard as extremely poor and deserving of aid. The difference is that the poor and rich in South Africa are inhabitants of the same country. It is this juxtaposition that shocks us (much as I am always shocked by a similar juxtaposition whenever I go to New York City).

This raises an interesting and important question in political philosophy. I wonder how many of the Americans who are prepared to condemn the inequality that exists in South Africa have asked themselves this question. The question is: Why is inequality worse when it exists between one South African and another South African than it is when it exists between inhabitants of Mexico and New Mexico? Few Americans think that the United States has a duty to allow unlimited immigration of Mexicans in order to relieve their poverty. But they do think, many of them, that it is wrong of the South African government to prevent internal migration with the same purpose. Why should this be so? Is it simply that the mere juxtaposition produces envy and moral indignation? But Mexico and New Mexico are contiguous. Or is there more to it?

There may be an answer to this question, but it raises further questions. The answer is that when poor and rich people live under the *same* government, that government may have the power, and therefore may have the responsibility, to decide whether to lessen the inequality. When people live under different governments, the power and the responsibility are much less. The question that arises next is: Is it possible, under modern conditions, to organize the governments of different parts of the world in any other way than by dividing up the world into territories of manageable size and letting the inhabitants of each get what government they can from the resources of leadership and political skill that they can muster? This is certainly what has actually happened in the world, since the demise or decline of imperialism everywhere except in the Soviet Union.

If this is really the only way of ordering things, it has certain consequences. It means that if there is economic inequality between the inhabitants of *different* countries, the power of the governments and peoples of the richer countries to do anything about it is limited by the capacity and willingness of the governments of the poorer countries to order their economic affairs in such a way that aid will not be wasted. I am not arguing that this makes aid altogether a waste of effort. There are some developing countries that have made good use of it. Nevertheless there is a limit.

But if this is so, it is a practical limit: and that perhaps shows us how we should address the problem of inequality within a single country, which is also a practical one. What *should* be done will depend, there too, on what *can* be done. Probably more can be done by a single government with rich and poor citizens than where they live under different governments. But here too there are practical limits, and what they are is the stuff of economic politics in all countries, including Britain and the USA. It is a question of how much by way of egalitarian policies the economy of a country will stand, and of what in particular they should be; and on that I am not an expert.

Some people have an intuition that economic equality ought to be sought at all costs. I do not agree with these people. I think that there are very strong utilitarian arguments for aiming at a high degree of equality (arguments based mainly on the diminishing marginal utility of most goods in most circumstances, and of money in nearly all circumstances, and on the disutility of occasioning envy (see pp. 195 f.)). These arguments do not support absolute equality, only moderate equality, though I am sure that they support a much higher degree of equality than exists in South Africa. But how this could be achieved, and how quickly, is a question I leave to those who know more about the country and about economics.

I now turn to political equality—that is, equality in political power. In one sense this is simply not achievable anywhere. All states will always be governed by oligarchies. Even in the extreme democracy of ancient Athens (disregarding the numerous slaves and resident aliens) the power was concentrated in the hands of the demagogues who could sway the Assembly by their rhetoric, and if you antagonized them you were in for trouble. What can be achieved is to establish between the rulers and the ruled a relation which makes the ruled content with the way things are ordered. For this it is necessary first that the rulers should have the ability to govern well, producing such conditions of life as please the citizens or as many of them as possible. But, secondly, it is necessary that the ruled should have confidence that the rulers have the ability and the desire to do this.

Some people have an intuition, as I said earlier, that one-person-one-vote democracy is the only acceptable form of government. I do not entirely agree with these people. What I do think is something less extreme: that representative democracy is, in societies that have the political skills to run it, and where conditions allow it, the best way of achieving these objectives (good government and the confidence of the people) simultaneously. The essence of representative democracy is the power of a majority of voters to turn the government out at a lawful election if they do not like what the government is doing. Normally they can do this only at stated intervals or under other stated conditions. A polity that does not confer this power is inherently unstable and exposed to *coups* and revolutions.

Democracy is the best sort of government for countries that can manage it. It is obvious from the recent history of Africa that not all countries can. It is very easy for representative democracy to slip into one-party democracy; and this can sometimes mean the domination of one section of the community, for example one tribe, over others. This in turn can give rise to military *coups* and dictatorships, thus destroying the advantages of democracy that I have mentioned. Not all these changes, however, are for the worse; the democracy that was supplanted may have been already corrupt or unstable, or a tyranny of the majority. It depends entirely on the conditions in a given country what kind of constitution is best for it. Such questions are to be settled not by intuition but by careful examination of the situation and prospects in the country one is considering.

If I am asked to say off the top of my head whether a representative democracy with universal adult suffrage would be a good idea in South Africa, I reply that, with effective constitutional safeguards for minorities, it would certainly be highly desirable, if the conditions could be brought into being under which such a democracy would be viable. This demands a good deal of careful preparation, which would take time, and it is only possible if those at both ends of the political spectrum cease to rely so much on their ingrained attitudes and intuitions (many of which are quite inappropriate to the situation), and use more critical thinking. I therefore do not think it can be introduced at once; but the example of India is not unhopeful, many as are the troubles of that huge country. The possibility of a qualified suffrage as an intermediate stage needs to be considered; there actually was one for certain groups in the Cape at one time, until the clock was put back.

Short of the eventual introduction of representative democracy with a wide suffrage, I cannot see how South Africa can avoid one of two alternatives. The first is a limited-franchise oligarchy such as there is at the moment, but with increasing violence and increasing repression in the attempt to contain it. The second is some kind of revolution (if, which I doubt, a revolution could succeed), ending up with rule by black leaders under threat of white terrorism, and even more bloodshed than at present. I do not think that either of these alternatives is preferable to the attempt to set up a full democracy. But can it successfully be done all at once? Cases in which it has been must be extremely rare. I shall return later to prognoses about what may actually happen.

I need to say a little about social equality; but only a little, because the principles of it are, or at least ought to be, well understood by now. In any society containing groups with different ways of life, there are two principles which have to be carefully distinguished, because one is a good one and the other a bad one. The first is the principle that we ought not to seek to impose uniformity. For one thing, variety is more attractive and interesting; for another, we can all learn from people who live differently from us. A more important reason is that if people are well satisfied with their own culture, you are likely to diminish preference-satisfactions if you bring pressure on them to change it.

The other, bad, principle creeps in when, as well as accepting variety, we take it as intuitively self-evident that our own way of life is superior and that of others inferior. If this degenerates into contempt for the cultures of others, it will lead to social inequalities of a pernicious sort, especially if those who think themselves superior have the political power to enforce discrimination and segregation and other humiliating practices. In short, we should accept social differences but reject social castes. It is a question of adopting the right attitudes and dispositions; and here, as elsewhere, the right dispositions are the ones whose acceptance is for the best for all in society treated impartially. I have shown this for the first of my principles; that the second (the caste principle) should be rejected is shown by the way in which it, perhaps more even than economic and political inequality, generates all kinds of social tensions which weaken the fraternity that I shall be speaking of later. Even where, as in India, it becomes institutionalized and accepted, the consequences are not for the best.

I have not had time to say nearly enough about economic, political, and social equality; but we must now turn to liberty. Liberty is always to some extent at odds with order, and one kind of liberty with another; indeed, if an excess of one kind of liberty impairs order, other kinds of liberty are bound to suffer. The liberty of some schoolchildren to disrupt their schools may take away the liberty of other schoolchildren to get an education. Though we have been made aware by Sir Isaiah Berlin (1958) and others that 'liberty' can have different meanings, in most ordinary senses of the word the only kind of order compatible with complete liberty is an order accepted without any coercion. As soon as the maintenance of order involves coercion, liberty is infringed. Only an anarchist, or somebody who believes that everybody is naturally and invariably law-abiding without compulsion, can say that this is not sometimes necessary.

The question therefore arises of how to strike a balance between liberty and order, and between liberty of different kinds and for different groups of people. If there is a danger of serious disorder, most people will after a time accept some deprivation of liberty. But they will not accept that liberty should be infringed when the order and the laws that are imposed are obviously intended to be in the interests of only a section of society. That is an additional argument for democracy, which gives, not a guarantee, but some hope, that the laws will be made in the interests of all impartially. But democracy may not work out well in societies that are deeply divided communally.

The consequence of all this is that we cannot say that liberty of all kinds is in practice desirable everywhere and under all conditions. The question will always be, how much liberty, and liberty for whom to do what, should be allowed under the law. It is very important that liberties should be allotted and regulated by law, and that the laws should be impartial and justly administered. This is not the case in South Africa, although there has been a good tradition of procedural justice in the courts, which South Africans should struggle to preserve.

There is also, unhappily, a fear that the police, unless brought more firmly under the law, may become a law to themselves. This tends to happen in all countries unless the government exercises control, and is a particular danger when there are serious public disorders, as now. At the best of times lawful and efficient policing is a difficult combination to achieve. One of the main constituents of it is a preservation of trust between police and public, and this can easily break down, as it has in South Africa. Restoring it sometimes involves a complete change of attitude on the part of the police, such as is, we hope, beginning to come about in America and Britain in the attempt to reduce racial tensions.

Here I must add a word about violence. I shall try to avoid using the word 'violence' itself, because its ambiguities have given scope for some very bad arguments in the mouths of the logically unscrupulous. I believe that reasons can be given for condemning the use of force in general. But I am not a pacifist (see pp. 74 ff.). I believe that the use of force can sometimes be justified. Critical thinking would clearly justify it for certain occasions, and indeed for certain general types of occasion, such as self-defence.

This has the consequence that when we are selecting prima facie principles for use in our day-to-day intuitive moral thinking, we shall select a principle, first, that forbids the use of force in general, and shall try to form in ourselves and others the disposition to abhor it; but, secondly, we shall make certain exceptions to this principle. What these exceptions should be requires a long argument. My own conclusion would be that the use of force by one member of society on another is justified within limits for preserving order under the law; but that forcible law-breaking by members of society, also within limits, can be justified if the laws are bad and they have no other effective means of protest (see pp. 25 ff.). I have the strong impression that both of these limits have in recent times in South Africa been far exceeded, not only by the police but also by some of those who live in the townships. Therefore both the government, which is supposed to control the police, and the people who are instigating the disturbances, are to be condemned in the strongest terms. Equally, those on both sides who try to restrain violence deserve the highest praise.

The government is to be condemned for another reason too: by cramming all those people into the townships and giving them no peaceful outlet for effective political protest, it made it inevitable that there should be this unrest. But though this explains the murders that are becoming frequent, it does not excuse those who have instigated them. Even on the narrowest political calculations they are counter-productive, as well as being morally evil. So, although I could not say that *all* political law-breaking is unjustified, I certainly think that the present wave of murders is. I would say the same of the actions of the government: they too can be *explained*, but not excused. If one says '*Tout comprendre c'est tout pardonner*' in one case but not in the other, one is using a double standard.

A question to which I do not know the answer, and did not

get one from anybody in South Africa, but which anybody who (rightly) condemns the actions of the police is bound to answer if he can, is 'How *should* the townships be policed?' No policing at all might be worse than the present situation, if it led to chaotic fighting between blacks and other blacks; but how can the situation be improved? How could there be a police force which enjoyed the confidence of the people there, and was subject to disciplined control under the law? Not, I am sure, without a complete change of attitude on the part of the government. The fact that so large a proportion of the ranks in the police are black should be a helpful factor; but it will not become so until both the police authorities and the local black leaders in the townships use it as one, and the latter stop encouraging the burning of black policemen and their houses.

If my approach to moral reasoning is right, the question that always has to be asked is: What compromise between liberty and order will, in a particular country in particular circumstances, most conduce to the furtherance of the interests of all its inhabitants, considered impartially? If I were satisfied that a government was asking that question, and had the necessary intelligence and understanding of the situation to answer it correctly and act accordingly, it would have my support. On the other hand, if one finds restraints on liberty which do not serve the interests of all treated impartially, and the government does not remove them, that is a reason for distrusting the government, and concluding that it is governing in the interests of a class. There is a great temptation to act thus when that class has the vote and others do not; and that is yet another argument for democracy. Because I am too ignorant about the situation in South Africa, I must leave others to judge *which* of the restraints on liberty that now obtain should be condemned by this criterion; but it seems fairly obvious that many should.

That is all I have time to say about civil liberty. Political liberty, so called, I have already dealt with under the heading of political equality. So I will now turn very briefly to the topic of fraternity. This, I need hardly say, is an extremely nebulous concept, very worthy of the French revolutionaries; but it is nevertheless an important one which it is therefore important to clarify. Perhaps the best way to start is to point out that one could be trying to bring about the maximum desirable degrees of equality and liberty, but fail because people had the wrong attitudes to one another. This is what notoriously happens in countries, or parts of countries, which are deeply divided communally. Northern Ireland is a very clear example; the Lebanon is another; and there are many more, such as Sri Lanka, the Punjab, even Belgium at least until recently. Switzerland is one of the few examples of a country which is divided by religion and language, but still has strong fraternity; and that is because citizens of Switzerland think of themselves as Swiss first and as French-speakers or Calvinists after that. So Switzerland is not really divided communally.

In order for a society to work and be governable, at least democratically, it is necessary that common citizenship should be cemented by a common loyalty. If that is lacking, no institutions, however admirable the principles of liberty and equality on which they are founded, can ever work. One of the strengths of the ruling party in South Africa seems to be the loyalty that it commands from an important section of the citizens—a loyalty which is in some ways exemplary. But of course, if loyalty is sectional in this way, it does nothing to win the allegiance of the rest of society. If the same kind of loyalty could be won from all, what a wonderful society it would be!

That is where fraternity comes in. The aim of statesmen in South Africa should be to bring about a situation in which common citizenship becomes a bond (I apologize for the pun—a *Broederbond*). Although this may seem an impossible ideal, it remains true that unless those who have the power are seen to be aiming at it, nothing can go well. But if it were aimed at and seen as a possibility which all can strive for, the future of the country would be hopeful. Fraternity was achieved between the British and the Afrikaners after all the evils of the Anglo-Boer War; and it should not be impossible between blacks and whites, when ideas the world over have changed so much. That at any rate is what our Christian religion should be teaching us. But, religion aside, moral philosophy, if I am right about it, tells us to cultivate those dispositions whose acceptance is for the best; and a fraternal disposition which extends to all members of society is one of the most important of these.

I must end by paying tribute to those South Africans who are trying to think rationally about these matters and to find truly universal principles on which they are prepared to act, even at great cost to themselves. They are among the people in the world whom I most admire. Would that there were more of them! One of them is sadly no longer with us, my dear friend Patrick Duncan the younger. Shortly before his tragic death nineteen years ago, he made a grim prediction to me, although I believe he hoped that the evil might be averted. He said that if the Nationalists took it into their heads to move further in the direction of Nazism and institute an out-and-out police state, they could survive for a very long time. It was not true then, and is not even now, that South Africa has yet gone all the way to Nazism; those who pretend that it has do not know from experience, as Patrick did and I do, what it was like in Nazi Germany. For example the courts and the press are much freer, though not free enough.

But if the whites, driven by fear (which is an even stronger motive than pride) took this path, I do not see what could stop them going all the way to a wholesale genocide of the blacks, or at least to a genuine apartheid, as contrasted with the present bogus kind. This would be achieved by driving all the blacks into reserves to starve, and replacing their labour by automation. It would involve very great sacrifices even for the whites. But the majority of these, who have nowhere else to escape to, might be prepared to suffer for the preservation of their tribe if they saw no other way; and, if they were determined to do this, nobody else is likely to be able to stop them. It will be said that power grows out of the barrel of a gun, and that political negotiations are a mirage. The trouble is that the whites have more and better guns, and the will to use them if driven to it. The wisdom of measures taken by people both inside and outside Africa is to be judged mainly by the effects they have in moving the white electorate, either in this direction, or in the more hopeful one I was indicating earlier. These effects can be monitored to some extent by watching the respective electoral fortunes and misfortunes of the extreme right-wing parties outside the government, and of the Progressive Federal Party at the other end of the parliamentary spectrum. It ought not to be the case that so much depends on the mood of the white minority; but unfortunately it does, because they have most of the power, and, revolution (in the sense of an overturn of the government by force) being practically speaking impossible at present, and terrorism only an annoyance which may even move them in the wrong direction, they are in a position to say whether reforms shall take place or not.

So this is how we should judge the relative wisdom of various pressures: diplomacy, votes in the United Nations, trade boycotts, divestment, loan refusals, ostracism in the arts and sport and by academics, supply of arms to terrorists, even threats of military intervention. It is by thinking critically about the effects of such measures that we should judge them, and not by a blanket ideology which says that anything which harms the white South Africans, or even which harms capitalists, must be good. It depends on who are harmed and how they will react. For example, I judge that the Nationalist government is positively pleased when academic exchanges between South Africa and other countries are stopped, because that cuts off one source of moral support and intellectual help from its opponents. This kind of ostracism, at any rate, does more harm than good. And the same might be said of Oliver Tambo's threat, when he met the businessmen at Lusaka, to nationalize their firms when he got into power. They did not need persuading to oppose the government, which they have been doing for years, but, if they did, this was hardly the way to go about it.

I have ended in this unhopeful way, mainly because it is what I think, but partly to avoid the charge that, in saying that philosophy could help, I have been too optimistic. I do indeed think that it could help, *if* people who influence events, on both sides of the political divide, would do more and better critical thinking. But as to whether many of them will, I am pessimistic in the extreme. Philosophy has been too much neglected.

14

Justice and Equality

THERE are several reasons why a philosopher of my persuasion should wish to write about justice. The first is the general one that ethical theory ought to be applied to practical issues, both for the sake of improving the theory and for any light it may shed on the practical issues, of which many of the most important involve questions of justice. This is shown by the frequency with which appeals are made to justice and fairness and related ideals when people are arguing about political or economic questions (about wages for example, or about schools policy, or about relations between races or sexes). If we do not know what 'just' and 'fair' mean (and it looks as if we do not) and therefore do not know what would settle questions involving these concepts, then we are unlikely to be able to sort out these very difficult moral problems. I have also a particular interest in the topic: I hold a view about moral reasoning which has at least strong affinities with utilitarianism (H 1976, *MT*); and there is commonly thought to be some kind of antagonism between justice and utility or, as it is sometimes called, expediency. I have therefore a special need to sort these questions out.

We must start by distinguishing between different kinds of justice, or between different senses or uses of the word 'just' (the distinction between these different ways of putting the matter need not now concern us). In distinguishing between different kinds of justice we shall have to make crucial use of a distinction between different levels of moral thinking which I have explained at length in other places (pp. 81 ff., H 1972*a* and *MT*). It is perhaps simplest to distinguish three levels of thought, one ethical or meta ethical and two moral or normative-ethical. At the meta ethical level we try to establish the meanings of the moral words, and thus the formal

From *Justice and Economic Distribution*, ed. J. Arthur and W. Shaw (Prentice-Hall, 1978).

properties of the moral concepts, including their logical properties. Without knowing these a theory of normative moral reasoning cannot begin. Then there are two levels of (normative) moral thinking which have often been in various ways distinguished. I have myself in the past called them 'level 2' and 'level 1'; but for ease of remembering I now think it best to give them names, and propose to call level 2 the *critical* level and level 1 the *intuitive* level. At the intuitive level we make use of prima facie moral principles of a fairly simple general sort, and do not question them but merely apply them to cases which we encounter. This level of thinking cannot be (as intuitionists commonly suppose) self-sustaining; there is a need for a critical level of thinking by which we select the prima facie principles for use at the intuitive level, settle conflicts between them, and give to the whole system of them a justification which intuition by itself can never provide. It will be one of the objects of this paper to distinguish those kinds of justice whose place is at the intuitive level and which are embodied in prima facie principles from those kinds which have a role in critical and indeed in meta ethical thinking.

The principal result of meta ethical enquiry in this field is to isolate a sense or kind of justice which has come to be known as 'formal justice'. Formal justice is a property of all moral principles (which is why Professor Rawls heads his chapter on this subject not 'Formal constraints of the concept of *just*' but 'Formal constraints of the concept of *right*' (1971: 130), and why his disciple David Richards is able to make a good attempt to found the whole of morality, and not merely a theory of justice, on a similar hypothetical-contract basis (1971)). Formal justice is simply another name for the formal requirement of universality in moral principles on which, as I have explained in detail elsewhere (*FR, MT*), golden-rule arguments are based. From the formal, logical properties of the moral words, and in particular from the logical prohibition of individual references in moral principles, it is possible to derive formal canons of moral argument, such as the rule that we are not allowed to discriminate morally between individuals unless there is some qualitative difference between them which is the ground for the discrimination; and the rule that the equal interests of different individuals have equal moral weight. Formal justice consists simply in the observance of these canons in our moral arguments; it is widely thought that this observance by itself is not enough to secure justice in some more substantial sense. As we shall see, one is not offending against the first rule if one says that extra privileges should be given to people just because they have white skins; and one is not offending against either rule if one says that one should take a penny from everybody and give it to the man with the biggest nose, provided that he benefits as much in total as they lose. The question is, How do we get from formal to substantial justice?

This question arises because there are various kinds of material or substantial justice whose content cannot be established directly by appeal to the uses of moral words or the formal properties of moral concepts (we shall see later how much can be done indirectly by appeal to these formal properties *in conjunction with* other premises or postulates or presuppositions). There is a number of different kinds of substantial justice, and we can hardly do better than begin with Aristotle's classification of them (1130b 31 ff.), since it is largely responsible for the different senses which the word 'just' still has in common use. This is a case where it is impossible to appeal to common use, at any rate of the word 'just' (the word 'fair' is better) in order to settle philosophical disputes, because the common use is itself the product of past philosophical theories. The expressions 'distributive' and 'retributive' justice go back to Aristotle, and the word 'just' itself occupies the place (or places) that it does in our language largely because of its place in earlier philosophical discussions.

Aristotle first separated off a generic sense of the Greek word commonly translated 'just', a sense which had been used a lot by Plato: the sense in which justice is the whole of virtue in so far as it concerns our relations with other people (1130a 8). The last qualification reminds us that this is not the most generic sense possible. Theognis had already used it to include the whole of virtue, full stop (147). These very generic senses of the word, as applied to men and acts, have survived into modern English to confuse philosophers. One of the sources of confusion is that, in the less generic sense of 'just' to be discussed in most of this paper, the judgement that an act would be unjust is sometimes fairly easily overridden by other moral considerations ('unjust', we may say, 'but right as an act of mercy'; or 'unjust, but right because necessary in order to avert an appalling calamity'). It is much more difficult for judgements that an act is required by justice in the generic sense, in which 'unjust' is almost equivalent to 'not right', to be overridden in this way.

Adherents of the '*fiat justitia ruat caelum*' school seldom make clear whether, when they say, 'Let justice be done though the heavens fall', they are using a more or a less generic sense of 'justice'; and they thus take advantage of its non-overridability in the more generic sense in order to claim unchallengeable sanctity for judgements made using one of the less generic senses. It must be right to do the just thing (whatever that may be) in the sense (if there still is one in English) in which 'just' *means* 'right'. In this sense, if it were right to cause the heavens to fall, and therefore just in the most generic sense, it would of course be right. But we might have to take into account, in deciding whether it would be right, the fact that the heavens would fall (that causing the heavens to fall would be one of the things we were doing if we did the action in question). On the other hand, if it were merely the just act in one of the less generic senses, we might hold that, though just, it was not right, because it would not be right to cause the heavens to fall merely in order to secure justice in this more limited sense; perhaps some concession to mercy, or even to common sense, would be in order.

This is an application of the 'two-level' structure of moral thinking sketched above. One of the theses I wish to maintain is that principles of justice in these less generic senses are all prima facie principles and therefore overridable. I shall later be giving a utilitarian account of justice which finds a place, at the intuitive level, for these prima facie principles of justice. At this level they have great importance and utility, but it is in accordance with utilitarianism, as indeed with common sense, to claim that they can on unusual occasions be overridden. Having said this, however, it is most important to stress that this does *not* involve conceding the overridability of either the generic kind of justice, which has its place at the critical level, or of formal justice, which operates at the meta ethical level. These are preserved intact, and therefore defenders of the sanctity of justice ought to be content, since these are the core of justice as of morality. We may call to mind here Aristotle's remarks about the 'better justice' or 'equity' which is required in order to rectify the crudities, giving rise to unacceptable results in particular cases, of a justice whose principles are, as they have to be, couched in general (i.e. simple) terms (1137b 8 ff.). The lawgiver who, according to Aristotle, 'would have' given a special prescription if he had been present at this particular case, and to whose prescription we must try to conform if we can, corresponds to the critical moral thinker, who operates under the constraints of formal justice and whose principles are not limited to simple general rules but can be specific enough to cover the peculiarities of unusual cases.

After speaking briefly of generic justice, Aristotle goes on to distinguish two main kinds of justice in the narrower or more particular sense in which it means 'fairness'. He calls these retributive and distributive justice. They have their place, respectively, in the fixing of penalties and rewards for bad and good actions, and in the distribution of goods and the opposite between the possible recipients. One of the most important questions is whether these two sorts of justice are reducible to a single sort. Rawls, for example (1971: 136), thinks that they are, and so do I. By using the expression 'justice as fairness', he implies that all justice can be reduced to kinds of distributive justice, which itself is founded on procedural justice (i.e. on the adoption of fair procedures) in distribution.

We may (without attempting complete accuracy in exposition) explain how Rawls might effect this reduction as follows. The parties in his 'original position' are prevented by his 'veil of ignorance' from knowing what their own positions are in the world in which they are to live; so they are unable when adopting principles of justice to tailor them to suit their own individual interests. Impartiality (a very important constituent, at least, of justice) is thus secured. Therefore the principles which govern *both* the distribution of wealth and power and other good things *and* the assignment of rewards and penalties (and indeed all other matters which have to be regulated by principles of justice) will be impartial as between individuals, and in this sense just. In this way Rawls in effect reduces the justice of acts of retribution to justice in distributing between the affected parties the good and bad effects of a system of retributions, and reduces this distributive justice in turn to the adoption of a just procedure for selecting the system of retribution to be used.

This can be illustrated by considering the case of a criminal facing a judge (Kant 1785: §2 *n.*) (a case which has been thought to give trouble to me too, though I dealt with it adequately, on the lines which I am about to repeat here, in *FR* 115–17; 124). A Rawlsian judge, when sentencing the criminal, could defend himself against the charge of injustice or unfairness by saying that he was faithfully observing the principles of justice which would be adopted in the original position, whose conditions are procedurally fair. What these principles would be requires, no doubt, a great deal of discussion, in the course of which I might find myself in disagreement with Rawls (see pp. 203 ff.). But my own view on how the judge should justify his action is, in its formal properties, very like his. On my view likewise, the judge can say that, when he asks himself what universal principles he is prepared to adopt for situations exactly like the one he is in, and considers examples of such logically possible situations in which *he* occupies, successively, the positions of judge, and of criminal, and of all those who are affected by the administration and enforcement of the law under which he is sentencing the criminal, including, of course, potential victims of possible future crimes—he can say that when he asks himself this, he has no hesitation in accepting the principle which bids him impose such and such a sentence in accordance with the law.

I am assuming that the judge is justifying himself at the critical level. If he were content with justifying himself at the intuitive level, his task would be easier, because, we hope, he, like most of us, has intuitions about the proper administration of justice in the courts, embodying prima facie principles of a sort whose inculcation in judges and in the rest of us has a high social utility. I say this while recognizing that *some* judges have intuitions about these matters which have a high social *dis*utility. The question of what intuitions judges ought to have about retributive justice is a matter for *critical* moral thinking.

On both Rawls's view and mine retributive justice has thus been reduced to distributive; on Rawls's view the principles of justice adopted are those which *distribute* fairly between those affected the good and the evil consequences of having or not having certain enforced criminal laws; on my own view likewise it is the impartiality secured by the requirement to universalize one's prescriptions which makes the judge say what he says, and here too it is an impartiality in distributing good and evil consequences between the affected parties. For the judge to let off the rapist would not be *fair* to all those who would be raped if the law were not enforced. I conclude that retributive justice can be reduced to distributive, and that therefore we shall have done what is required of us if we can give an adequate account of the latter.

What is common to Rawls's method and my own is the recognition that to get solutions to particular questions about what is just or unjust, we have to have a way of selecting principles of justice to answer such questions, and that to ask them in default of such principles is senseless. This measure of agreement can extend to the method of selecting principles of distributive justice as well as retributive. Neither Rawls nor I need be put off our stride by an objector who says that we have not addressed ourselves to the question of what acts are just, but have divagated on to the quite different question of how to select principles of justice. The point is that the first question cannot be answered without answering the second. Most of the apparently intractable conflicts about justice and rights that plague the world have been generated by taking certain answers to the first question as obvious and requiring no argument. We shall resolve these conflicts only by asking what arguments are available for the principles by which questions about the justice of individual acts are to be answered. In short, we need to ascend from intuitive to critical thinking; as I have argued in my review of his book (H 1973*a*), Rawls is to be reproached with not *completing* the ascent.

Nozick, however, seems hardly to have begun it (1974).

Neither Rawls nor I have anything to fear from him, so long as we stick to the formal part of our systems which we in effect share. When it comes to the application of this formal method to produce substantial principles of justice, I might, as I said, find myself in disagreement with Rawls, because he relies much too much on his own intuitions which are open to question. Nozick's intuitions differ from Rawls's, and sometimes differ from, sometimes agree with mine. This sort of question is simply not to be settled by appeal to intuitions, and it is time that the whole controversy ascended to a more serious, critical level. At this level, the answer which both Rawls and I should give to Nozick is that whatever sort of principles of justice we are after, whether structural principles, as Rawls thinks, or historical principles, as Nozick maintains, they have to be supported by critical thinking, of which Nozick seems hardly to see the necessity. This point is quite independent of the structural-historical disagreement.

For example, if Nozick thinks that it is just for people to retain whatever property they have acquired by voluntary exchange which benefited all parties, starting from a position of equality but perhaps ending up with a position of gross inequality, and if Rawls, by contrast, thinks that such inequality should be rectified in order to make the position of the least advantaged in society as good as possible, how are we to decide between them? Not by intuition, because there seems to be a deadlock between their intuitions. Rawls has a procedure, which *need* not appeal to intuition, for justifying distributions; this would give him the game, if he were to base the procedure on firm logical grounds, and if he followed it correctly. Actually he does not so base it, and mixes up so many intuitions in the argument that the conclusions he reaches are not such as the procedure really justifies. But Nozick has no procedure at all: only a variety of considerations of different sorts, all in the end based on intuition. Sometimes he seems to be telling us what arrangements in society would be arrived at if bargaining took place in accordance with games-theory between mutually disinterested parties; sometimes what arrangements would maximize the welfare of members of society; and sometimes what arrangements would strike them as fair. He does not often warn us when he is switching from one of these grounds to another; and he does little to convince us by argument that the arrangements so selected would be in accordance with justice. He hopes that we will think what he thinks; but Rawls at least thinks otherwise.

How then do we get from formal to substantial justice? We have had an example of how this is done in the sphere of retributive justice; but how is this method to be extended to cover distributive justice as a whole, and its relation, if any, to equality in distribution? The difficulty of using formal justice in order to establish principles of substantial justice can indeed be illustrated very well by asking whether, and in what sense, justice demands equality in distribution. The complaint is often made that a certain distribution is unfair or unjust because unequal; so it looks, at least, as if the substantial principle that goods ought to be distributed equally in default of reasons to the contrary forms part of some people's conception of justice. Yet, it is argued, this substantial principle cannot be established simply on the basis of the formal notions we have mentioned. The following kind of schematic example is often adduced: consider two possible distributions of a given finite stock of goods, in one of which the goods are distributed equally, and in the other of which a few of the recipients have nearly all the goods, and the rest have what little remains. It is claimed with some plausibility that the second distribution is unfair, and the first fair. But it might also be claimed that impartiality and formal justice alone will not establish that we ought to distribute the goods equally.

There are two reasons which might be given for this second claim, the first of them a bad one, the other more cogent. The bad reason rests on an under-estimate of the powers of golden-rule arguments. It is objected, for example, that people with white skins, if they claimed privileges in distribution purely on the ground of skin-colour, would not be offending against the formal principle of impartiality or universalizability, because no individual reference need enter into the principle to which they are appealing. Thus the principle that blacks ought to be subservient to whites is impartial as between *individuals*; any individual whatever who has the bad luck to find himself with a black skin or the good luck to find himself with a white skin is impartially placed by the principle in the appropriate social rank. But if the whites are faced with the decision, not merely of whether to frame this principle, but of whether to prescribe its adoption universally in all cases, including hypothetical ones in which their own skins turn black, they will at once reject it (*FR* 106 f.; H 1978).

The other, more cogent-sounding argument is often used as an argument against utilitarians by those who think that justice has a lot to do with equality. It could also, at first sight, be used as an argument against the adequacy of formal justice or impartiality as a basis for distributive justice. That the argument could be levelled against both these methods is no accident; as I have tried to show elsewhere (*MT*), utilitarianism of a certain sort is the embodiment of—the method of moral reasoning which fulfils in practice—the requirement of universalizability or formal justice. Having shown that neither. of these methods can produce a direct justification for equal distribution, I shall then show that both can produce indirect justifications, which depend, not on a priori reasoning alone, but on likely assumptions about what the world and the people in it are like.

The argument is this. Formal impartiality only requires us to treat everybody's interest as of equal weight. Imagine, then, a situation in which utilities are equally distributed. (There is a complication here which we can for the moment avoid by choosing a suitable example. Shortly I shall be mentioning the so-called principle of diminishing marginal utility, and shall indeed be making important use of it. But for now let us take a case in which it does not operate, so that we can, for ease of illustration, treat money as a linear measure of utility.) Suppose that we can vary the equal distribution that we started with by taking a dollar each away from everybody in the town, and that the loss of purchasing power is so small that they hardly notice it, and therefore the utility enjoyed by each is not much diminished. However, when we give the resulting large sum to one man, he is able to buy himself a holiday in Acapulco, which gives him so much pleasure that his access of utility is equal to the sum of the small losses suffered by all the others. Many would say that this redistribution was unfair. But we were, in the required sense, being impartial between the equal interests of all the parties; we were treating an equal access or loss of utility to any party as of equal value or disvalue. For, on our suppositions, the taking away of a dollar from one of the unfortunate parties deprived him of just as much utility as the addition of that dollar gave to the fortunate one. But if we are completely impartial, we have to regard *who has* the dollar or that access of utility as irrelevant. So there will be nothing to choose, from an impartial point of view, between our original equal distribution and our later highly unequal one, in which everybody else is deprived of a dollar in order to give one person a holiday in Acapulco. And that is why people say that formal impartiality alone is not enough to secure social justice, nor even to secure impartiality itself in some more substantial sense.

What is needed, in the opinion of these people, is some principle which says that it is unjust to give a person more when he already has more than the others—some sort of egalitarian principle. Egalitarian principles are only one possible kind of principles of distributive justice; and it is so far an open question whether they are to be preferred to alternative inegalitarian principles. It is fairly clear as a matter of history that different principles of justice have been accepted in different societies. As Aristotle says, 'Everybody agrees that the just distribution is one in accordance with desert of some kind; but they do not call desert the same thing, but the democrats say it is being a free citizen, the oligarchs being rich, others good lineage, and the aristocrats virtue' (1131a 25). It is not difficult to think of some societies in which it would be thought unjust for one man to have privileges not possessed by all men, and of others in which it would be thought unjust for a slave to have privileges which a free man would take for granted, or for a commoner to have the sort of house which a nobleman could aspire to. Even Aristotle's democrats did not think that slaves, but only citizens, had equal rights; and Plato complains of democracy that it 'bestows equality of a sort on equals and unequals alike' (*Republic* 558c). We have to ask, therefore, whether there are any reasons for preferring one of these attitudes to another.

At this point some philosophers will be ready to step in with their intuitions, and tell us that some distributions or ways of achieving distributions are *obviously* more just than others, or that *everyone will agree on reflection* that they are. These philosophers appeal to our intuitions or prejudices in support of the most widely divergent methods or patterns of distribution. But this is a way of arguing which should be abjured by anybody who wishes to have rational grounds for his moral judgements. Intuitions prove nothing; general consensus proves nothing; both have been used to support conclusions which *our* intuitions and our consensus may well find outrageous. We want arguments, and in this field seldom get them.

However, it is too early to despair of finding some. The utilitarian, and the formalist like me, still have some moves to make. I am supposing that we have already made the major move suggested above, and have ruled out discrimination on grounds of skin colour and the like, in so far as such discrimination could not be accepted by all for cases where they were the ones discriminated against. I am supposing that our society has absorbed this move, and contains no racists, sexists, or in general discriminators, but does still contain economic men who do not think it wrong, in pursuit of Nozickian economic liberty, to get what they can, even if the resulting distribution is grotesquely unequal. Has the egalitarian any moves to make against them, and are they moves which can be supported by appeal to formal justice, in conjunction with the empirical facts?

He has two. The first is based on that good old prop of egalitarian policies, the diminishing marginal utility, within the ranges that matter, of money and of nearly all goods. Almost always, if money or goods are taken away from someone who has a lot of them already, and given to someone who has little, total utility is increased, other things being equal. As we shall see, they hardly ever are equal; but the principle is all right. Its ground is that the poor man will get more utility out of what he is given than the rich man from whom it is taken would have got. A millionaire minds less about the gain or loss of a dollar than I do, and I than a pauper.

It must be noted that this is not an a priori principle. It is an empirical fact (if it is) that people are so disposed. The most important thing I have to say in this paper is that when we are, as we now are, trying to establish prima facie principles of distributive justice, it is enough if they can be justified in the world as it actually is, among people as they actually are. It is a wholly illegitimate argument against formalists or utilitarians that states of society or of the people in it could be *conceived of* in which gross inequalities could be justified by formal or utilitarian arguments. We are seeking principles for practical use in the world as it is (see p. 163). The same applies when we ask what qualifications are required to the principles.

Diminishing marginal utility is the firmest support for policies of progressive taxation of the rich and other egalitarian measures. However, as I said above, other things are seldom equal, and there are severe empirical, practical restraints on the equality that can sensibly be imposed by governments. To mention just a few of these hackneyed other things; the removal of incentives to effort may diminish the total stock of goods to be divided up; abrupt confiscation or even very steep progressive taxation may antagonize the victims so much that a whole class turns from a useful element in society to a hostile and dangerous one; or, even if that does not happen, it may merely become demoralized and either lose all enterprise and readiness to take business risks, or else just emigrate if it can. Perhaps one main cause of what is called the English sickness is the alienation of the middle class. It is an empirical question, just when egalitarian measures get to the stage of having these effects; and serious political argument on this subject should concentrate on such empirical questions, instead of indulging in the rhetoric of equal (or for that matter of unequal) rights. Rights are the offspring of prima facie, intuitive principles, and I have nothing against them; but the question is, What prima facie principles ought we to adopt? What intuitions ought we to have? On these questions the rhetoric of rights sheds no light whatever, any more than do appeals to intuition (i.e. to prejudice, i.e. to the prima facie principles, good or bad, which our upbringings happen to have implanted in us). The worth of intuitions is to be known by their fruits; as in the case of the principles to be followed by judges in administering the law, the best principles are those with the highest acceptance-utility, i.e. those whose general acceptance maximizes the furtherance of the interests, in sum, of all the affected parties, treating all those interests as of equal weight, i.e. impartially, i.e. with formal justice.

We have seen that, given the empirical assumption of diminishing marginal utility, such a method provides a justification for moderately egalitarian policies. The justification is strengthened by a second move that the egalitarian can make. This is to point out that inequality itself has a tendency to produce envy, which is a disagreeable state of mind and leads people to do disagreeable things. It makes no difference to the argument whether the envy is a good or a bad quality, nor whether it is justified or unjustified—any more than it makes a difference whether the alienation of the middle class which I mentioned above is to be condemned or excused. These states of mind are facts, and moral judgements have to be made in the light of the facts as they are. We have to take account of the actual state of the world and of the people in it. We can very easily think of societies which are highly unequal, but in which the more fortunate members have contrived to find some real or metaphorical opium or some Platonic noble lie (*Republic* 414b) to keep the people quiet, so that the people feel no envy of privileges which we should consider outrageous. Imagine, for example, a society consisting of happy slave-owners and of happy slaves, all of whom know their places and do not have ideas above their station. Since there is *ex hypothesi* no envy, this source of disutility does not exist, and the whole argument from envy collapses (on slavery, see pp. 148 ff.).

It is salutary to remember this. It may make us stop looking for purely formal, a priori reasons for demanding equality, and look instead at the actual conditions which obtain in particular societies. To make the investigation more concrete, albeit over-simplified, let us ask what would have to be the case before we ought to be ready to push this happy slave-owning society into a revolution—peaceful or violent—which would turn the slaves into free and moderately equal wage-earners. I shall be able only to sketch my answer to this question, without doing nearly enough to justify it.

First of all, as with all moral questions, we should have to ask what would be the actual consequences of what we were doing—which is the same as to ask what we should be *doing*, so that accusations of 'consequentialism' need not be taken very seriously (Anscombe 1958; Williams 1973: 82). Suppose, to simplify matters outrageously, that we can actually predict the consequences of the revolution and what will happen during its course. We can then consider two societies (one actual and one possible) and a possible process of transition from one to the other. And we have to ask whether the transition from one to the other will, all in all, promote the interests of all those affected more than to stay as they are, or rather, to develop as they would develop if the revolution did not occur. The question can be divided into questions about the process of transition and questions about the relative merits of the actual society (including its probable subsequent 'natural' development) and the possible society which would be produced by the revolution.

We have supposed that the slaves in the existing society feel no envy, and that therefore the disutility of envy cannot be used as an argument for change. If there *were* envy, as in actual cases is probable, this argument *could* be employed; but let us see what can be done without it. We have the fact that there is gross inequality in the actual society and much greater equality in the possible one. The principle of diminishing marginal utility will therefore support the change, provided that its effects are not outweighed by a reduction in total utility resulting from the change and the way it comes about. But we have to be sure that this condition is fulfilled. Suppose, for example, that the actual society is a happy bucolic one and is likely to remain so, but that the transition to the possible society initiates the growth of an industrial economy in which everybody has to engage in a rat race and is far less happy. We might in that case pronounce the actual society better. In general it is not self-evident that the access of what is called wealth makes people happier, although they nearly always think that it will.

Let us suppose, however, that we are satisfied that the people in the possible society will be better off all-round than in the actual. There is also the point that there will be more generations to enjoy the new regime than suffer in the transition from the old. At least, this is what revolutionaries often say; and we have set them at liberty to say it by assuming, contrary to what is likely to be the case, that the future state of society is predictable. In actual fact, revolutions usually produce states of society very different from, and in most cases worse than, what their authors expected—which does not always stop them being better than what went before, once things have settled down. However, let us waive these difficulties and suppose that the future state of society can be predicted, and that it is markedly better than the existing state, because a greater equality of distribution has, owing to diminishing marginal utility, resulted in greater total utility.

Let us suppose that the more enterprising economic structure which results leads to increased production without causing a rat race. There will then be more wealth to go round and the revolution will have additional justification. Other benefits of the same general kind may also be adduced; and what is perhaps the greatest benefit of all, namely liberty itself. That people like having this is an empirical fact; it may not be a fact universally, but it is at least *likely* that by freeing slaves we shall *pro tanto* promote their interests. Philosophers who ask for a priori arguments for liberty or equality often talk as if empirical facts like this were totally irrelevant to the question. Genuine egalitarians and liberals ought to abjure the aid of these philosophers, because they have taken away the main ground for such views, namely the fact that people are as they are.

The arguments so far adduced support the call for a revolution. They will have to be balanced against the disutilities which will probably be caused by the process of transition. If heads roll, that is contrary to the interests of their owners; and no doubt the economy will be disrupted at least temporarily, and the new rulers, whoever they are, may infringe liberty just as much as the old, and possibly in an even more arbitrary manner. Few revolutions are pleasant while they are going on. But if the revolution can be more or less smooth or even peaceful, it may well be that (given the arguments already adduced about the desirability of the future society thereby achieved) revolution can have a utilitarian justification, and therefore a justification on grounds of formal impartiality between people's interests. But it is likely to be better for all if the same changes can be achieved less abruptly by an evolutionary process, and those who try to persuade us that this is not so are often merely giving way to impatience and showing a curious indifference to the interests of those for whom they purport to be concerned.

The argument in favour of change from a slave-owning society to a wage-earning one has been extremely superficial, and has served only to illustrate the lines on which a utilitarian or a formalist might argue. If we considered instead the transition from a capitalist society to a socialist one, the same forms of argument would have to be employed, but might not yield the same result. Even if the introduction of a fully socialist economy would promote greater equality, or more equal liberties (and I can see no reason for supposing this, but rather the reverse; for socialism tends to produce very great inequalities of *power*), it needs to be argued what the consequences would be, and then an assessment has to be made of the relative benefits and harms accruing from leaving matters alone and from having various sorts of bloody or bloodless change. Here again the rhetoric of rights will provide nothing but inflammatory material for agitators on both sides. It is designed to lead to, not to resolve, conflicts.

But we must now leave this argument and attend to a methodological point which has become pressing. We have not, in the last few pages, been arguing about what state of society would be just, but about what state of society would best promote the interests of its members. All the arguments have been utilitarian. Where then does justice come in? It is likely to come into the propaganda of revolutionaries, as I have already hinted. But so far as I can see it has no direct bearing on the question of what would be the better society. It has, however, an important indirect bearing which I shall now try to explain. Our prima facie moral principles and intuitions are, as I have already said, the products of our upbringings; and it is a very important question *what* principles and intuitions it is best to bring up people to have. I have been arguing on the assumption that this question is to be decided by looking at the consequences for society, and the effects on the interests of people in society, of inculcating different principles. We are looking for the set of principles with the highest acceptance-utility.

Will these include principles of justice? The answer is obviously 'Yes', if we think that society and the people in it are better off with *some* principles of justice than without any. A 'land without justice' (to use the title of Milovan Djilas's book, 1958) is almost bound to be an unhappy one. But what are the principles to be? Are we, for example, to inculcate the principle that it is just for people to perform the duties of their station and not envy those of higher social rank? Or the principle that all inequalities of any sort are unjust and ought to be removed? For my part, I would think that neither of these principles has a very high acceptance-utility. It may be that the principle with the highest acceptance-utility is one which makes just reward vary (but not immoderately) with desert, and assesses desert according to service to the interests of one's fellow men. It would have to be supplemented by a principle securing equality of opportunity. But it is a partly empirical question what principles would have the highest acceptance-utility, and in any case beyond the scope of this paper. If some such principle is adopted and inculcated, people will *call* breaches of it unjust. Will they *be* unjust? Only in the sense that they will be contrary to a prima facie principle of distributive justice which we ought to adopt (not because it is itself a just principle, but because it is the best principle). The only sense that can be given to the question of whether it is a just principle (apart from the purely circular or tautological question of whether the principle obeys itself), is by asking whether the procedure by which we have selected the principle satisfies the logical requirements of critical moral thinking, i.e. is *formally* just. We might add that the adoption of such a formally just procedure and of the principles it selects is just in the *generic* sense mentioned at the beginning of this paper; it is the right thing to do; we morally ought to do it. The reason is that critical thinking, because it follows the requirements of formal justice based on the logical properties of the moral concepts, especially 'ought' and 'right', can therefore not fail, if pursued correctly in the light of the empirical facts, to lead to principles of justice which are in accord with morality. But because the requirements are all formal, they do not by themselves determine the content of the principles of justice. We have to do the thinking.

What principles of justice are best to try to inculcate will depend on the circumstances of particular societies, and especially on psychological facts about their members. One of these facts is their readiness to accept the principles themselves. There might be a principle of justice which it would be highly desirable to inculcate, but which we have no chance of successfully inculcating. The best principles for a society to *have* are, as I said, those with the highest acceptance-utility. But the best principles to *try to inculcate* will not necessarily be these, if these are impossible to inculcate. Imagine that in our happy slave-society both slaves and slave-owners are obstinately conservative and know their places, and that the attempt to get the slaves to have revolutionary or egalitarian thoughts will result only in a very few of them becoming discontented, and probably going to the gallows as a result, and the vast majority merely becoming unsettled and therefore more unhappy. Then we ought not to try to inculcate such an egalitarian principle. On the other hand, if, as is much more likely, the principle stood a good chance of catching on, and the revolution was likely to be as advantageous as we have supposed, then we ought. The difference lies in the dispositions of the inhabitants. I am not saying that the probability of being accepted is the same thing as acceptance-utility; only that the rationality of trying to inculcate a principle (like the rationality of trying to do anything else) varies with the likelihood of success. In this sense the advisability of trying to inculcate principles of justice (though not their merit) is relative to the states of mind of those who, it is hoped, will hold them.

It is important to be clear about the extent to which what I am advocating is a kind of relativism. It is certainly not relativistic in any strong sense. Relativism is the doctrine that the truth of some moral statement depends on whether people accept it. A typical example would be the thesis that if in a certain society people think that they ought to get their male children circumcised, then they ought to get them circumcised, full stop. Needless to say, I am not supporting any such doctrine, which is usually the result of confusion, and against which there are well-known arguments. It is, however, nearly always the case that among the facts relevant to a moral decision are facts about people's thoughts or dispositions. For example, if I am wondering whether I ought to take my wife for a holiday in Acapulco, it is relevant to ask whether she would like it. What I have been saying is to be assimilated to this last example. If we take as given certain dispositions in the members of society (namely dispositions not to accept a certain principle of justice however hard we work at propagating it) then we have to decide whether, in the light of these facts, we ought to propagate it. What principles of justice we ought to propagate will vary with the probable effects of propagating them. The answer to this 'ought'-question is not relative to what we, who are asking it, think about the matter; it is to be arrived at by moral thought on the basis of the facts of the situation. But among these facts are facts about the dispositions of people in the society in question.

The moral I wish to draw from the whole argument is that ethical reasoning *can* provide us with a way of conducting political arguments about justice and rights rationally and with hope of agreement; that such rational arguments have to rest on an understanding of the concepts being used, *and* of the facts of our actual situation. The key question is 'What principles of justice, what attitudes towards the distribution of goods, what ascriptions of rights, are such that their acceptance is in the general interest?' I advocate the asking of this question as a substitute for one which is much more commonly asked, namely 'What rights do I have?' For people who ask this latter question will, being human, nearly always answer that they have just those rights, whatever they are, which will promote a distribution of goods which is in the interest of their own social group. The rhetoric of rights, which is engendered by this question, is a recipe for class war, and civil war. In pursuit of these rights, people will, because they have convinced themselves that justice demands it, inflict almost any harms on the rest of society and on themselves. To live at peace, we need principles such as critical thinking can provide, based on formal justice and on the facts of the actual world in which we have to live. It is possible for all to practice this critical thinking in co-operation, if only they would learn how; for all share the same moral concepts with the same logic, if they could but understand them and follow it.

15
Punishment and Retributive Justice

ALTHOUGH the problem of the justification of punishment, and particular problems about the justification of particular punishments, remain as pressing as ever, and crucial political decisions depend on the solutions to them, the philosophical study of the subject has not advanced as much as could have been hoped in the last thirty years. This is my excuse for starting by discussing a famous early paper (1953) by Lord Quinton (as he now is) which is still widely read, and, more surprisingly, even accepted as the prevailing orthodoxy, in spite of its containing a very obvious mistake, which has indeed been pointed out by others long ago (e.g. Baier 1955). This makes me think that, in spite of the mistake, there must be something important in the paper which deserves to be rescued; and this we can do by looking carefully at the mistake and seeing whether Quinton's main thesis can survive its correction.

His main thesis is that the moral justification of punishment as an institution is utilitarian, and that the truth in retributivism is a purely logical truth. A utilitarian myself, I should naturally like to defend such a thesis, although, as should be evident from my other writings, I do not accept the common dogma that utilitarianism has to be at odds with Kantianism or even with tenable forms of deontology (H 1985). When all these positions are carefully formulated, they cease to be in disagreement. However, I shall in this paper argue, like Quinton, as a utilitarian. Since punishment is thought to be a prime example of a question on which utilitarians disagree with Kantians and deontologists, it will be useful to point out that they need not. Quinton himself has done a lot to help resolve this dispute.

Quinton claims that what is true and essential in the so-

From *Philosophical Topics* 14, *Value Theory*, ed. J. Adler and R. N. Lee (U. of Arkansas P., 1986).

called retributive theory of punishment is analytically true in virtue of the meaning of the word 'punish'. He says,

For the necessity of not punishing the innocent is not moral but logical. It is not, as some retributivists think, that we *may* not punish the innocent and *ought* only to punish the guilty, but that we *cannot* punish the innocent and *must* only punish the guilty ... The infliction of suffering on a person is only properly described as punishment if that person is guilty. The retributivist thesis, therefore, is not a moral doctrine, but an account of the meaning of the word 'punishment' (1953: 137).

It is because I agree with the general tendency of Quinton's argument, and with most of the utilitarian conclusions that he supports with this premiss about the *logical* character of the retributivist thesis, that I wish, by amending the premiss in one particular, to plug one hole in his argument. For as it stands the claim that one logically cannot punish the innocent seems to me wholly unconvincing. Logical theses of this sort rest on linguistic intuitions (*MT* 9), and my linguistic intuitions do not at all tally with Quinton's.

Quinton does consider the objection that 'the innocent can be punished and scapegoats are not logical impossibilities' (1953: 138). And Professor Flew, who maintains a similar thesis, also tries to answer this objection, though in a different way. Flew appeals to the vagueness of the term 'punish', and calls such cases as I shall mention later 'metaphorical, secondary or non-standard' (1954: 138; cf. Hart 1968: 5). The question is, however, whether the word 'punish' is *ever* used in the restricted way that he and Quinton maintained. Quinton, on the other hand, puts his main reliance on a comparison between 'punish' and 'that now familiar class of verbs whose first-person-present use is significantly different from the rest' (1953: 138). But he does not succeed in showing that the verb 'punish' belongs to this class; it is certainly not a performative verb, as are the examples he quotes (one cannot punish someone by *saying* 'I hereby punish you', as one can make a promise to someone by saying 'I hereby promise you that . . .'). However, since this argument of his has been dealt with satisfactorily by Professor Baier (1955: 30), I shall not amplify this criticism now.

Consider the statement 'I am punishing you for something

that you have not done.' I can see nothing *logically* wrong with saying this, and the use does not seem to me in any way peripheral. We can well imagine a member of the Tsarist secret police saying it to an unfortunate prisoner; for it is said to have been a maxim of theirs that it is better to shoot the wrong man than not to shoot anybody. Indeed, it is not even a sign of wickedness to say this: as Baier points out (ibid.), a conscientious hangman, convinced that there has been a miscarriage of justice, might say it to his victim.

What may have misled Quinton and Flew is this. Punishment is always, in virtue of the meaning of the word, *for* something. In legal punishments, it is aways *for* the offence for which it is appointed by law. It is easy, but wrong, to infer from this that the person who is punished for something must, logically, have done it. But we can know that a person has been punished for an offence without knowing whether he actually committed it or not. The argument went on in Britain for many years about whether Timothy Evans had actually committed a murder for which he had undoubtedly been punished by hanging. When in the end it was accepted that he had not, we did not stop saying that he had been punished; nor did we start using 'punish' in a different sense from that in which both parties had been using it all along—those who thought he had done the murder and those who did not.

It may help if we compare the use of the word 'pay'. A payment is always *for* something. If I hand somebody (say a beggar) some of my money to keep for himself, for nothing, it is not a payment but a gift. The *Oxford English Dictionary* defines 'payment' as '. . . the giving of money, etc., in return for something or in discharge of a debt'. But this does not mean that it is logically impossible to pay money that is not due, or even money that you know is not due. If I am presented often enough with a bill for goods which I never had, and am threatened with proceedings, I may, if the sum involved is not large, pay the bill (and not in scare quotes either). The words in the definition 'in return for something' do not necessarily imply that the something has to exist. Similarly, when the *OED* says that a punishment is 'the infliction of a penalty in retribution *for* an offence', this does not imply that the offence must actually have been committed by the man who is punished, nor even at all, nor even that the people who do the punishing think so. Quinton has made an illegitimate step from 'Punishment must be for an offence' to 'Punishment must be of a person who committed the offence.' Admittedly, when I say, 'He was punished for the murder', I imply that there was a murder; but that is in virtue of the use of the definite description 'the murder', and has nothing to do with the word 'punished'. I could have said, without changing the meaning of 'punished', 'He was punished for the alleged murder'; and then I should not have implied that there was a murder at all.

Part of the source of Quinton's confusion is to be traced to some typically hyperbolic and rhetorical remarks by Bradley, in a well known essay to which Quinton refers. Notice that Bradley, a fine specimen of a retributivist, does not cleave consistently to the view which Quinton fathers on the retributivists. Bradley's central view is, rather, that punishment of the innocent must be wrong and unjust. But he confuses this with a quite different view, that no harm inflicted on an innocent man can be *called* punishment. The two views indeed seem incompatible; for what logically cannot exist (punishment of the innocent, on Quinton's view) can hardly be unjust. I have, in the quotation from Bradley that follows, put in italics the words that express what I shall call the standard retributivist view that punishment of the innocent is wrong; and I have put the words that express the Quintonian version of retributivism (that there logically cannot be punishment of the innocent) in capitals.

If there is any opinion to which the man of uncultivated morals is attached, it is the belief in the necessary connexion of punishment and guilt. PUNISHMENT IS PUNISHMENT, ONLY WHERE IT IS DESERVED. We pay the penalty, because we owe it, and for no other reason; and *if punishment is inflicted for any other reason whatever than because it is merited by wrong, it is a gross immorality, a crying unjustice, an abominable crime* and NOT WHAT IT PRETENDS TO BE . . . Having once the right to punish, we may modify the punishment according to the useful and the pleasant; but these are external to the matter, they cannot give us a right to punish, and *nothing can do that but criminal desert . . . I am not to be punished, on the ordinary view, unless I deserve it* (1876: 26 f.).

Note that Bradley does not say here, 'I am not punished unless I deserve it' (which would support Quinton's interpretation), but 'I am not *to be* punished.' My own guess as to Bradley's meaning is that the passages in capitals, which seem to support Quinton's view, are confused pieces of rhetoric, and that the other passages represent Bradley's real position.

Quinton's own text is not immune from this confusion. He can say things like, 'Essentially, then, retributivism is the view that only the guilty *are to be* punished', but slides from this, via 'guilt is the necessary condition of punishment' (which is equivocal), to the view, which is his central one, that 'we cannot punish the innocent' (1953: 137).

However, leaving Bradley, something a bit like Quinton's thesis might be truly maintained, not about the word 'punishment', but about the word 'penalty'. The difference in meaning between these two words was first pointed out to me by Baier, and is of great importance. A penalty is, according to the *OED*, 'a loss, disability, or disadvantage of some kind . . . *ordained by law* to be inflicted for an offence'. Punishment, on the other hand, is defined as '[t]he *action* of punishing or the fact of being punished, the *infliction* of a penalty in retribution for an offence' (emphasis added). Thus we might say that penalties are hypothetical, punishments actual. There is a penalty for a certain offence if it is the law that *if* the offence be committed a certain sort of punishment shall be inflicted. Thus there can be penalties even if there are no punishments. Somebody might say without self-contradiction, of a country with Draconian laws, 'In that country they never have any punishments, because all the penalties are so atrocious that nobody commits any crimes.' Note also the oddness of the question put to a schoolboy after an interview with the headmaster at an old-fashioned school, 'Did your penalty hurt very much?'

Now it is true of penalties that they cannot be ordained for *not* committing offences against the law to which they are attached. That is indeed a logical impossibility, and the promulgation of the penalty would be self-contradictory; and this would be a good way of rephrasing the point which Quinton ought to have been making. One could not consistently put up in the park a notice saying, 'Do not pick the flowers:

penalty for not picking the flowers £10'. This logical impossibility is of some importance in the controversy between the retributivists and the utilitarians; for it lends some support to the often-canvassed compromise between the two views which allows the retributivists to have their way with regard to individual acts of punishing (they ought, that is to say, to be inflicted only where the law has been broken) but allows the utilitarians to have *their* way with regard to the so-called 'legislator's question' of what penalties we ought to have, and for what. Thus it is possible to combine a utilitarian theory about penalties with a retributive theory about punishments. This would suit Quinton's book, and I shall shortly be elaborating a form of this compromise, in terms of my own two-level theory of moral thinking (see *MT*). Reflection on the problem of punishment was one of the things which led me to develop the theory.

Another way of putting essentially the same point as I have just been making about punishments and penalties is in terms of what I have called functional words (*LM* 100 f.). These are words such that, if we know their meaning, we know at least something about the function of an object or person of the kind in question. Thus to know what an auger is, or what the word 'auger' means, is to know that augers are carpenters' tools for boring holes in wood, and thus to know that, if an auger will not bore holes in wood, it cannot be a good one. Similarly to know what a carpenter is, is to know that carpenters have as their function the making of things out of wood shaped and fastened together; so if a carpenter (otherwise than temporarily) cannot do this, he cannot be a good carpenter.

'Punishment' is at least rather like a functional word: punishment, in order to fulfil its function, has to be in retribution for an offence, and, if there has been no offence by the person punished, the punishment cannot be a just one. (I leave out of consideration vicarious punishments, which in any case are usually considered unjust.) The major change is that from 'good' to 'just'; and this is important. But it gives us what may be a correct way of putting the point incorrectly formulated by Quinton. Quinton's way of putting it is like saying of the word 'auger' that in virtue of its meaning augers

logically cannot be used for digging up potatoes. But if I use
an auger for digging up potatoes, it is still an auger, though I
am not using it *as* an auger (not using it in the function for
which augers are designed). There is nothing *logically* improper
in saying; 'I am going to use (or am using) this auger for
digging up the potatoes.' But it is true in virtue of the meaning
of 'auger' that this would be an improper use of an auger. It
would be technically improper, not logically improper, though
it is a logical truth that it *would* be technically improper.

Similarly with 'payment'. If I pay money which is not due,
I am not doing the logically impossible; but it is logically
impossible to be properly required to pay money which is not
due. In the same way, if I use a tool-for-boring-holes not for
boring holes, I am not using it for what it is for; and if I inflict
on someone suffering which should only be inflicted on him if
he has committed an offence, I am inflicting on him suffering which I should not inflict. The 'should' here is moral
or legal, depending on the context; but the consequence
is a logical one, arising out of the meaning of the word
'punish'.

Another parallel is this: If I am awarding the prize for the
biggest pumpkin, it is perfectly possible for me to award it to
someone who has not entered the biggest pumpkin; but it is
not logically possible for me *properly* so to award it.

We might be tempted at this point to find here an easy way
of deriving an 'ought' from an 'is', but it will not work. The
argument would go, 'A prize is by definition *for* a certain
achievement; but this person has not achieved the achievement;
therefore it ought not to be awarded to him.' And similarly,
substituting 'punishment' for 'prize' and 'offence' for 'achievement'. Here the first premiss is supposed to be about
language; the second is an ordinary statement of fact; and the
third is a moral or other evaluative judgement.

But this is too easy. The situation is rather like that out of
which Professor Searle got so much mileage in his notorious
paper 'How to Derive "Ought" from "Is" ', about promises
(1964), to which I replied in my almost equally notorious
paper 'The Promising Game' (H 1964). The point there was
that, if we are going to have the word 'promise' in our
language (i.e. have the institution of promising), we have to

have a prior commitment to a certain moral principle according to which there is a moral obligation to keep promises. And from the fact that having such a moral principle is a necessary condition for the adoption of the use of a certain word, it does not follow that the moral principle itself has the necessity that it would have if it were true by definition. It is not necessary, logically or otherwise, for us to adopt the use of the word 'promise' or the word 'punishment'. If we do adopt them, we shall be showing our adherence to the principle that there is an obligation to keep promises, or to punish only the guilty. But we could decide (at a cost) to do without those words.

It is a very common mistake in philosophy, committed among others by Wittgenstein in what he said about pain, or at least by some of his disciples in expounding him, to think that, if a certain word cannot be introduced unless a certain assumption is made, then the assumption logically has to be made. This is simply not so. We can perhaps do without the word. We have to assume a certain view about other people's experiences if we are to teach children the use of the word 'pain'; but it may be that we only *think* that we have been successful in teaching it: they do not have pains, but have only learnt to mouth the word on the occasions on which we think they have pains. But it would be too much of a digression to pursue this point (see H 1964).

The upshot is that we have established certain logical features of the word 'punish'; but, as we have seen, these do not suffice (and this is indeed the useful part of Quinton's thesis) to prove any *moral* conclusions about when it is right to punish. We need a totally different approach in order to show this. That is to say, if we are to have the word 'punish' in our language in the sense that it currently has, we have to agree that only offenders can justly be punished; but why should we have it in language in that sense? More generally: there are certain logical relations between the language and the institution, and between both and the obligation to obey the principle constitutive of the institution. But why have we a duty to adopt any of these? To have the institution of punishing entails having principles of a certain form. But why should we have that institution or that kind of principles? And, even given that they have to be of that form, why should they have one *content* rather than another? That is to say, even given that we have, by adopting the word, taken on the formal obligation to punish only for offences, how do we decide what, if anything, is to be an offence, and what is to be the punishment for it?

Nobody should be surprised if I now say that these questions can be answered satisfactorily by a theory like mine, which divides moral thinking into two levels (*MT*). The theory is able to achieve this because it is at one and the same time Kantian and utilitarian. The problem of retributive justice is generally thought to be a crucial area of disagreement between Kantians and utilitarians; but, as I have already hinted, a carefully formulated Kantian theory and a carefully formulated utilitarianism do not need to disagree.

To show this, let us first look at the scene as it is. We find ordinary people, including ordinary judges, legislators, policemen, etc., firmly wedded (at least we hope so) to a set of principles of retributive justice. By 'firmly wedded' I mean not merely that they have moral opinions in the sense of being ready to express them when asked. I mean that they have what are called 'consciences': if they feel tempted to break these principles, they at once experience a strong feeling of repugnance; if others break them, they experience feelings of what Sir Stuart Hampshire calls 'outrage or shock' (1978). We can if we wish dignify these experiences by the name of 'moral intuitions'. They are what Courts of Human Rights are apt to appeal to, with good results provided (and it is a big proviso) that their members have been brought up, or have schooled themselves, in the light of sound critical moral thinking.

In such a situation, everything will proceed just as intuitionists say it does, at the intuitive level. However, what are we to say to the citizens of a country where they believe in arbitrary sentencing and atrocious penalties? What are we to say even among ourselves when some particular principle in the administration of the law, or some particular piece of legislation, is questioned? For this, we shall need to do some critical thinking. I have tried to show elsewhere (*MT*) that the critical thinking has to be utilitarian in method; but my way of showing this owes almost everything to Kant. I argued on a basis similar to what Kant called 'the groundwork of the metaphysic of morals', but which I like to call the logic of the moral concepts.

Suppose that we start asking moral questions about punishment. We are not, as I have admitted, logically bound to do this, though there are strong non-logical reasons for doing it. But *if* we ask these moral questions, the rules of critical thinking imposed by the logic of the words we are using in our questions will compel us to try to assess the acceptance-utility of various moral principles about punishment that we might adopt. These will include, first of all principles about the practice of courts in arriving at their verdicts and their sentences; then, proceeding in one direction, principles about the conduct of the police in trying to bring offenders before the courts; and in the other, principles to be followed by the legislature when deciding what criminal laws to make and what penalties to attach to them.

Are the attitudes which judges, legislators, and ordinary people generally have in Western countries with regard to the administration of justice able to stand up to such a scrutiny? On the whole they are; but no doubt there is room for improvement; in some respects there might be better arrangements. But it is no use our thinking about this if we have no method for determining what *would* be better. I am suggesting that proposed new principles of conduct in these matters should be judged in the light of the utility of bringing them into use. This involves seeing how the bringing into use of various principles would affect the satisfaction of the preferences of all those affected. In other words the best principles will be the ones whose general adoption will have the best consequences all told for all those affected, considered impartially.

As I hope I made clear in *MT* 4, such a suggestion is at once Kantian and utilitarian. Kant himself did not distinguish clearly enough between the two levels, and this is one of the sources of the widespread misunderstanding of his intentions. But in the suggestion just made, Kantian elements appear at both levels. At the critical level, when selecting the principles which we are to use at the intuitive level, we are treating everybody equally as an end (that is, willing as our own ends what they (rationally) will as their ends, and giving equal weight impartially to everybody's ends). Thus we are, as legislating members of the kingdom of ends, selecting those maxims for general use which we can will to be universal law, no matter who is at the receiving end. In so doing, we are trying to maximize the realization of the ends of those affected, i.e. what recent utilitarians have called the satisfaction of their (rational) preferences.

The maxims themselves cannot be of unlimited specificity, for good practical reasons—above all the reason that they have to be built into our characters, and for this purpose a certain degree of generality is requisite. But the thought that goes to their selection could, if we had the time and the knowledge, be as specific as was needed to establish their acceptance-utility. Kant wanted his maxims to be highly general and simple (perhaps, because of his rigorist upbringing, more simple than his method will really justify). But we can agree that they have to be *fairly* general, just because to be useful they have to apply to many situations which resemble one another in important respects, and have to be a suitable guide for moral education, which cannot cope with principles of infinite specificity.

It would be out of place here to examine the text of Kant in any more detail. My point is merely that, by applying Kantian universalizing impartiality at the critical level, we are able to select, for use at the intuitive level in our ordinary moral thinking, general, fairly simple principles or maxims such as Kant desired. And, without labouring the point, the resemblance of this scheme to the kind of act-cum-rule-utilitarianism advocated in my *MT* will be obvious.

Such a utilitarian proposal is not open to the vulgar objections that are commonly brought against it by intuitionists, and in particular not to those which relate to punishment and retributive justice. These consist in alleging that a utilitarian judge would have, in consistency with his theory, to sentence entirely on the strength of the consequences in the particular case, rather narrowly delimited. For example, if it would have the best consequences in a particular case to send an innocent man to prison, this is what, it is alleged, the utilitarian judge would do (see *MT* 48). And, the objection goes on, this runs counter to our deepest moral convictions (which is what these objectors call their intuitions when they are pulling the rhetorical stops out, as was Bradley in the passage I quoted earlier). The objection is usually based on highly artificial examples, for the good reason that no real ones are forthcoming which support the objectors' case.

But now we can see that the objection misses the point. A thoroughgoing and well informed act-utilitarian (the arch-angel as I have called him, *MT* 44) would know that more harm than good would come in the long run from breakdown of public confidence in the fairness of our judicial procedures, or of the police, than could ever be compensated for by the good achieved by sentencing an innocent man. The same applies in general to any kind of (as we should call it, having been brought up the way we have) judicial malpractice. In the real world, as opposed to the examples provided by philo-sophers with axes to grind, it is rather obvious that the principles of retributive justice in which we all believe have a very high acceptance-utility.

I am far less confident in the general principles about legislation that are currently accepted—if indeed we can say that any are. Act-utilitarianism of the two-level kind that I am advocating can give good guidance to legislators too, and they need it. What they should consider, when contemplating setting up a new offence, or altering the penalties for an existing one (rape for example), is again the acceptance-utility of the principle on which they act, and indeed, since the law itself is a kind of principle, of the actual law which is being proposed. In considering, for example, the abolition or the restoration of capital or corporal punishment, what we should be considering are the consequences for the preference-satisfactions of all, treated impartially, of various possible laws about these matters, and of various possible public attitudes.

I hope it will not be said that I have *abandoned* justice in favour of utility. The foundation of moral thinking (in essentials a Kantian foundation) is the impartiality required by the demand that we will universally in making our moral judgements. This impartiality requires us to treat the equal (rational) preferences (or as Kant put it, wills) of all affected parties as of equal weight i.e. to be fair to them all. This is the formal principle of justice on which everything else depends. In judging proposed pieces of legislation by their acceptance-utility, we are following this requirement of equal concern, or formal justice in one of the senses of that expression. Those who live in a society have varying and often conflicting interests, which are a function of what they rationally will. Between these we have to be fair. We shall be fair if we do not give anybody's interest extra weight for any other reason than that it is greater.

This approach leads us to treat retributive justice as, basically, a form of distributive justice (*MT* 161 f.). We are distributing fairly between the members of society the benefits and harms which come from living in that society subject to those laws. This is to be fair and just to all, viewing their interests with equal concern. If this impartial view leads us to assign certain rights to certain classes of people, as having the highest acceptance-utility, those are the rights they should have, for that is the most just allocation of benefits and harms.

It is fairly obvious that, in society as we know it, the right to a fair trial will be one of these. So will the right to equality before the law, and to a democratic voice in legislation. There is no room here to justify the according of these rights, or to spell out in detail what will be their precise content; but I have shown how we should decide this. We should do it by counting everybody for one and nobody for more than one (Bentham, cited in Mill 1861 *s.f.*) and treating humanity, whether our own or other people's, always as an end and never merely as a means (Kant 1785: ch. 2, *s.f.*), and so seeking to do the best impartially for all—whether we are choosing principles for courts or police to follow, or attitudes for them and the public to adopt, or laws for the legislators to enact.

The purpose of a system of retributive justice is to further impartially the interests of those affected. What *will* most further them (deterrence, or all the other many consequences of a system of punishments, or attempts to rehabilitate criminals and fit them back into society, or no penalties at all) is a factual question, depending on what people will or would rationally prefer, and on what would conduce to this. It can be clearly addressed only by those who have understood the point of punishment, which is, like the point of all moral action, the impartial furthering of interests.

16
Contrasting Methods of Environmental Planning

IN planning the conduct of his affairs in relation to nature, man is faced with many problems which are so complex and so intermeshed that it is hard to say at first even what kind of problems they are. We are all familiar with the distinction between factual and evaluative questions, and I do not doubt that there is this distinction; but the actual problems with which we are faced are always an amalgam of these two kinds of questions. The various methods used by environmental planners are all attempts to separate out this amalgam, as we have to do if we are ever to understand the problems—let alone solve them. I wish in this essay to give examples of, and appraise, two such methods. I shall draw from this appraisal not only theoretical lessons which may interest the moral philosopher but also practical lessons which, I am sure, those who try to plan our environment ought to absorb. Though my examples come mostly from urban planning because that is the kind of planning with whose problems (although only an amateur) I am most familiar, what I have to say will apply also to problems about the countryside and the environment in general.

Suppose that I am a single person living by myself in a flat and have decided to remodel my kitchen. I can please myself—questions about other people's interests are unlikely to arise, and in any case let us ignore them. Even in this simple situation it is possible to illustrate some of the pitfalls that practical thinking can fall into. What I have to do, according to the first method that I am going to consider, is to decide upon certain ends or goals, and then look for means to them. I shall call this way of doing things the *means–end* model. Its disadvantages are obvious. What are the ends that I am

From *Nature and Conduct*, ed. R. S. Peters (Royal Inst. of Ph. Lectures, 1974, Macmillan, 1975).

setting myself in remodelling the kitchen? It is not difficult to make a list of them: convenience, economy, beauty, hygiene, and so on. But this is going to be of not much use for my purposes, for several reasons. The first is that even if we confine ourselves to one of these ends it may be difficult to say *how much* of the quality in question is required or even to find a way of measuring how much of it has been provided. This is obviously true of beauty; but even if we take economy, which looks more promising, because we can at least measure how much gas, and at what price, it takes to boil a pint of water, we are still in difficulties because we do not know how small a gas consumption would satisfy us. Similarly with convenience; it is possible to do ergonomic studies—and very useful ones have been done—to determine how many steps or arm-movements are required on a certain layout in order to wash a given collection of dishes. But how many is too many?

However, it is when we come to comparisons and trade-offs between the various desiderata that we are in real trouble. We should need to know how much convenience we are prepared to sacrifice for how much economy, or how much beauty for how much hygiene. For example, if the old copper pans which we keep on the shelf just for show collect the dust and harbour flies, are we going to put up with this because they look so good? Economists discuss this sort of problem and help with it up to a point; but the philosophical problems about method remain, and I can illustrate them without doing more than the simplest economics, if any.

One of the things that tend to happen if we use the means–end model is that the goals whose attainment is in some degree measurable, and which can therefore easily be put into cost–benefit calculations, tend to get taken care of, whereas the ones that are not measurable, like beauty, tend to get left out. It may help us to understand the problem if we contrast the means–end model with another model which I am going to call the *trial-design* model. It is the one in fact used by nearly all architects in dealing with their clients because it is so much more helpful than the means–end model. In this way of doing things, the designer just produces more or less detailed particular designs for the client to look at, all of which he certifies as at least feasible, and attaches perhaps a rough costing to them; and the client then chooses the one that he prefers. The process of choice is then in its logical aspects very similar to that which I go through when I go to a shop and choose a pair of shoes, except that I cannot actually try on the shoes, but have to choose them from drawings.

This difference is, however, of very great practical consequence. For clients are often not very good at understanding from the drawings what the finished product is going to be like to live with (in our example, what it is going to be like cooking in this kitchen); and some designers are not very good at explaining it to them. However, the system can work and is not in principle different from choosing goods from a mail-order catalogue when you are not allowed to have them on approval.

It is important not to exaggerate the difference between the two models. No doubt even in the trial-design model the designer will have had some idea, obtained by preliminary questioning, of what the client's goals and preferences are; so the alternative designs he produces for the client to choose from are not churned out at random. Knowing the client's preferences, he gives him a short list of designs, or in the first instance just one, which he thinks the client will like. A certain amount of means–end reasoning has gone into this process. And even in a means–end system there may be trial-designs produced in the later stages. It may be that in a complete and adequate procedure both models would play a part. But it is still important to distinguish between them, and above all not to think that the means–end model by itself is enough.

I want now to illustrate the important difference between these two models or methods by contrasting two studies in which they are employed, each in a fairly pure form. These are, first, the book *Urban Transportation Planning*, by Roger Creighton (1970), an American transportation engineer, which advocates a certain method in transport planning and illustrates its use in two important studies which his team did for Chicago and Buffalo; and secondly, Sir Colin Buchanan's Edinburgh study published in two books *Alternatives for Edinburgh* (1971) and *Edinburgh: The Recommended Plan* (1972).

The first of these studies uses the means–end model. Before I go into detail, I must repeat that one of the chief things that all planning procedures have to do, if the thinking is going to be clear and unconfused, is to distinguish questions of fact from questions of value. I am not going here to try to justify this remark; anybody who spends much time reading about planning problems cannot help noticing the terrible confusions which result when people think, either that they can answer factual questions by making value-judgements (which we call 'wishful thinking') or that they can answer evaluative questions by elaborate observation of the facts. It is neither the case that you will make a certain proposed road network lead to a certain reduction in traffic in some environmentally sensitive area just by thinking how nice it would be if it did have this result; nor that you can by traffic statistics prove that it is the *best* solution to the problem. You can prove, perhaps, within certain limits of error, that *this* is what the traffic will do when you have built the network; but the public still has to decide what kind of city it prefers to have.

The two methods that I am discussing are essentially two rival ways of separating factual from evaluative judgements. The means–end model used in Creighton's book strikes many people at first as an obvious way of achieving this separation. We incorporate all our value-judgements at the beginning of the planning process into statements of what are called 'goals'. Having thus, as it were, put all our values into the machine once for all, we cause the machine to turn out various plans and to evaluate them with reference to these goals, and the best plan will automatically be chosen. This process is represented schematically in Creighton 1970: 136:

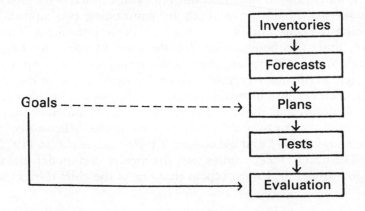

We first make our factual enquiry into the inventories, that is to say, into the actual statistics of the present situation: existing road networks, traffic counts on them, the same for rail and other public transport networks, distribution of population and of places of work, and so on. We also check one of these groups of statistics against the other; there are certain reasonably reliable models which allow one to predict the distribution of travel over a network given the distribution, as to places of residence and of work, of the people who are going to use it. So we can test these models for their predictive accuracy by seeing whether, by using them, the existing population- and work-distribution can be made to generate the observed existing traffic flows. All this is common to both the methods I am considering, so I shall not have to repeat it.

So is the step called 'forecasts'. This consists in making predictions, on sociological, economic, and other grounds, of the *future* distribution of population and places of work, and thus of the 'desire for travel', in the future, along various lines within the area to be covered by the plan. A date is normally set for which the plan is being made; twenty years is thought to be about the limit of human prescience by existing methods.

The two methods now start to diverge. The Creighton method, having made its inventories and forecasts, requires the determining at this point, once and for all, of a number of 'goals'. The approach of the author is well illustrated by this excerpt:

Scientific Method: Objectivity. In great part due to the influence of Carroll, the transportation studies adopted the scientific method as the standard for their work. The features of observation, advancement of hypotheses, and replicability of calculations were considered to be the proper guidelines for all the analysis and development of theory which were done by transportation studies. Although the preparation of plans necessarily included the subjective element of human goals, even this part of the planning operation was treated with extreme objectivity once the list of goals was adopted. And even in selecting goals, attempts were made to deduce goals from an observation of what people actually choose to do. In short, judgement was out and the rules of evidence and demonstration were in as the standards by which decisions were made (1970: 146).

In order to fit into this method, the goals have also to be stated in very simple terms, and such that the extent to which they are realized is not only quantifiable but quantifiable in a way that enables us to compare the realization of one goal with that of another on a common scale (which in practice has to be that of money). For example, if one goal is saving of time and another saving of lives, we have to find a way of measuring both these benefits in money terms. The same applies to even more difficult items like the enhancement of the quality of life in cities or the preservation or improvement of their visual quality.

When we come to look at the actual goals listed in Creighton's book, we see how difficult the task is going to be. Eleven are listed (overlapping with one another to some extent): safety; saving time in travel; reducing operating costs; increasing efficiency; mobility; beauty; comfort and absence of strain, noise, or nuisance; reducing air pollution; minimizing disruption; increasing productivity of the economy; and ability to move about without an automobile (1970: 199 ff.). In the Chicago study in which the author was involved, says Creighton,

One of the tasks the staff set for itself was to build a formal bridge between goals and plan. *We wanted to be able to prove that the plan we recommended for the Chicago area would be the best.* If the Policy Committee to whom we reported approved our statement of goals and objectives, and our reasoning processes were correct, then they would almost automatically approve the plan, because the one had to follow from the other. The ultimate extension of this idea, of course, would be one in which a computer would be given a statement of goals for a given metropolitan area, together with the facts describing that metropolitan area, and then it would be programmed to produce the best plan for the area automatically. We later achieved this, though only at very small scale (emphasis added) (1970: 201).

The restrictions which I mentioned earlier on the kinds of goal that the machine can cope with lead in practice to the simple omission of goals the extent of whose realization is not measurable in terms of money. Thus in the two studies taken as examples by Creighton, concerned with Chicago and the environs of Buffalo, only the first four goals which occur in the list I quoted were used in evaluating the alternative plans: safety, reduction of travel time, operating costs, and capital costs. The last three of these are easily expressible in money terms; safety is so expressible if we apply to the accident statistics (actual and predicted) the values set upon loss of life, injury, and damage to property by the courts, though the basis of such valuations is quite unclear.

The other goals simply get omitted. Economists have tried to find theoretical ways around this difficulty (Munby 1970), but in practice a means–end model which insists on prior statement of goals and a mechanical operation of the evaluation process thereafter is almost bound to have this result; and the outcome of such thinking is to be seen in typical American cities. It was also to be seen in the majority report on the third London airport (Roskill 1971), in which the cost–benefit analyses were expressed in money terms, and everything that was going to be considered had to have a money value set on it—the commission was in difficulties as to whether the value of an irreplaceable Norman church was to be taken as the sum it was insured for.

Is there an alternative? I think there is, and that planners are beginning to use it, although I doubt whether they really yet understand how different the new method is from the old. Perhaps I am exaggerating; perhaps traces of the new kind of thinking are to be found in Creighton's book (1970: 318, 343). In one place we have a trial-design method used: 'The "modal model" described in the preceding chapter was used in 1966 to test eleven different combinations of transit and highway systems for the Niagara Frontier. These tests were released to the public in December that year, but without recommendation.' And on another page a diagram ends:

Publish both Risks and Gains

↓

Hold Public Referendum

And perhaps traces of the means–end model are to be found in the Buchanan study which I am going to consider in a moment. But I have somewhat schematized the methods in order to make the contrast clearer.

Buchanan's team was called in to report on Edinburgh after a plan proposed by the corporation had aroused a lot of opposition because of the very obtrusive character of the new roads proposed in it and the destruction of the environment, especially its visual qualities, that would be entailed. What the team did, after doing the factual analyses and forecasts which, as I said, are common to both the methods, was to prepare in skeleton form a number of different plans (including an adaptation of the one which had caused the fuss), involving different degrees of reliance on public transport, different scales of road expenditure, and different amounts of restriction of access for private cars to the centre. I will not say that goals were not considered at all before the plans were made (as I said, I do not want to exaggerate the break between the two methods or to represent the transition between them as having occurred suddenly). Obviously, in selecting just *these* plans for elaboration and evaluation the team had some idea in mind of what they and the public were after (just as, even in Sir Karl Popper's theory of scientific method (1934; 1963), the scientist, though he may adopt a hypothesis for testing on a mere hunch, normally has more to go on than that). But Buchanan's study is, so far as I can see, altogether free of the doctrine that goals or ends have to be stated once and for all at the beginning, the rest of the evaluation being done mechanically by application of these goals to the facts.

Instead, what the study does is to predict the factual consequences of building each of the schemes in turn, describe these in some detail and in as clear and quantified a way as the nature of the facts allows, and then ask the public (that is, the inhabitants of Edinburgh and their elected representatives) to discuss the various alternatives in the light of these facts, and, ultimately, say which they prefer. The crucial evaluation comes at the end of the process, not at the beginning. After it had received the comments of the public, the team then produced a recommended plan in the light of them which was also to be the subject of public evaluation.

This method at one blow avoids all the disadvantages of the previous one. Goals do not have to be tied up in advance.

Nothing is in principle presupposed about goals until the time comes to opt for one or another of the plans. The public can just look at the plans and say which it prefers. The point of all the analysis of consequences of the plans is not to *prove* an evaluative conclusion, namely, that one of them is the best, as Creighton's method tries to do; it is, rather, to make the ultimate choice as well-informed as possible, in that the public will have a clear idea of what it is choosing between. Therefore, it is not necessary to express all the goals in terms which allow of a financial comparison; they do not have to be commensurable at all, any more than the fit of shoes has to be commensurable with their cost. Thus, Buchanan's team estimated the environmental effects of the various proposals quite independently of the economic cost–benefit analysis. These environmental effects were predicted by working out what volumes of traffic would be present in the various streets. Then these volumes were compared with what is called the 'environmental capacity' of the streets—that is, the amount of traffic that there can be in the streets without disrupting the environment to more than a certain degree. This degree is measured in terms of the amount of noise, the amount of visual intrusion of vehicles and road structures, and so on. Where precisely the 'environmental capacity' is fixed is of course an evaluative matter. However, the method employed does (for me at any rate) considerably clarify the evaluative process so that, when I come to choose between the plans, I feel that I know much more clearly what I am choosing between. In principle the choice is left to me; nobody is trying to prove anything to me, except that those would be the consequences of the adoption of a certain plan.

The two methods lead to two very different sorts of plans. Buchanan, unlike Creighton, is led, after the public discussion, to propose a plan which requires quite a high degree of restriction of private cars for commuting, with closure of streets in the centre, restriction of some existing and new streets to buses, fairly low road expenditure, and large reliance on public transport. He does not, indeed, go as far as some people would like, and the debate in Edinburgh continues. It is also alleged that the terms of reference which he was given compelled him to concentrate too much on the scheme's effects in the central area of the city and not enough on those in the suburbs. But at least he has displayed a method which enables the debate to be conducted rationally. Those of us who on the whole share his preferences have a right to insist that those who do not, work out the factual consequences of *their* preferred schemes as conscientiously and try to convince the public that these consequences would prove in practice more acceptable.

The difference between the outcomes of the two methods is not entirely due to the difference between the methods themselves; but it partly is. Another factor is a greater readiness of the British public than of the American to contemplate restrictions on private cars (due perhaps to our lower degree of motorization). The second of the two methods, if followed in America, might lead to a choice by the public of solutions involving higher road expenditure and less restriction on private cars than is likely to be acceptable in Edinburgh. And, of course, Edinburgh is an outstandingly beautiful city. Nor do I want to suggest that all Americans adhere to the means–end model in their thinking—even all professional planners.

The means–end model is naturally congenial to the engineer; the trial-design model to the architect. Buchanan is both. Engineers usually get, when they are designing a bridge, a fairly cut-and-dried statement of goals (e.g. that it should have a certain traffic capacity, take a certain maximum load, and cost as little as possible); and they can exercise their science and prove that the design which they recommend is superior in these respects to others. The architect, on the other hand, normally produces sketches and then more worked-out plans of alternative layouts, and the client has to say which he wants. Though I am convinced that the engineer is an indispensable member of the planning team, I am equally convinced that the 'architectural' overall method is the better one.

I have been speaking mainly about urban problems; but what I have said is obviously applicable to all decisions about environmental planning, including those that affect nature in the narrow sense. But these latter problems are likely to bring out, even more than those of city planning, a distinction which

I have not yet mentioned. This is the distinction between the work of the architect or the engineer on the one hand and that of the planner on the other. The architect and the engineer are likely to have just one client who is going to choose the final design and pay for its execution. I have been speaking as if this were so in city planning; but it is not. The planner has to satisfy great numbers of 'clients' whose interests are often in conflict.

The difference is not merely a difference in complexity. I started by considering a problem about planning a kitchen. Architectural problems like this could become extremely complex without becoming a battlefield for conflicting interests. Suppose, for example, that some rich landowner is redesigning his entire mansion and perhaps a vast estate too; the problems may then be as complex as a great many planning problems. But provided that the landowner is concerned solely with his own interest, and not at all with the interests of the others affected (he is quite ready, say, to shift a whole village to improve his view, as Lord Harcourt did at Nuneham[1]), he will be able to proceed just as in the 'kitchen' case. He will, that is to say, if he follows the trial-design model, get Vanbrugh or Capability Brown to give him some alternative designs, and choose between them. He will not have to consult anybody else.

In planning decisions, however, almost by definition, other people are involved and will have, in any democratic system, to be consulted. There are first of all the many different people who are going to live or work in or visit frequently the piece of land whose use is being decided; then there are the neighbours who will live where they are affected by that use; then there are other members of the public who will see it; and those who, though they will not see it, will use, or be affected by the use of, whatever is produced there (gravel for example); and so on.

There are two questions—both of them moral questions—which at once arise when many people are concerned like this. The first is about procedure. What is the most just way of arranging for the decision to be made so that the interests of

---

[1] It has been suggested that Oliver Goldsmith's poem *The Deserted Village* is about this eviction.

all these people get their due consideration and they have some say in the decision proportionate to their interests? The second is about the substance of the decision arrived at. What makes a decision a just or a right one in such cases?

On the first question: it is obvious that whatever procedure we adopt will be some kind of *political* process. In this it is different from the 'kitchen' case or even the 'mansion' case; the addition of all these different people whose interests have to be considered has made politics inescapable, as it is not for our bachelor who is consulting with his architect. Even in the extreme case of a dictator who just says, 'Pull down the old quarter in front of St Peter's and build the Via della Conciliazione instead,' this is a political act, and it is only because the *polity* is like that (namely a dictatorship) that he can make the decision and get it executed without taking anybody else's views into consideration. If anybody objects that this is true of the landowner too, I shall not argue the point. At any rate, in normal polities, even some quite undemocratic ones, there has to be some process whereby the interests of different people are taken into account, and the question is (a moral question): Which of these arrangements is most just in the circumstances of a particular society?

The second question would arise even if the first did not. Suppose, again, that there is a dictator; or suppose, less extremely, that a particular person (say the Minister for the Environment) has the sole decision about some particular issue (for example whether, or on what route, to build the extension of the motorway from Oxford to Birmingham). Suppose that *that* is the political procedure which has in fact been adopted. The first question has then been answered, but the second question still has to be answered by this dictator or minister, if he is a moral man and is trying to do the fair or the just thing.

I will only indicate my own view, without arguing for it, about how the second question is to be answered. As it happens, an answer to it is implicit in the theory about the nature and logical properties of the moral concepts which I have worked out in my books. To be prepared to say, 'That is the solution which ought to be adopted' is to be prepared to prescribe it for universal adoption in cases just like this. I have argued elsewhere (p. 46; H 1972*a* 1973*a*) that this way of putting the matter comes to the same thing as two other theories which have had a wide currency: the so-called ideal observer theory and the so-called rational contractor theory—but only in certain of their forms, and in the latter case *not* in the form preferred by its best-known advocate, Professor Rawls. Certain forms of utilitarianism lead to the same conclusions, as do certain interpretations of the Kantian doctrine and of the Christian injunction to do unto others as we want them to do to us. So the method which I am advocating ought to have the support of a fairly wide spectrum of philosophers.

What it comes to is this. If I am prescribing universally for all situations just like this one, I shall be prescribing for situations in which I myself occupy the roles of all the persons affected by the decision. If we like to dramatize the method, we can adopt C. I. Lewis's device of imagining that I am going to occupy, seriatim in random order, the positions of all these people in identical corresponding situations (1946: 547). If I do this, I am bound to accord equal weight to the equal interests of each individual affected (and of course the weight will vary according to the degree to which they are affected).

So then, the first thing that the person making the decision has to do is to find out, by factual enquiry, how various alternative decisions *will* affect the interests of the various parties. And this question is divisible into two elements. He has first to find out (as precisely as needs be) what will happen if one decision or the other is taken. This includes questions like: how many aircraft will use the proposed airport; how much noise they will make and over what areas; how many passengers will travel by them, and how far they will travel, and by what means, to reach the airport; how much land and how many buildings of what sorts will be taken over or destroyed; how much the whole thing will cost; how much the passengers will have to pay in transport costs; and so on. And secondly he has to find out how all these facts will affect people's interests; the people whose homes will be destroyed or disturbed; the people who travel by air; the people who send or receive freight by air; the people who pay taxes which are used to finance the construction; and so on. The facts here are facts about the desires and likes or dislikes of these people, how much they mind what is being done to them, or how much they appreciate what is done for them. It must be emphasized that facts about people's likes and dislikes are still facts, although to have a certain like or dislike is not to state any fact. From these facts, we can get conclusions about what the people's interests are.

One of the arguments for 'participation' and for democratic ways of deciding questions about planning is that they automatically give those concerned a certain voice so that they can make known how they think their interests are affected. But a procedure may be procedurally just, or be accepted as being so, but still not achieve a just solution to the substantial problem. This is because people (usually because they lack foresight) do not always use the procedure wisely in even their own interests. Shopkeepers have in the past often opposed the creation of pedestrian precincts or the building of bypasses to their towns, in the mistaken belief that this would result in loss of trade. Actually, when this is done, it seems usually to improve trade because people like shopping where they are not disturbed by traffic. So if you had tried to follow procedural justice by giving traders a big voice commensurate with the extent to which their interests are affected, they would have actually used this voice to bring about a decision (the maintenance of the status quo) which was against their interest. The same applies to members of the general public, who may object to certain features of planning schemes as against their interest simply because they are unable to foresee or visualize the actual effects of the schemes.

Another objection is that it is extraordinarily difficult by democratic procedures to ensure that people get a say in proportion to the degree to which their interests are affected. In theory, the people who are going to suffer most will howl the loudest, so if we had an instrument for measuring in decibels the loudness of howls *and* people were always the best judges of their own interests, and if posterity could howl, we could use this instrument as a just procedural means of ensuring justice in the result. But in fact it may be the people who are best organized, or who have most money, who succeed in making the most noise, and the resulting political pressures may be an extremely imperfect reflection of the degree to which people's interests are actually going to be affected. For these two reasons (ignorance and the imperfection of the participatory process), there is almost bound to have to be a certain amount of paternalism in these decisions if they are going to be just ones; one can do one's best to bring the facts before the public and to get those whose corns will be trodden on the hardest to make the most noise and the rest to pipe down a bit; but probably someone in the machine will have always to be looking after the interests of those who lack the knowledge, or the power, to stand up for their own real interests.

It is at this point that both the uses and the limitations of cost–benefit analysis are most clearly revealed (see Self 1975: 298). In the cases considered previously, in which one person only was concerned in the choice of a design (the 'kitchen' case, for example) there was no need for cost–benefit analysis at all; when the client was fully apprised of the factual consequences of adopting each of the different designs, he could just choose. There was no need to express the alternatives in terms of costs or benefits measured by some common scale (for example, money). We compared the choice with that of shoes at a shoe shop; in order to choose rationally between pairs of shoes at different prices one does not have to *price* the value to oneself of good fit, smart appearance, etc., although one may show *by one's choice* what monetary value one attaches to these qualities. The monetary value thus derived is a *deduction from* the choice made, not an *aid to making* the choice rationally.

But where many people are affected, as in most planning decisions, there is the problem of balancing their interests fairly against one another. So it looks as if it might help to work out the costs and benefits to all the parties on some common scale and thus make the adjudication fairly. One would then not be imposing a cost on one person unless a greater benefit was thereby secured to another; and thus one would be maximizing utility. Alternatively, if one were an adherent of some non-utilitarian system of distributive justice, one would seek to distribute costs and benefits in some other way considered just. Any of these processes, however, depends on knowing what value, on a common scale, each of the individuals affected attaches to the 'costs' and 'benefits' in question. And this, as before, can only be a deduction from the choices which are made (see Creighton 1970: 146), or which it is predicted would be made, by these individuals.[2] Cost–benefit analysis can therefore not be a substitute for making these choices. It can never altogether take the place of voting and other political procedures or of selective purchase and other economic procedures. We can observe how people do vote, what they do buy, whether they go by car or bus when travelling from A to B, and so on, and thus make inductive inferences about what choices they and people like them *would* make in relevantly similar circumstances. But they have to do the initial choosing.

The element of paternalism, therefore, which I said is inevitably involved in planning if the ill-informed are to be protected from making choices which they will regret, is of a very limited sort. It consists in predicting what choices the ill-informed would make if they were more fully informed. For example, it might be legitimate, if the planner could get away with it politically and if he were sure of his facts, for him to make the traffic-free shopping precinct referred to in my earlier example; if in the end the shopkeepers and the public liked it, he would have been proved right even if he went against their wishes at the time. But it is not open to the planner to dictate to them what they *shall* like or dislike or choose or reject; he can only make more or less hazardous predictions about what they *will* like or *would* choose, and an item can appear as a 'cost' or a 'benefit' in his calculations only on the basis of these predictions. And, if the public were much better informed than it is about the consequences of different planning policies, participation and democratic voting would be a better means of choosing politics than bureaucratic direction. If, therefore, the public wants not to be paternalized, it has to some extent to learn (or at least learn from) the planner's predictive skills. Even so, however, there are difficulties, familiar to political theorists, but beyond the scope of this essay, about whether distributively just solutions are likely to be arrived at by democratic processes however well oiled (see p. 247).

[2] On cost–benefit analysis see p. 246 and Sen 1970, Munby 1970, and Self 1975.

Behind these again lurk further difficulties, familiar to philosophers and economists, of how to determine the interests of the parties given information about their desires and likings and choices in actual and hypothetical situations, and of how to make desires and likings interpersonally commensurable. Without wishing to make light of these difficulties, I may perhaps say two things. The first is that these are not difficulties peculiar to utilitarians. They affect anybody whose moral thinking contains any element or principle of benevolence; for we cannot tell how much good on the whole we have done unless we are able to compare the good we have done to one person with that which we have done to another. Philosophers, therefore, who wish to avoid this difficulty will have to abjure all reasons for action which have to do with the walfare of others; so they must not, like the pluralist Sir David Ross, make benevolence or beneficence only one of their principles. The second is that such difficulties are solved in practice, all the time, in simple cases; we are able to judge which of our children wants a certain toy most. Cost–benefit analysis is an attempt, on the basis of data about people's actual choices and predictions about hypothetical ones, to do this sort of thing on a bigger scale—an exercise which we cannot avoid if we are to do the best we can, in sum, for competing claimants.

Let us, however, suppose that the two kinds of facts that I mentioned (about the consequences of planning decisions and about how these will affect people's interests) have been ascertained. We have then a number of trial designs, each of them accompanied by an array of these two kinds of facts. The decision has, however, still to be taken. It does not follow logically from these facts. If a dictator were interested only in the glory of his national airline or, more commendably, in the preservation of the countryside just as it is, and so made his decision regardless of all the other factors, we should not be able to fault his logic. However, if he, or if the people who are making the decision, ask what they can prescribe universally for situations just like this, they are bound, as I said, to give equal weight to the equal interests of all those affected and so will choose a solution that does the best for those interests taken as a whole. And this is what planners should do.

I wish to contrast this essentially utilitarian solution, which is that adopted by the best planners, with the sort of solution that is likely to get adopted if we follow some less adequate methods. They are nearly all less adequate for the same reason, which is that they have taken a highly selective view of the facts. But this can be for a number of different reasons. First we have those who, obsessed with the need to be scientific, take into account only those facts which can be measured. I have said enough about them already. On the other hand, we have those who take a selective view of the facts for entirely non-scientific (e.g. for political) reasons, and ignore, for example, economic factors. I know people whose views on planning all stem from a pathological hatred of the automobile (sometimes because it is anachronistically taken to represent middle-class values), and others who are led to the opposite extreme by an insane love of this useful but dangerous machine. It is the one-sided character of most of what most people say about planning and conservation that makes me despair of our getting many wise decisions.

What is the philosophical interest in all this? First of all, it is an excellent illustration of the necessity for understanding ethical theory if we are going to think rationally about our practical moral problems. I have mentioned, and I hope exemplified, the usefulness of carefully distinguishing factual from evaluative questions. The most harmful theorists of all are those who say (without producing any good arguments) that this cannot be done and that therefore we are condemned to argue endlessly in terms which bend as we use them, reducing the discussion of these issues to a contest between rhetoricians. If we can separate out the questions of fact from the others, we can at least obtain reliable answers to *them*. But when we have done this, we then have to resist the seductions of the second most dangerous set of theorists—those who say that since only facts are 'objective,' and values are merely 'subjective,' there can still be no rational process for deciding questions of value, which all questions of planning to some extent are.

I have tried to explain how, having separated out the two kinds of questions, it is possible to use our knowledge of the facts in order to present ourselves with an informed choice between possible solutions. If only one party is affected by the choice, then that is all there is to be said, and his choice, if fully informed, is as rational as it could be. But if many people are affected, as in planning decisions they are, we need also a rational means of adjudicating between their interests; and this, I have claimed, ethical theory can supply. The difficulty remains of finding a political procedure which will make this rational adjudication possible; but since this difficulty takes us into the heart of all the as yet unsolved problems of political philosophy, I will not now embark on a discussion of it. I have perhaps done enough to show that moral philosophers can both profit from, and contribute to, thought about concrete environmental problems.

17

Moral Reasoning about the Environment

THOUGH philosophers can make a modest but useful contribution to environmental problems, it is important to be clear what this contribution is. Philosophers are above all students of arguments (how to tell the good from the bad ones); and they have their own techniques for achieving this, all part of logic in a wide sense. They ought to be able to sort arguments out with more expertise than many of them manage. And non-philosophers who address this essentially philosophical task often, in their innocence, simply fail to notice on what thin logical ice they are skating; and no amount of enthusiasm or commitment will make up for the blunders they then commit. What we need is some account of the way in which one should reason about environmental issues, and the principles that such reasoning leads to. It might go on to suggest political and administrative procedures to make the public argument run clear. Both conservationists and their opponents ought to be trying to make their arguments hold water. Unless they can do this, how can they expect reasonable people, who do not want just to listen to a lot of rhetoric, to be convinced by them?

I shall not be able in this paper to complete such an account, but I will discuss just two or three very crucial questions with which it would have to deal. First, since environmental planning is a way of adjudicating conflicts between various interests, we need a careful delimitation of the interests that have to be considered: and then we need to ask by what method of moral thinking the adjudication should be done. Since it is moral reasoning that we are discussing, we need consider only those interests which can generate moral duties and rights. I shall call these 'morally relevant interests', and sometimes in what follows abbreviate this to 'interests'.

From *Journal of Applied Philosophy* 4 (1987).

As we shall see later, there may be some kinds of entities (trees and bicycles for example) which have interests of a sort, or in a sense, that is not morally relevant. This complication I will ignore for the present.

In the literature a lot of things are credited with interests, and the first task should be to decide which of these things actually have morally relevant interests. Some people speak of the interests of 'Nature'. Others speak of the interests of the biosphere, of the ecosystem, and of non-living things in it, such as lakes, valleys, and mountains. It is a controversial question whether such non-living things can have interests. Others, while denying that such things have interests, assign interests to plants and non-sentient animals, which are living indeed, but have no conscious experiences.

We could rule all these latter classes of things out of court if it is impossible to have interests without having desires for their furtherance or regrets if they are not preserved; for desires and regrets are conscious experiences which non-sentient things cannot have. One might be inclined to answer that it is not impossible, because obviously a small child might be harmed if its trustees made away with some of its money, and it never found out about the defalcation, and, because there was plenty of money left, never noticed the diminution in spending power even when it grew up. So the child would have interests without having any desires or regrets. This answer, however, misses the point I am trying to make. Presumably the child, when grown up, will have *some* desires which would have been realized if there had been more money, but as it was could not be realized. If this were not so, there really would be no harm to the child's interests. So even in this case the frustration of desire, now or in the future or possible future, is a necessary condition of harm to interests. Even if the child, in the event, dies before it has the desire that would have been frustrated, it might not have, and therefore its *expectation* of desire-satisfaction has been diminished, and that is harm.

I shall assume provisionally (leaving for later consideration an argument against this view) that there can be no harm to morally relevant interests without at least potential prevention of desire-satisfaction. So, on this showing, we ought not to attribute such interests to creatures such as plants and the lower animals, which could not have desires. Next, we have to ask about the interests of the higher animals, who do have conscious experiences including desires (or at least I presume they do), and lastly of people. The general question is, where in this list do we draw the line and say that, since the things below the line have no interests (at least of the kind that generate moral duties) questions about duties to them, and of their rights, do not arise?

A second dimension of controversy emerges when we ask, of things of any of these sorts, whether to have interests they have already to exist, or at least be definitely going to exist. It is easiest to take people as an example, though the question arises in principle for any of the things I have been listing. It seems reasonable to say that if it is the case that a certain person is definitely going to exist (say the person that the foetus in this normal pregnancy will turn into when born), then he or she will have interests in what happens to him or her after becoming a normal adult. But it is not possible to generalize from this clear case to the interests of posterity in general. The reason is that almost any adoption of an environmental or planning policy is going to affect people's actions in the future, and in particular the *times* at which they copulate to produce children. This in turn will affect the precise sperms and ova that unite to produce the children, and so the individual identities of those children (Parfit 1982: 115, 1984: ch. 16).

The consequence is that there is no such thing as an identifiable set of people that we can label as 'posterity'—as if those and only those people were the ones that were going to be born. 'Posterity' is a set of people whose identities are not yet fixed, because they depend on actions not yet taken and policies not yet decided. If therefore (as some philosophers have done) we claim that no interests are harmed or rights infringed unless there already exists, or is definitely going to exist, an identifiable individual person whose interests and rights these are going to be, posterity in general will have no interests or rights and we can do what we please about the future of the world.

A particular case of this problem is that of whether we have a duty to bring people into existence. Most people think that we do not have a duty to bring into existence all the people we could—and there are arguments for this view which I shall not have room to go into. But have we a duty to bring *any* people into existence? Could we rightly, if it suited us, just stop having children altogether? I do not myself accept the view that, just because posterity does not consist of now identifiable individuals who could have interests and rights, posterity in general has no interests or rights. I do think that we have duties to posterity, and these may even include the duty to ensure that there is a posterity; but I shall not here give my arguments for this view, which I have set out in full in a forthcoming paper (H 1988*b*).

There is a relation between having an interest and valuing, which is a special case of that between having an interest and desiring. If *a* values *b* (or in other words if *b* is of value to *a*), then *a* has an interest (*pro tanto* and *ceteris paribus*) in the existence of *b*. And this implies that (again *ceteris paribus*) *a* desires, or will under certain conditions desire, that *b* exist. Valuing is one kind (I am not committed to saying that it is the only kind) of desiring. This relation between interests and values may help us in delimiting the class of entities which have interests, and to which, therefore, there is a point in attributing rights.

It does not follow, from the fact that an entity can value other entities, that it itself has positive value, even to itself. It is not self-contradictory to speak of a valueless valuer. A very unhappy man might value his childrens' continued existence, even though he did not value his own, and neither did anyone else. So, in classifying entities that have value, we do not need to include any entity just because it is capable of valu*ing*. The class of entities which have interests may therefore contain members which do not have value; for these members may value other entities though they themselves are of no value to any entity, even to themselves.

We must distinguish three classes of entities which can be said to have value. I shall call these classes *alpha*, *beta*, and *gamma*.

Alpha. Pre-eminently, something has value if it has value *to* itself, as when *a* values the existence of *a*. Most humans fall into this class, because they value, and therefore have an interest in, their own continued existence. The same may be true of other higher animals. For example, it seems likely that cows, as sentient creatures, value their own existence. At the other end of the scale God, if he exists, values and has an interest in his own existence. To borrow a phrase from Aristotle, to all these things 'their own existence is good and pleasant; for they take pleasure in being conscious of [their own] intrinsic good' (1170b 4). We may say that such entities are valuable to themselves.

Beta. There are other entities of which this cannot be said, but which, though not valuable *to* themselves, are valuable *in* themselves *to* other entities (e.g. to those in class *alpha*, or to other entities which can value). As examples of *beta* entities, we may give inanimate objects which are valued in themselves. For example, someone may value Wastwater in itself, and want it to exist for its own sake, even when he is no longer alive to enjoy the beauty of the lake. I am not discussing whether there could be any good reason for thinking like this about Wastwater, but only claiming that if somebody said it, we would understand him. The same might be said of some kind of tree of which we make no use: somebody might want giant sequoias to go on growing in California even after he is no longer there to see them, and perhaps even when there is *nobody* there to see them. But Wastwater is of no value *to Wastwater*, and the sequoias are of no value *to the sequoias*, because they are not entities that can value.

Gamma. Lastly, there are entities which do not value their own existence like those in class *alpha*, and which are not of value in themselves to other entities as are those in class *beta*, but which are valued by, or of value to, other entities *instrumentally*, for the use made of them. Into this class fall crops, natural commodities like gravel, and some artefacts.

It might be objected that we are prejudging an important issue if we say that these are the only classes of things that have value. May there not be a class (let us call it *omega*) of entities which have value (are valuable) though they do not have value (are not valuable) *to* anything, even to themselves? I wish to argue that class *omega* must be empty, because to think that an entity has value although nothing is valuing it is incoherent. For to think that something has value is either to value it oneself, or to think that it has value to something else. To think that something has value although nobody and nothing, not even oneself, values it is like thinking that some statement is true although nobody, not even oneself, believes it. In thinking it true one *is* believing it. It is important, however, not to confuse this argument with the view, to which I can attach no sense that makes it acceptable, that we somehow *make* things valuable by valuing them. This is like saying that we make statements true by believing them.

Even if it be granted that it is incoherent to say that something is valuable though valued by nobody, does it follow (an objector might ask) that it is incoherent to *suppose* that there might be something that was valuable although valued by nobody? There could after all be a statement that was true although believed by nobody (not even the person who made it). I would answer that it is incoherent, because it is incoherent to suppose that the supposition could be true. For if it were true, we should be able to say of the thing in question that it was valuable, and in so doing we should either be valuing it ourselves, or claiming that something else valued it, and therefore could not, without the same pragmatic inconsistency as before, say that nobody was valuing it. In any case, such *supposed* valuable entities are not going to have a bearing on practical decisions unless and until it is established that they might *become* actual if certain decisions were taken.

It is true that we can coherently suppose the existence of an entity having certain specific properties, and say that it *would* be valuable *if* it existed. Then we should be valuing its existence hypothetically, and could not consistently say in the same breath that this was not valued by anybody. Hypothetical valuing as inescapably accompanies the hypothetical existence of valuable things as actual valuing does their actual existence. In each case we are valuing the existence of a thing having *those* properties *because* it has them. If, however, we merely suppose the existence of something valuable without specifying the properties that make it valuable, we do not know what we are supposing to exist, and our valuation is empty, because we do not know what we are valuing, nor on what grounds. Even if such a supposition makes sense (which

I doubt) it is at any rate clear that it is not going to affect any practical decision, because that would have to be grounded in our valuation of the properties that do, or would, make the thing valuable.

I conclude that the class *omega* is empty. I may add that if we are talking not about values but about interests, then the argument has even more obvious force. For even if it made sense to speak of something that had value although nothing valued it, it would make no sense to speak of there being interests which were the interests of nothing.

Reverting now to the problem of delimiting the class of beings that can have morally relevant interests and rights, I will suggest a possible way of solving it which looks promising. It is a generalization of the method of moral argument known as the Golden Rule. We have to ask what we wish should be done to us, were we in the position of the victim of a certain action. The method, as a way of deciding moral questions, has a very strong affinity, not only with the Christian law of *agape* of which it is one expression, but also with the Kantian and utilitarian traditions in moral philosophy, which are supposed by some to be opponents, but actually come to the same thing, at least in this area (*MT* 4).

It certainly seems possible to ask what I want to be done to me if I am one of the people who occupy my house and garden when I have vacated it on my death. These are not yet identifiable people; but that does not stop me having regard to their interests; not, for example, polluting the garden by burying hazardous waste in it. I know what it would be like for this to be done to me, so I know what it would be like for my successors, whoever they may be, to have it done to them.

Though some will make objections, I myself do not find any difficulty in extending this argument to sentient animals who may suffer if I do not keep the garden free of pollution. I am not claiming that all sentient animals suffer from the same causes or to the same extent. For example, if the land is to be taken over by a farmer and occupied by cows, they will not mind, as a human occupant might, if the land is infested with some weed that is anathema to gardeners but delicious to cattle. But what about non-sentient animals and plants? If I ask myself whether I mind what happens to me if I become a tree in the garden, I answer (holding the view that I do about the physiology of trees and their lack of a nervous system, which I think to be a necessary condition of sentience) that I could not care less what happens to me if I am a tree, any more than I care if someone cuts off my limbs after I am dead. In consequence, a 'golden-rule' method of moral reasoning will not ascribe any morally relevant interests to trees, nor any rights that we have a duty to respect.

No doubt some will deny that the supposition that I could become a tree has any sense. If this were accepted, it would do equally well for my present argument; but since I do not actually think this, and wish in any case to give the opposition a run for its money, I shall not take advantage of this move. In my own view, the reason why I do not care what happens to me if I become a tree is not that it makes no sense to suppose this, but that when I do suppose it, as I certainly can, I know that in the tree's position I shall have no sentience, and therefore no suffering, any more than I shall when I am dead, and so what happens to me in the role of tree will not affect my experience for better or worse.

The crucial point here is that in making the moral judgement that we ought (or ought not) to treat something in a certain way, we are prescribing that anything of an exactly similar sort ought (or ought not) to be so treated in exactly similar circumstances. Where the thing in question is sentient, we shall be unwilling (*ceteris paribus*) to prescribe that we ourselves should, if in that situation with that sentience (including those desires), be so treated, if the treatment runs counter to the desires. So this will stop us saying that we ought to treat *sentient* creatures in a way that runs counter to their desires (unless there are countervailing considerations arising out of the desires of other beings in whose places we imagine ourselves). But in the case of non-sentient creatures that have no desires, this argument will not work, and we shall not be stopped from treating them in any way consistent with the furtherance of the desires and interests of sentient creatures. If I am right about this (and I have had to leave out a lot of the argument) it gives us a fairly clear cut-off point at which we can stop speaking of the morally relevant interests of the classes of beings I listed at the beginning: non-sentient animals, plants, ecosystems, the biosphere, and the universe or Nature.

There is an argument against this cut-off point sometimes used by conservationists, which is Aristotelian in inspiration. It is an argument for including in the class which has morally relevant interests not only sentient, but also non-sentient living beings, while still excluding non-living beings. It is said, for example, that we morally ought to consider the interests of trees. We do, perhaps, speak of the good of trees. Trees have a nature, and grow in accordance with it, even if they are not conscious. The interest of the acorn is to become a full-grown oak, for example. That is what it would be for the tree to realize its own good. Robin Attfield, who maintains a view of this sort (1981), has told me in conversation that he does not wish to go as far as Aristotle, and attribute *desires* to trees, or say that they are *trying* to become full-grown. There would indeed be no harm in saying this, in Aristotle's senses of 'desire' and 'trying' which do not imply consciousness.

But the question is whether such interests, desires, and tryings have moral relevance, in that they constitute moral reasons for treating trees in one way rather than another. For it is possible to agree that we do speak of the good of trees without admitting that this has any moral relevance for environmental policy. If the basis of morality is the Golden Rule to do to others as we wish that they should do to us, then if, as I have said, I could not care less what happens to me if I am a tree, I shall not care in particular whether, if I am the tree, it realizes its peculiar good or not. I no more care what happens to me if I am the tree than I do what happens to me if I am the bicycle that I knock over. The bicycle too has a good; one can harm it by knocking it over. But that does not entail that the bicycle has interests of the sort that could generate moral rights or duties.

From the premiss that we have no duties *to* trees or lakes or the biosphere, it does not follow that we have no duties *with regard to* these things. Harm to them may harm sentient beings including people, to whom we have duties. It is up to the conservationists, and not so difficult as some people think, to show that these inanimate things, though they themselves have no morally relevant interests, ought to be conserved in the interests of beings that do have such interests. Wise conservationists try to show this, instead of taking the short cut of assuming illegitimately that all kinds of things have morally relevant interests, and thus rights, which could not have them.

I suspect that what is happening when people attribute morally relevant interests and rights to non-sentient creatures is this. They are projecting their own values (their ideals) on to the things in question. They, the environmentalists, think certain natural objects like mountains valuable 'in themselves', as they would say; that is, they value them highly, which they are perfectly at liberty to do. Through a confusion between classes *alpha* and *beta* above, they slip from expressing their own valuation of the mountain in itself, which puts it only into class *beta*, to attributing an act of valuation to the mountain itself, thus mistakenly including it in class *alpha*. Entities in class *alpha*, it will be remembered, must be capable of having interests, because they can value; but this is not true of entities in class *beta*.

Although I would be the last person to rely on moral intuitions as proof of moral theses, it is perhaps worth saying that the classification I have suggested does seem to be in accord with the intuitive opinions of most people about where to draw the line between the entities to which we have moral duties and those to which we have not. If we ask, for example, why most people think it worse to devastate Wastwater than some lake in the remote Yukon which hardly anybody will ever see, the answer seems to be that we are giving weight to the interests of the people that will enjoy the lakes. No doubt we should add the interests of the sentient wildlife that can enjoy them; and of course the preservation of the Yukon may be important environmentally because of its wider environmental effects, and because of the value it may have for posterity. But when all these interests, including the immediate interests of sentient creatures that can enjoy the lakes, are added up, it looks as if Wastwater wins. The same kind of reasoning explains why we value the preservation of some rare and beautiful species of butterfly over the preservation of the smallpox virus. Part of the reason may be that we think that the butterfly is sentient and the virus not; but more importantly, we think that the preservation of the virus, except for a few specimens safely locked up, would harm sentient creatures, whereas the preservation of the butterfly adds to their pleasure.

I should like at this point to refer to the preceding paper, and take up some problems that I did not there have room to deal with. I did deal at length with the problems of choosing between environmental options when only one party's interests are affected; and I suggested two contrasting models of how this should be done. In the first, the *means–end* model, what are called 'goals' are specified right at the start, and then it is determined on a factual basis, without further evaluative judgements, which option would most fully realize these goals. In the second, the *trial-design* model, the factual predictions come first; it is determined in sufficient detail what would actually happen, or what it would be like, if each of the various options were realized, and after that an informed evaluative choice can be made between the options, because we then know clearly in factual terms what we are choosing between.

The assumption that a single entity called 'the public' could make these choices would be too simple. Where there really is just one individual making the choices, he can proceed by the trial-design method, and need do no cost–benefit analysis; he can just choose, knowing what he is choosing between. But where the conflicting interests of individuals are affected, the question of what morally ought to be done cannot be answered without comparing the strength of the interests, and this involves some kind of cost–benefit analysis. Anti-utilitarians may not like this; but it is hard to see how else we can be fair to the different parties. Not only utilitarians, but anyone who needs to assess the amount of harm or good done to those affected (Rawls for example, with his difference principle (1971: 76 ff.), or Ross with his duties of beneficence and non-maleficence (1930: 21)), has to have a method for assessing it; and this will be cost–benefit analysis under another name.

The reason why even the trial-design method does not obviate the need for cost–benefit analysis altogether is that after we have put it into operation—i.e. after it has become clear to everybody just what the various options will be like in practice, which is of course a very difficult thing to achieve— the person or body that makes an environmental decision will have to find out from all the people affected, as best he can, *how much* they would like or dislike the various options, and then translate those likes and dislikes into a decision which is fair. I suggested jocularly (p. 230) that if everybody affected howled, and one could measure howls in decibels, one might thus arrive at a fair solution by choosing the option with the minimum of decibels against it. This too would be a kind of cost–benefit analysis. It would however be defective, because it would ignore posterity, which cannot howl yet, and also would give a false picture if, as is likely, the howlers were not accurately envisaging what the various options would be like in practice even for them.

Even less satisfactory, in theory, is any pure democratic method, not only because posterity cannot vote any more than howl, but because votes do not measure strengths of preferences. I shall later be using the example of the proposed construction of a new road. It might be that a huge majority was in favour of the road, because each member of the majority would benefit to a relatively small degree, but that enormous harm would be done to a few people who would be affected severely by the road, but who would be voted down because they had only one vote each. In some cases this could result in injustice; for it might be that the enormous harms to the few outweighed the relatively minor benefits, in time and money saved, to the many. This indeed is what the opponents of new roads sometimes argue. As a utilitarian, I am able to invoke justice here, because it is of dominant utility in a society that justice should be seen to be done, and also because it will actually *be* done in a particular case if interests are weighed in proportion to their strength, as utilitarianism requires.

In theory this problem could be overcome if people were able to buy votes and thus proportion the number of votes they had to the strength of their preferences. In the interests of social justice one would have to make the price paid for a vote proportionate to the voter's net income. I cannot see such a system working in practice; and perhaps it is a misuse of the democratic principle. What democracies ought rather to do is to vote for laws setting up principles for deciding such environmental questions—principles which would be accepted by all as just. The principles would include procedures for choosing the wise men who make or prepare the decisions (whether officials, or ministers, or inspectors at public inquiries), and, after choosing them, seeing to it that they decide fairly. This involves the power of the voters to turn them out if they do not satisfy the requirements of justice, as perceived by the voters.

We have then to ask what the procedures ought to be in our own society—procedures for ascertaining the various interests affected and adjudicating between them when they conflict. The first thing, obviously, that the procedure has to establish is the relative strengths of the interests. There is an excellent device used in the United States for this purpose, which we do not have in Britain, called the Environmental Impact Statement (EIS), which has to be prepared and published at an early stage before approval is given for major projects. This is then made the subject of a public hearing about the project. If either the statement or the procedure at the hearing has been defective, the project can later be challenged in the courts.

Our British system is not so good; government agencies have a habit of preparing schemes in the secrecy of their offices and only revealing them at a later stage when it is hard to change them; the 'public inquiries' that then take place often cannot have so much effect as the public process does in America. The necessity for publishing an EIS secures the *early* consideration of environmental dangers, and may result in greater care being taken at this early stage to avoid them, when it is not too late.

I know of a case in Britain where day-to-day intervention by a keen and influential environmentalist during the construction of a motorway, right up to the time of its opening, resulted in great improvements being made in the design and execution of a short length of it, but at very great expense, which could have been saved if the matter had been considered more carefully by the engineers who prepared the original design. But this is not likely to happen often, because such people are rare. The American system also does a lot more than the British to educate the public, so that these matters may be intelligently discussed.

The purpose of an EIS should be to make clear what environmental interests would be affected by a project, and to what extent. This at least sets the stage for an adjudication. Without going into a lot of ethical theory I shall not be able to substantiate this; but it seems natural to say that the strengths of the various interests, environmental and other, and the degree to which they are affected, should be the determining factor. We have to balance the interests against one another. A good procedure for adjudication would see to it that the interests were safeguarded, all in all, to the maximum degree possible, treating impartially all those affected.

It is sure to be claimed by some people that this way of looking at the matter leaves out the quality of the interests, and considers only their quantity, i.e. the strengths of the preferences. Imagine, for example, that it is proposed to develop a certain part of the sea-shore, adding various attractions, and that hordes of people will go there and enjoy it, but at the cost of entirely destroying its former natural beauty. It will be said (in many cases rightly as I think) that it ought not to be done. But it is very important to get the reasons for this right; for bad arguments in the long run defeat themselves politically. One reason is that the beauty of the shore is destroyed for ever and cannot be restored. So there is in principle an unlimited number of people whom you are depriving of that beauty in the future.

It might be said that there is also an unlimited, and larger, number of people in the future who could enjoy the popular attractions. Part of the answer is that the enjoyment of *these* people is often achievable without going near any shore. There are plenty of places which can be developed with these attractions without harming much natural beauty. So good planning would preserve the shore for those (we hope an increasing number within its capacity) who will enjoy it in times to come; and the others, even if more numerous, can be accommodated elsewhere. The only reason in the first place for proposing the development of the shore may have been a wholly mistaken belief that, to the people it would cater for, spoilt or even still beautiful shores have anything to offer that cannot be provided elsewhere. In that case, the interests of all parties could be preserved by keeping the shore as it is.

In Florida where I spend the winters there is a case which illustrates this argument. If the developers of Disney World had chosen a site on the coast, as they easily might have, then that huge attraction, which gives innocent pleasure to vast numbers of people, would have had a far more adverse environmental impact than it has had. I might have said 'even than it has had'; this is a matter for dispute.

However, when all of that has been said, the environmental planning of the coastline remains a difficult task. Any theory that makes it sound easy must be wrong. It may be that there are large numbers of people who have a legitimate interest in spending their holidays by the sea, and enjoy them more when the attractions are provided. Fortunately coastlines are quite long, and it should not be impossible to preserve the wilder and more beautiful parts of them, while still providing agreeable recreation for the hordes (who luckily do not mind a lot of company). We can have Blackpool *and* Skokholm. This kind of decision is the stuff of environmental planning; and if the planner has been fair to all the interests affected, he has done his job.

I am going to end with another typical example of an environmentally damaging land use which illustrates the problems of planners even better: the building of new roads. This is a question which still excites enormous bitterness in Britain, but, I believe, less so now in America. In Britain there must be at the moment a half dozen or so major road schemes, and no doubt dozens of smaller ones, which are being bitterly contested. It may be that Americans are more tolerant of roads and automobiles; or that they have in general more room for roads, and so can avoid environmentally sensitive areas more easily than we can in Britain. Or is it just that they have been coping with the problem for longer and have arrived at a *modus vivendi* which satisfies most people?

I am not saying that new roads never excite controversy in America, where many more appalling things have been done by way of road-building than would ever be countenanced in

Britain; but only that they now (perhaps as a result of past errors) seem to be better at resolving the controversies. The wiser part of the environmental lobby in America now rightly spends more effort getting the roads that have to be built put in the right places and made environmentally acceptable, than in trying to stop them altogether. What is most needed there is the kind of control of access to *all* highways that in Britain, since the Ribbon Development Act in the Thirties, has prevented the dangerous and disfiguring development that mars most American roads on the outskirts of cities.

What has to be done in this case, as in all cases of environmentally damaging land uses, is to do justice between the various interests affected; and I have already suggested, though only in principle, a method of doing this. We have to find out what the interests are, and then protect them to the maximal extent, treating the interests of all those affected impartially, strength for strength.

To see the problem of road construction in perspective, it is helpful to think, perhaps while one is driving along one of these new roads, what the great volume of traffic on them would be doing if the road had not been built. Would it be trying to force its way through the cities and towns which the road now avoids? That, I am sure, would harm more interests more severely than any road through open country, however beautiful the landscape through which it passes. Or would the freight and passengers that are now conveyed along the road be using alternative modes of transport? I am not going to have room to argue this, but I do not believe that there *are* any alternative modes of transport which could convey the same amount of freight and passengers to the same places without prohibitive cost. Or are the opponents of new roads just wanting there not to be this amount of transport of freight and passengers? So far as the freight goes, this entails accepting a sharply reduced level of economic activity, with all that that implies. I do not believe that even these people would like it if that had happened: they would have found their interests as adversely affected as everybody else's. They are only pretending to favour a life-style such as we would have if this freight were not transported.

As for the passengers, I am again convinced that interests

would be more adversely affected by forcing nearly everybody to travel by public transport than by constructing roads. I am talking about motorways and major trunk roads through open country. It may be different when we speak of roads *through* and *into* towns and cities, though the extreme views on that question are, as I think, both wrong. No doubt a good case can be made for more provision of public transport in large cities, and indeed for the preservation of a viable and efficient railway system. But even if both these things were achieved, they could not possibly enable us to dispense with more than a small fraction of the traffic that now goes by road.

Those who oppose new roads simply because they impinge on the landscape are in effect asking that people should not make the journeys which now, for good purposes of their own, they wish to make. And that is to affect their interests adversely. I believe that if these people could not go in their own cars, they would not in most cases go at all. We have only to compare the state of affairs that obtained when no more than a few rich people owned cars (and I can remember that time). Though the majority who had no cars did travel sometimes by train, this did not happen often, and so they did not see each other, or see things they wanted to see, so much, or in general do things they wanted to. So I think that to prevent them now travelling by car would be a deprivation more severe than any suffered by people who do not like looking at roads or having them built across their land. And many activities would just cease. For example, would the Royal Horticultural Society's gardens at Wisley be financially viable if people could not get there by road?

It is generally agreed even among conservationists that, at the time when the railways were built, it was on the whole beneficial to build them. The great increase in general living standards that occurred in the course of the nineteenth century would have been impossible without them. Yet in Britain at least there was just as much opposition to the building of the railways in the nineteenth century as there is in the twentieth to the building of roads. We should remember Ruskin who thought it monstrous to build a railway so that every fool in Buxton could be at Bakewell in half an hour and every fool in Bakewell at Buxton. That line was built, and conservationists fought its recent closure, just as they do that of the line from Leeds to Carlisle across the Ribblehead viaduct.

I am very ready to admit that a lot of roads in Britain, and no doubt elsewhere too, have been built in the wrong places. And I am prepared to admit that, even when they were put in the right places, they were built sometimes with great insensitivity to the landscape. In the early days when these roads were planned, the economics of road location and the aesthetics of road design were little studied. But we are learning more about how to get these things right. If those who oppose all roads on principle would instead spend more time studying how the job could best be done, and less saying that it should not be done at all, it might be that it would be done better. I think that this is beginning to happen even in Britain.

REFERENCES AND BIBLIOGRAPHY

References are to the date and page number, unless otherwise indicated. Dates of forthcoming works are conjectural. References beginning '*LM*', '*FR*', and '*MT*' are to *The Language of Morals* (H 1952), *Freedom and Reason* (H 1963), and *Moral Thinking* (H 1981*a*) respectively. References beginning with 'H' are to the first part of the bibliography; the rest, beginning with the author's name unless this is clear from the context, are to the second. Full bibliographies of the writings of R. M. Hare are to be found in H 1971*a* (to 1971), *MT* (1971–81) and H 1988*a* (1981–7).

1. Writings of R. M. Hare

1952 *The Language of Morals* (Oxford UP). Translations: Italian, *Il linguaggio della morale* (Ubaldini, 1968); German, *Die Sprache der Moral* (Suhrkamp, 1972); Spanish, *El lenguaje de la moral* (Mexico UP, 1975). Also Chinese and Japanese.

1963 *Freedom and Reason* (Oxford UP). Translations: Italian, *Libertà e ragione* (Il Saggiatore, 1971); German, *Freiheit und Vernunft* (Patmos, 1973; Suhrkamp). Also Japanese.

1964 'The Promising Game', *Rev. Int. de Ph.* 70. Repr. in *Theories of Ethics*, ed. P. Foot (Oxford UP, 1967), in *The Is–Ought Question*, ed. W. D. Hudson (Macmillan, 1979), and in H 1988*c*.

1966 'Peace', RSA Lecture, Australian National University, Canberra. Repr. in H 1972*c*.

1969 'Community and Communication', in *People and Cities*, ed. S. Verney (Collins). Repr. in H 1972*c*.

1971*a Practical Inferences* (Macmillan).

1971*b Essays on Philosophical Method* (Macmillan). Italian translation: *Studi sul metodo filosofico* (Armando, 1978).

1972*a* 'Principles', *Ar. Soc.* 73. Repr. in H 1989.

1972*b Essays on the Moral Concepts* (Macmillan).

1972*c Applications of Moral Philosophy* (Macmillan). Also Japanese translation.

1973*a* Critical Study: 'Rawls' Theory of Justice—I and II', *Ph.Q.* 23. Repr. in *Reading Rawls*, ed. N. Daniels (Blackwell, 1975) and in H 1989.

1973*b* 'Language and Moral Education', in *New Essays in the*

Philosophy of Education, ed. G. Langford and D. J. O'Connor (Routledge). Repr. with criticism by G. J. Warnock and reply in *The Domain of Moral Education*, ed. D. B. Cochrane *et al.* (Paulist P. and Ontario Inst. for St. in Edn., 1979).

1975 'Abortion and the Golden Rule', *Ph. and Pub. Aff.* 4. Repr. in *Philosophy and Sex*, ed. R. Baker and F. Elliston (Prometheus, 1975).

1976 'Ethical Theory and Utilitarianism', in *Contemporary British Philosophy* 4, ed. H. D. Lewis (Allen and Unwin). Repr. in *Utilitarianism and Beyond*, ed. A. K. Sen and B. A. O. Williams (Cambridge UP, 1982) and in H 1989.

1977 'Opportunity for What?: Some Remarks on Current Disputes about Equality in Education', *Oxford Rev. of Edn.* 3.

1978 'Relevance', in *Values and Morals*, ed. A. I. Goldman and J. Kim (Reidel). Repr. in H 1989.

1979 'Utilitarianism and the Vicarious Affects', in *The Philosophy of Nicholas Rescher*, ed. E. Sosa (Reidel). Repr. in H 1989.

1981*a* *Moral Thinking: Its Levels, Method, and Point*, containing bibliography of writings of R. M. Hare, 1971–80 (Oxford UP).

1981*b* Review of *The Expanding Circle*, by P. Singer, *New Republic* (February).

1984 'Supervenience', *Ar. Soc.* suppl. 58. Repr. in H 1989.

1985 'The Ethics of Clinical Experimentation on Human Children', in *Logic, Methodology and Philosophy of Science* 7, Proc. of 7th Int. Congress of Logic, M. and Ph. of Sc., Salzburg, 1983, ed. R. B. Marcus *et al.* (N. Holland).

1988*a* Replies to critics in *Hare and Critics*, ed. N. Fotion and D. Seanor (Oxford UP).

1988*b* 'Possible People', forthcoming in *Bioethics*.

1989 *Essays in Ethical Theory* (Oxford UP).

2. Other Writings

ALEXANDER, Mrs C. F. (1848), 'All Things Bright and Beautiful', in *Hymns Ancient and Modern*.

ANSCOMBE, G. E. M. (1958), 'Modern Moral Philosophy', *Phil.* 33. Repr. in *The Is–Ought Question*, ed. W. D. Hudson (Macmillan, 1969).

ARISTOTLE, *Nicomachean Ethics* (refs. to Bekker pages).

ATTFIELD, R. (1981), 'The Good of Trees', *J. Val. Inquiry* 15. Repr. (abridged) in *People, Penguins and Plastic Trees*, ed. D. Van de Veer and C. Pierce (Wadsworth, 1986).

AUSTIN, J. L. (1961), *Philosophical Papers* (Oxford UP).

—— (1962), *How to Do Things with Words* (Oxford UP).

AYER, Sir ALFRED (1936), *Language, Truth and Logic* (Gollancz; refs. to 2nd edn.).

BAIER, K. (1955), 'Is Punishment Retributive?', *Analysis* 16.

BAKER, J. A. (1982), chairman, *The Church and the Bomb*, Report of Church of England Working Party (Hodder and Stoughton).

BARRY, B. (1973), *The Liberal Theory of Justice* (Oxford UP).

BERLIN, Sir ISAIAH (1958), *Two Concepts of Liberty* (Oxford UP). Rev. in *Four Essays on Liberty* (Oxford UP, 1969).

BOSWELL, J. (1759), *Life of Johnson*. Refs. to edn. of G. B. Hill and L. F. Powell (Oxford UP, 1934).

BRADLEY, F. H. (1876), *Ethical Studies* (Oxford UP).

BRANDT, R. B. (1955), 'Definition of an Ideal Observer Theory in Ethics', *Phil. and Ph. Res.* 15.

—— (1959), *Ethical Theory* (Prentice Hall).

—— (1972), 'Utilitarianism and the Rules of War', *Ph. and Pub. Aff.* 1.

—— (1979), *A Theory of the Good and the Right* (Oxford UP).

BROCK, W. R. (1977), *Conflict and Transformation: The United States 1844–1877* (Penguin).

BUCHANAN, Sir COLIN (1971, 1972), *Alternatives for Edinburgh* and *Edinburgh: the Recommended Plan* (Edinburgh Corpn.).

CREIGHTON, R. L. (1970), *Urban Transportation Planning* (U. of Illinois P.).

DALLAS, R. C. (1803), *The History of the Maroons* (Longman; repr. Cass, 1968).

DJILAS, M. (1958), *Land Without Justice* (Methuen).

DWORKIN, R. M. (1977), *Taking Rights Seriously* (Harvard UP).

—— (1981), 'Is There a Right to Pornography', *Oxford J. Leg. St.* 1.

ELKINS, S. M. (1959), *Slavery* (U. of Chicago P.).

European Court of Human Rights (1981), Judgement in case of *Young, James, and Webster* (Strasbourg, 13 Aug.).

FLEW A. G. N. (1954), 'The Justification of Punishment', *Philosophy* 29.

GOLDSMITH, O. (1770), *The Deserted Village* (Griffin).

GRICE, H. P. (1961), 'The Causal Theory of Perception', *Ar. Soc.* suppl. 35.

HAMPSHIRE, Sir STUART (1972), 'A New Philosophy of the Just Society', *NY Rev. of Books* (24 Feb.).

—— (1978), 'Morality and Pessimism', in his *Public and Private Morality* (Cambridge UP, 1978). (Originally published as Leslie Stephen Lecture, Cambridge UP, 1972).

HARSANYI, J. (1975), 'Can the Maximin Principle Serve as a Basis for Morality?', *Am. Pol. Sc. Rev.* 69.

HART, H. L. A. (1968), *Punishment and Responsibility* (Oxford UP).

HOBBES, T. (1651), *Leviathan*.

HOHFELD, W. (1923), *Fundamental Legal Conceptions* (Yale UP and Oxford UP).

HOMER, *Iliad*.

KANT, I. (1785), *Grundlegung zur Metaphysik der Sitten* (*Groundwork of the Metaphysic of Morals*), trans. as *The Moral Law* by H. J. Paton (Hutchinson and Barnes and Noble, 1948).

LEWIS, C. I. (1946), *An Analysis of Knowledge and Valuation* (Open Court).

LONGFORD, E. (1969), *Wellington: The Years of the Sword* (Weidenfeld and Nicholson).

LYONS, D. (1965), *Forms and Limits of Utilitarianism* (Oxford UP).

—— (1984) 'Utility and Rights', *Nomos* 24.

MACKIE, J. L. (1984), 'Rights, Utility and Universalization', in *Utility and Rights*, ed. R. Frey (U. of Minnesota P.).

MANSFIELD, Lord (1772); Judgement in Sommersett's case, King's Bench, 12 Geo. III, repr. in *Howells' State Trials* 20, pp. 1 ff. See also summing up for defence.

MILL, J. S. (1861), *Utilitarianism*.

MOORE, G. E. (1903), *Principia Ethica* (Cambridge UP).

MUNBY, D. L. (1970), 'Faith and Facts: Quantity and Quality', in *Humane Gesellschaft*, ed. T. Rendtorff and A. Rich (Zurich).

NAGEL, T. (1972), 'War and Massacre', *Ph. and Pub. Aff.* 1.

NOZICK, R. (1974), *Anarchy, State and Utopia* (Basic Books).

PARFIT, D. L. (1982), 'Future Generations: Further Problems', *Ph. and Pub. Aff.* 11.

—— (1984), *Reasons and Persons* (Oxford UP).

PATTERSON, O. (1967), *The Sociology of Slavery* (MacGibbon and Kee).

PLATO, *Meno* and *Republic* (refs. to Stephanus pages).

POPPER, Sir KARL (1934), *Logik der Forschung*, rev. as *The Logic of Scientific Discovery*, (Hutchinson, 1959).

—— (1963), *Conjectures and Refutations* (Routledge).

PRIOR, A. N. (1955), *Formal Logic* (Oxford UP).

QUINTON, Lord (1953), 'On Punishment', *Analysis* 14.

RAWLS, J. (1955) 'Two Concepts of Rules', *Ph. Rev.* 64.

—— (1971), *A Theory of Justice* (Harvard UP and Oxford UP).

RICHARDS, D. A. J. (1971), *A Theory of Reasons for Action* (Oxford UP).

ROSKILL, Lord (1971), chairman, *Report of Commission on Third London Airport* (HMSO). See also Bucks. County Council (1971), Memorandum, *The Third London Airport*.

ROSS, A. (1968), *Directives and Norms* (Routledge).

ROSS, Sir DAVID (1930), *The Right and the Good* (Oxford UP).

SALISBURY, Bishop of, see BAKER, J. A.

SAMPSON, A. (1956), *Drum* (Collins).

SEARLE, J. R. (1964), 'How to Derive "Ought" from "Is" ', *Ph. Rev.* 73. Repr. in *The Is–Ought Question*, ed. W. D. Hudson (London, Macmillan, 1969) and in *Readings in Ethical Theory*, 2nd edn., ed. W. Sellars and J. Hospers (Appleton).

SELF, P. (1975), 'Techniques and Values in Policy Decisions', in *Nature and Conduct*, ed. R. S. Peters (Royal Inst. of Ph. Lectures, 1974, Macmillan).

SEN, A. (1970), *Collective Choice and Social Welfare* (Oliver and Boyd).

SINGER, P. (1973), *Democracy and Disobedience* (Oxford UP).

—— (1981), *The Expanding Circle* (Oxford UP).

SMART, J. J. C. (1973), in Smart and Williams, *Utilitarianism: For and Against* (Cambridge UP).

STEVENSON, C. L. (1944), *Ethics and Language* (Yale UP).

THEOGNIS, *Poems.*

THOMSON, J. J. (1971), 'A Defense of Abortion', *Ph. and Pub. Aff.* 1.

US Commission on Obscenity and Pornography (1970), *Report* (Comm. Print).

WESTERMANN, W. L. (1955), *The Slave Systems of Greek and Roman Antiquity* (Am. Philological Soc.).

WILLIAMS, B. A. O. (1973), in Smart and Williams, *Utilitarianism: For and Against* (Cambridge UP).

—— (1979), chairman, *Report of Committee on Obscenity and Film Censorship* (London, HMSO Cmnd. 7772). Repr. Cambridge UP, 1981.

XENOPHON, *Memorabilia Socratis.*

INDEX